50 Hikes in Michigan

50 *Hikes*

In Michigan

Sixty Walks, Day Trips & Backpacks
in the Lower Peninsula

JIM DUFRESNE

Third Edition

THE COUNTRYMAN PRESS
Woodstock, Vermont

AN INVITATION TO THE READER

Over time trails can be rerouted and signs and
landmarks altered. If you find that changes have
occurred on the routes described in this book,
please let us know so that corrections may be
made in future editions. The author and publisher
also welcome other comments and suggestions.
Address all correspondence to:

  Editor, 50 Hikes Series
  The Countryman Press
  P.O. Box 748
  Woodstock, VT 05091

Maps by MichiganTrailMaps.com
Book design by Glenn Suokko
Text composition by PerfecType, Nashville, TN
Interior photographs by the author unless
otherwise specified

Published by The Countryman Press,
P.O. Box 748, Woodstock, VT 05091
Distributed by W. W. Norton & Company, Inc.,
500 Fifth Avenue, New York, NY 10110
Printed in the United States of America

10 9 8 7 6 5 4 3 2 1

To Donna,

And her enthusiasm for new adventures, her quest for adventure, her passion for the wilderness. Routines are for the everyday people.

60 Hikes in Michigan at a Glance

HIKE	REGION
1. Graham Lakes Trail	SE Michigan
2. Springlake Trail	SE Michigan
3. Wilderness Trail	SE Michigan
4. Haven Hill Natural Area	SE Michigan
5. Penosha Trail	SE Michigan
6. River and Blue Trails	SE Michigan
7. Crooked Lake Trail	SE Michigan
8. Lakeview and Oak Woods Loop	SE Michigan
9. Port Crescent Trails	Lake Huron
10. Tobico Marsh Trail	Lake Huron
11. Sandy Hook Trail	Lake Huron
12. Highbanks Trail	Lake Huron
13. Reid Lake Foot Travel Area	Lake Huron
14. Hoist Lakes Foot Travel Area	Lake Huron
15. Chippewa Trail	Lake Huron
16. Bishop's Bog Preserve Trail	Heartland
17. Hall Lake Trail	Heartland
18. Green Trail	Heartland
19. Ledges Trail	Heartland
20. Maple River	Heartland

DISTANCE (in miles)	BACKCOUNTRY CAMPING	FISHING OPPORTUNITIES	GOOD FOR KIDS	GREAT LAKE BEACH	NOTES
3.6		★	★		Lakes, scenic vistas
3.1		★	★		Nature center at trailhead
5.2					McGinnis Lake and hardwood-forested hills
4.8			★		History of Edsel Ford
5.0					Great fall colors
5.75		★	★		Huron River and great spring wildflowers
5.1			★		Scenic vistas of inland lakes
3.6			★		Geology center and Mill Lake
2.3			★	★	Sand dunes, overlooks
4.8			★	★	Birding, nature center
1.5			★	★	Birding, scenic beaches
4.0			★		Au Sable River, scenic vistas, largo Springs
5.25	★	★	★		Interesting beaver ponds
11.0	★	★			Scenic vistas and inland lakes
7.0			★	★	Shoreline views, beautiful beaches
4.6			★		Floating trail through bogs
3.4			★		Unusual geological formations
3.3			★		Interpretive displays, wetlands
2.4			★		Ancient rock cliffs
2.3					Birding blind and tower

60 Hikes in Michigan at a Glance

HIKE	REGION
21. Birch Grove Trail	Heartland
22. Pine Valleys Pathway	Heartland
23. Silver Creek Pathway	Heartland
24. Lost Twin Lakes Pathway	Heartland
25. Mt. Randal Trail	Lake Michigan
26. Warren Woods	Lake Michigan
27. Baldtop	Lake Michigan
28. Livingston Trail Loop	Lake Michigan
29. Homestead Trail	Lake Michigan
30. Dune Ridge Trail	Lake Michigan
31. Silver Lake Dunes Route	Lake Michigan
32. Ridge & Island Trails	Lake Michigan
33. Lighthouse Trail	Lake Michigan
34. Nordhouse Dunes	Lake Michigan
35. Old Indian Trail	Sleeping Bear
36. Platte Plains Trail	Sleeping Bear
37. Empire Bluff Trail	Sleeping Bear
38. Dunes Trail	Sleeping Bear
39. Dunes Trail–Sleeping Bear Point	Sleeping Bear
40. Alligator Hill Trail	Sleeping Bear

DISTANCE (in miles)	BACKCOUNTRY CAMPING	FISHING OPPORTUNITIES	GOOD FOR KIDS	GREAT LAKE BEACH	NOTES
9.8	★				Loda Lake Wildflower Sanctuary
4.1	★	★	★		Inland lakes
4.0	★	★			Trout fishing on Pine River
3.4			★		Old Growth pines
4.0			★	★	Sand dunes, beach walking
2.0			★		Virgin beech forest, birding
2.0			★	★	Scenic vistas, sand dunes
3.4			★	★	Sand dunes, scenic vistas
2.7			★	★	Nature center, beach walking
4.2			★		Open dunes, scenic views
7.0			★		Open dunes, beach walking
4.8					Scenic views, sand dunes
4.3				★	Historic lighthouse, beach walking
6.5	★			★	Sand dunes, scenic overlooks
3.2			★	★	Remote beach
7.2	★		★	★	Remote beach, scenic views
1.5			★	★	Interpretive trail, scenic vistas
4.0				★	Sand dunes, steep climbs
2.8			★	★	Open dunes, ghost forests, remote beach
4.3					Scenic vistas

60 Hikes in Michigan at a Glance

HIKE	REGION
41. Pyramid Point Trail	Sleeping Bear
42. South Manitou Island	Sleeping Bear
43. North Manitou Island	Sleeping Bear
44. Lake Michigan and Mud Lake Loop	Sleeping Bear
45. Manistee River Trail	Pere Marquette
46. NCT–Manistee Segment	Pere Marquette
47. Marl Lake Trail	Pere Marquette
48. Lake Ann Pathway	Pere Marquette
49. Old Mission Point	Pere Marquette
50. Wakeley Lake	Pere Marquette
51. Mason Tract Pathway	Pere Marquette
52. Au Sable River Foot Trail	Pere Marquette
53. Platte River Springs Pathway	Pere Marquette
54. Thompson's Harbor	Tip of the Mitt
55. Sinkholes Pathway	Tip of the Mitt
56. Ocqueoc Falls Bicentennial Pathway	Tip of the Mitt
57. Jordan River Pathway	Tip of the Mitt
58. Shingle Mill Pathway	Tip of the Mitt
59. Lighthouse Ruins Trail	Tip of the Mitt
60. Nebo Trail Loop	Tip of the Mitt

DISTANCE (in miles)	BACKCOUNTRY CAMPING	FISHING OPPORTUNITIES	GOOD FOR KIDS	GREAT LAKE BEACH	NOTES
2.6				★	Lake Michigan vistas
9.7	★	★		★	Shipwrecks, open dunes, beach walking
8.8	★	★		★	Lake Manitou, historic relics
5.0				★	Remote beach, scenic overlook
11.0	★	★			Combines with NCT–Manistee to form 20-mile loop
12.0	★	★			Rugged terrain, scenic vistas
5.5		★	★		Inland lake, some mountain biking
3.4		★	★		Views of lakes and Platte River
5.0			★		Historic lighthouse, Grand Traverse Bay
3.9	★	★	★		Superb warm water fishery, birding
9.5		★			Blue-ribbon trout stream
3.1		★	★		Trout stream, virgin pines
1.6		★	★		Platte River, old growth maple and beech trees
5.2			★	★	Wildflowers, orchids
2.0			★		Unusual geological formations
6.0		★	★		Ocqueoc River and Falls
18.0	★	★			Superb backpacking adventure, trout streams
10.0	★	★			Overlooks, trout streams
5.5	★		★	★	Lighthouse ruins, rental cabins
8.35	★			★	Rental cabin

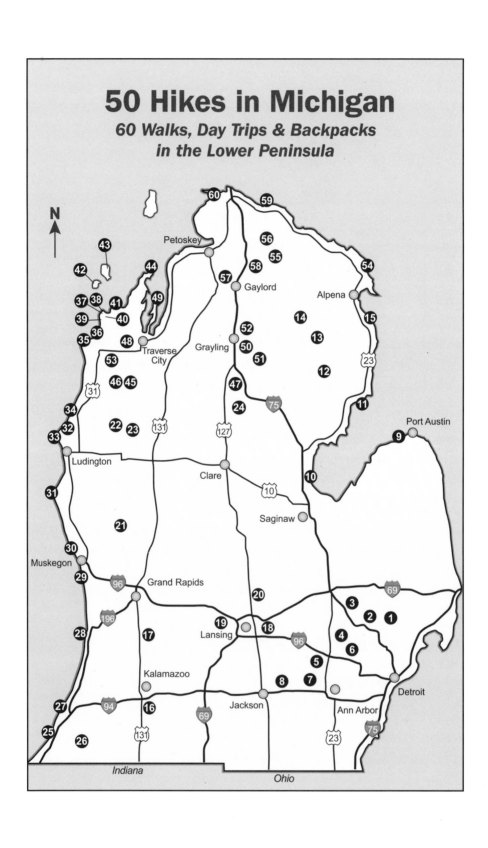

50 Hikes in Michigan

60 Walks, Day Trips & Backpacks
in the Lower Peninsula

Contents

Foreword

When Jim DuFresne first told me that he was writing a guide to 60 hikes in Michigan's Lower Peninsula, I said, "You've got to be kidding. There aren't that many."

Being a hiker and having lived in southern Michigan most of my life, I thought Jim was starting to suffer from a little too much fresh air. But what is clear after reading through the following pages is that this guide is an eminently useful resource.

Outdoor pursuits have never been as diverse and as widely popular as they are today. With the increasing urbanization of lower Michigan and growing complexity of living in a society steadily moving away from the land, there are corresponding stresses that prompt in many of us a need to return to a natural environment.

Social scientists and bioengineers have long understood that the presence of plants can have a soothing effect on the human psyche. In recent years the findings from their research have led corporate leaders and city planners to incorporate more of nature into the day-to-day scheme of things, whether by encouraging workers to bring plants to the office, building lush atriums for coffee breaks in corporate headquarters, or giving increased attention to landscape planning on corporate grounds and in city and neighborhood parks. Today, even at the somewhat sterile NASA laboratories of Johnson Space Center in Houston, research is under way on how greenery might be incorporated into future space stations to take advantage of the many benefits it provides.

That is where this book comes in—as an easily read and carried window of opportunity for those who periodically feel the need to get away. For people who like to hike occasionally, the first question is usually where to go. *Fifty Hikes in Michigan* provides the answers, whether you have time for only a two-hour jaunt nearby or can take a day or weekend to visit some of Michigan's most scenic walks.

For the hiker who enjoys getting away from city life regularly, this book will provide still other benefits. With its topographic trail maps and detailed descriptions of the topography, trails, and how to get to them, it offers a quick reference to the qualities of various hikes and what hikers might observe on them. A compilation of information important to hikers, it is easy to carry along in a day pack and will serve well as a guide on the trail.

Anyone who has spent time and money on stamps, envelopes, or long-distance calls to obtain trail maps and information from various land-managing agencies knows what a hassle that can be. Easy to use, thorough, and very readable, this book eliminates the misery of rummaging through file boxes or drawers of stray maps and trail information. When Saturday or Sunday morning arrives and the urge hits to be on a trail, you can just flip through the pages and pack a lunch, toss your boots in the car, and go.

—Howard L. Meyerson, Outdoors Editor
Grand Rapids Press and Mlive.com

Acknowledgments

I like to hike. More than any other outdoor activity, more than tossing a dry fly in the Au Sable, skiing on a groomed trail, or kayaking around Isle Royale's rugged coast, what I enjoy most in the outdoors is a quiet walk in the woods. It is simple enjoyment that sets free the soul and allows the mind to escape the daily routines of life in the city. This project, now in its third edition, was never just another book in the ongoing effort to pay the bills but always an opportunity for me to share with others what I love most about Michigan.

I'm deeply indebted to many people who have assisted me in this book. As always thanks to Sandy Graham of Backcountry North for encouraging me to write and then selling my guidebooks for the past 30 years.

I appreciate all the help I have received over the years from various government agencies but particularly Ron Welton of the Newaygo Parks and Recreation, both a friend and a confidant of mine. Thanks to Phil Akers, chief ranger at Sleeping Bear Dunes National Lakeshore, a man who knows any outdoor adventure can always be improved with a good microbrew.

But most of all, I will always remember fondly my hiking partners and the others I met along these trails, if only for a brief instant to share information or swap exaggerated tales. Topping that list is my daughter, Jessica, who makes any trail look better, and Jim Walters, who is so enthused about hiking that I need to find a way to slow him down.

Introduction

Walking in the woods with my son, I suddenly stopped, stared at the two paths that confronted me, looked around for a trail sign, and finally pulled out the map.

Michael stared at me before asking the inevitable question, "Are we lost?"

"Absolutely not, I know where we are."

"Where?"

"In Michigan," I said, and then told my son to pipe down while I studied the map we had picked up at the Department of Natural Resources field office in Baldwin.

Lost in the woods? No, as my old scoutmaster used to say, just "geographically displaced." And it shouldn't really have surprised me. We were hiking along Pine Valleys Pathway in Pere Marquette State Forest, planning to spend a night at the walk-in campsites on the shores of . . . Lost Lake. As with many foot travel areas in Michigan's state forests, hikers share the area with horseback riders, mountain bikers, and skiers, while snowmobilers have their own trail passing through. Throw in a couple of old logging two-tracks and the dirt road to Stewart Lake, and it's quite understandable why we were geographically displaced.

No problem. One nice feature of this 8-mile trail network is how well it's been posted with trail signs. We merely retreated 100 yards to the last blue boot print we passed and corrected our error.

Another nice aspect of this pathway was that we didn't see another person on the trail that afternoon. Three wild turkeys, a ruffed grouse, and deer prints by the dozens, but no other backpackers. But the best part of the trip was emerging on the edge of a wooded bluff and "finding" Lost Lake for the first time. There wasn't a soul on the small lake. It was all ours. We descended to the shoreline, pitched our tent so we could view the whole lake from our sleeping bags, and spent most of the evening sitting on the bank watching our bobbers on the still surface.

While enjoying our own little lake, for the first time that day we truly felt lost . . . from everybody and everything. And isn't that what hiking is all about?

HIKING IN SOUTHERN MICHIGAN

It should be no surprise that Michigan, with the world's greatest collection of freshwater sand dunes, with the best trout streams east of the Mississippi, with 3,200 miles of Great Lake shoreline, has the trail network and scenery every hiker dreams about. A hike in the Great Lakes State is not just a walk down a dirt path but the means to see some of the country's most spectacular natural treasures. From sand dunes without even a blade of grass to the towering monarchs of Hartwick Pines' virgin forests, from miles of beach that turn to gold with every Lake Michigan sunset to one of the 11,000 inland lakes where on a still evening bass rise to the surface like trout, all these wonders of the Midwest can be reached by hiking foot trails.

The scenery is as varied as anywhere in the country, and so are the trails. Michigan's paths include a fourth of what, when completed, will be the longest trail in the country, the 4,600-mile North Country Trail, and range down to a walk of less than a mile to the towering bluffs above Lake Michigan at the end of the Empire Bluff Trail. The hikes can be classified as walks, short and easy trails that are usually under 3 miles in length; trails, which include a variety of terrain and are often 5 to 8 miles in length; and foot travel areas, a network of trails that usually offers backcountry camping.

All three types of trails are in this book, which seeks to reveal the best 60 hikes in Michigan's Lower Peninsula. The Straits of Mackinac make for a natural line to divide the state as far as hikers are concerned. The only link between the Lower and Upper Peninsula is human-made: the 5-mile Mackinac Bridge.

But driving time also separates the two peninsulas. From Michigan's major urban areas—Detroit, Grand Rapids, Lansing, Flint, Jackson, and Kalamazoo—most of the hikes in this book are within a two- to three-hour drive and are almost always under five hours away. The majority of them are thus possible day hikes, and almost all can be weekend destinations. But hikers in southern Michigan cannot reach and return from any trail in the Upper Peninsula in a day and even on a weekend outing would be spending most of their time driving, not walking.

TOPOGRAPHY AND TERRAIN

There are no mountains in southern Michigan, but there are hills (some steep ones), many ridges, and, of course, sand dunes. All of them are the results of the several continental glaciers that covered Michigan during the Pleistocene epoch, which ended only 12,000 years ago. The forward movement of the glaciers rounded off the tops of hills, gouged out the Great Lakes, and deepened valleys to give them their U-shapes.

As the great Ice Age melted northward, water was everywhere. New river channels cut through sands and gravel, carving sculptures—such as the ledges of the Grand River—before draining into broad lowlands and filling the Great Lakes. Massive chunks of ice became kettle lakes, while winds and waves gathered up glacial drift and created the beaches along the Great Lakes and the dunes bordering Lake Michigan.

Today in southern Michigan, hikers find a region with a variety of topography—from the broad river valleys in the heart of the state to the vast stretches of wetlands that border Saginaw Bay and the state's most famous stretches of dunes. Within this region is the dividing line between the hardwood forests of broadleaf trees, whose leaves turn brilliant colors in the fall, and the transitional forest. Commonly referred to as the North Woods, here beech and sugar maples of the southern forest grow side by side with red pine, white pine, and hemlock, trees typical of the boreal forests of Canada.

Because of this variety, the 60 hikes in this book have been divided into seven areas:

Southeast: Although dominated by Detroit, an urban wasteland to most hikers, the edges of this seven-county region contain some excellent hiking opportunities. It's not wilderness, not by any means, and sometimes it's hard to escape the sights and sounds of a mushrooming metropolitan area, but many people are surprised at the rugged terrain, scenic lakes, and rewarding trails they can find within an hour's drive of the city. *Best short hike into the history of the Motorcity:* Haven Hill Natural Area, a 4.8-mile loop in the Highland Recreation Area that includes the ruins of the Edsel Ford Haven Hill estate (Hike 4).

Lake Huron: This region extends from the Thumb and Saginaw Bay north along the Great Lake and includes most of Huron National Forest. It's characterized by the

Taking in Lake Michigan from the top of a dune in Sleeping Bear Dunes National Lakeshore. The national park offers the best hiking in the Lower Peninsula.

wetlands along the Saginaw Bay, the Au Sable River and other fine trout streams, and the most undeveloped Great Lake shoreline found anywhere in the southern half of the state. Included in this book are seven trails in this area, several with backcountry camping opportunities. *Best backpacking trip:* the Chippewa Trail to South Point in Negwegon State Park (Hike 15). *Most unusual day hike:* The 4-mile trek along the Highbanks Trail in the Huron National Forest from Lumberman's Monument to Iargo Springs (Hike 12).

Heartland: The only region not abutted by a Great Lake, this section of Michigan extends from the borders with Ohio and Indiana to Roscommon County, the heart of the Lower Peninsula. The area is characterized by numerous rivers and the broad valleys they flow through on their way to the Lakes, including the Grand River, the longest waterway in Michigan at 260 miles. Three of the

nine hikes border rivers, including the Grand. *Best hike for children:* The 2.4-mile Ledges Trail along lower Michigan's most famous stone cliffs in Grand Ledge (Hike 19). *Best trail for birding:* The Maple River State Game Area north of Lansing, which includes an observation tower and a photographer's blind overlooking vast wetlands (Hike 20).

Lake Michigan: This is dune country. Michigan's shoreline is a showcase of 275,000 acres of freshwater sand dunes, and the vast majority of them are found here and in the Sleeping Bear Dunes region. These towering hills of sand, which often rise to almost 200 feet above Lake Michigan, make for an intriguing topography and for outstanding hiking. There are 10 hikes featured in this region, and 8 of them wind through the coastal dunes along the Great Lake, where it's often possible to combine a trek in the morning with stretching out on a remote beach in the afternoon.

Best backpacking adventure: Following the incredibly beautiful shoreline trail of the Nordhouse Dunes to spend a night in the backcountry (Hike 34). *Best hike through dune country:* the route to Lake Michigan in Silver Lake State Park (Hike 31).

Sleeping Bear Dunes: This is the smallest region in the book, covering only Benzie and Leelanau Counties, but it includes Sleeping Bear Dunes National Lakeshore. Stretching from Crystal Lake to North Manitou Island offshore of Leland, Sleeping Bear is one of Michigan's four great hiking areas. The other three, Pictured Rocks National Lakeshore, Porcupine Mountains Wilderness State Park, and Isle Royale National Park, are all located in the Upper Peninsula.

Nine of the 10 hikes described lie in Sleeping Bear Dunes National Lakeshore, whose towering mountains of sand may be the most famous dunes in the country. Trails often climb 100 feet or more to scenic vistas, where you can gaze over the rugged coastline to the islands out on Lake Michigan or, if you time it right, toward a sunset melting into a watery horizon. *Best island adventure:* South Manitou Island (Hike 42). *Best hike through dune country:* the 2.8-mile Sleeping Bear Point Trail through open dunes and ghost forests (Hike 39).

Pere Marquette: Hiking abounds in this seven-county region, for much of it has been preserved in two great forests: the Pere Marquette State Forest and the Manistee National Forest. To most people in Michigan, here is where you enter the North Woods, that fabled spot where pines lean over banks of crystal-clear streams and trout are rising just around the bend. Vast forests, spring-fed rivers, and trout characterize this area, home of such scenic and wild rivers as the Pere Marquette, Little Manistee, Pine, and Boardman. *Best backpacking adventure:* Manistee River Trail in the Manistee National

Forest (Hike 45). *Best hike along a fabled trout stream:* The 9.6-mile Mason Tract Pathway along the South Branch of the Au Sable River ((Hike 51).

Tip of the Mitt: This rugged region is the only one that borders two Great Lakes: Michigan and Huron. There are beach hikes on both lakes as well as treks in the hills and ridges that form the rolling topography at the northern tip of the Lower Peninsula. For most hikers in southern Michigan, the drive to the Tip of the Mitt is too far to be a day trip. The region is a favorite for weekend backpacking trips, however, as four of the seven hikes included offer opportunities to overnight on the trail. *Best weekend adventure:* Jordan River Pathway (Hike 57). *Best shoreline hike:* Lighthouse Ruins Trail in Cheboygan State Park (Hike 59).

WHEN TO HIKE

You can undertake these trails any time of the year, and during a mild winter you need not even worry about encountering much snow south of Lansing. Most people, though, regard the hiking season in the Lower Peninsula as extending from late April to early November. Depending on the year, there is often good hiking in April and early May. Streams may be swollen and trails a little muddy in places, but the wildflowers are blooming in profusion, fiddleheads are emerging from a damp layer of leaves, and ducks and geese are migrating through the region. Everything in the forest seems to be awakening, hikers included. Best of all, there are no bugs, not yet. Temperatures can be cool—in the 50s and 60s—and rain showers are a frequent occurrence. Pack rain gear and don't worry about getting your boots muddy.

June through August is summer hiking, the most popular time if only because children are out of school and treks into the woods are often part of family vacation or camping trips. Temperatures can range anywhere from a pleasant 70 degrees in June to a blistering 90 in August. Sunny weather and blue skies are the norm, but keep an eye out for sudden thunderstorms that roll off Lake Michigan or across the state. Many state park campgrounds are filled for the weekend by Thursday night, and, of course, summer is insect season. Mosquitoes begin appearing by mid-May in southern Michigan and usually peak sometime in late June. Deerflies filter through later (how convenient!) and seem to be most annoying in late July and early August.

If bugs and crowds annoy you, there are trails that provide an escape from both. The dune country is an excellent choice. Step out of the woods and into the open dunes and watch the bugs diminish. Hike a mile or two from the road, and there's a beach to stretch out on or a walk-in campsite without a single recreational vehicle.

Few argue, however, that the best time to hike Michigan's Lower Peninsula is September through October. Temperatures return to those pleasant levels below 70 degrees. Showers are common (especially on the weekends, it seems), but so are those glorious Indian summer days when the sky is a deep blue, the forest is dry, and the temperature peaks in the mid-60s. And then there are the fall colors. The hardwoods in this part of the state begin changing in mid-September and peak anywhere from the first week of October around Petoskey to the end of the month at the Warren Woods Natural Area (Hike 26) near the Indiana border.

There are no bugs, there's great color, it's common to spot deer and other wildlife, and on a Saturday afternoon, half the state is glued to the television watching the University of Michigan football game. Without a doubt, Michigan autumns were made for

hikers. The unofficial end of the hiking season for many is November 15, the first day of the firearm deer season. Not caring to add hunter orange to their wardrobes, people tend to put the boots away; by the time the 16-day season is over, they are too busy with other activities to return to the woods.

CLOTHING AND EQUIPMENT

Too often people undertake a day hike with little or no equipment and then, two hours from the trailhead, get caught in a rain shower while wearing only a flimsy cotton jacket. Or, in the worst possible scenario, they get lost and are forced to spend a night in the woods without food, matches, or warm clothing. To hike without a soft day pack or rucksack containing the essential equipment is like driving your car without putting on the seat belt. The risk just isn't worth it.

Always carry what many refer to as the 10 essentials. They are (1) food, either lunch or high-energy snacks such as trail mix, chocolate, or protein bars; (2) rain protection in the form of a windbreaker or Gore-Tex garment and, depending on the season, extra warm clothing, especially a wool hat and mittens; (3) water; (4) a pocket-sized flashlight; (5) a compass or GPS unit; (6) an appropriate map; (7) matches in a waterproof container; (8) insect repellent; (9) a small folding knife (the Swiss Army knife being the classic choice); and (10) a small first-aid kit that contains items (moleskin, bandages) to take care of blisters that suddenly develop 3 miles from the trailhead.

Perhaps the most important piece of equipment is your footwear. In the past, the traditional choice was the heavy, all-leather hiking boot that was smeared on the outside with half a can of beeswax. Today most hikers opt for the ultralight nylon boots made by sporting-shoe companies such as Lowa, Merrell, and Vasque. These are easier on the feet, do not need half as much time to break in, and provide enough foot protection for the trails in Michigan's Lower Peninsula. Normal tennis or running shoes, on the other hand, do not provide sufficient ankle support for most trails.

Depending on the season, other gear might be necessary. In the summer, you will want to carry along sunscreen, sunglasses, and a wide-brim hat, especially when hiking the trails in dune country. In November or December, mittens, stocking cap, and a warm sweater or sweatshirt are needed to avoid chilling when you stop for a break or lunch. If it's deer season, whether the firearm or the archery hunt, which extends from October 1 to December 31, add a piece of hunter orange clothing, if only a stocking cap.

BACKPACKING AND CAMPING

Backpacking opportunities, off-trail camping, walk-in campsites, and trailside cabin rentals are described for 16 of the 60 trails included here. The "highlights" listing at the beginning of each chapter indicates which trails offer such camping opportunities. Backcountry camping offers hikers a rustic setting that can be reached only by trail, with sites containing at most a fire ring, a hand pump for water, and maybe a vault toilet. Many spots are simply a scenic place to pitch a tent. When considering such an adventure, follow the new wilderness ethic of minimum-impact camping being promoted by the USDA Forest Service and many other groups.

Either pitch the tent in designated campsites or select a level area with adequate water runoff. Use a plastic ground cloth to stay dry rather than making a ditch around the tent. Position the tent so that it blends in with the environment, and never set up camp within 200 feet of natural water or the trail. Wash, brush teeth, and clean dishes 100 feet from all water sources. Never use soap or clean up directly in streams or lakes. Cook on pack stoves and, if you must have a fire, keep it small, using only downed wood. Totally dismantle the rocks used for the pit and cover up the ashes with natural material. Leave the ax at home.

It's best to hike and camp in small groups that have less impact on wildlife and terrain. Forgo the boom boxes and radios. And, most important, don't just pack out all your own garbage but pick up and carry out any litter you encounter on the trail. If hikers don't pick it up, who will?

TRAIL MAPS

Maps listed are what is available at the park headquarters or nearest ranger station or what is available online from MichiganTrailMaps.com (www.michigantrailmaps.com), the Michigan-based cartography publisher that produced all the maps included in this book.

USGS topos are not listed because while they are detailed, the information is far from being current. Most of the trails described in these hikes are not on the topos, while many former roads and traditional trails are displayed even though they have long since been absorbed by the woods. If you're looking for USGS topos, a good online source is MyTopo (www.mytopo.com). Trail maps produced by parks and government agencies are usually more up to date but often too simplistic to satisfy the needs of hikers and backpackers on long trails. Many, but certainly not all, are available online, including those from the Michigan Department of Natural Resources (www.michigan.gov/dnr), the Huron-Manistee National Forests (www.fs.usda.gov/hmnf), and Sleeping Bear Dunes National Lakeshore (www.nps.gov/slbe).

A hiker enjoys the panaromic view from a trail in Sleeping Bear Dunes National Lakeshore.

WATER AND TICKS

Unless the water comes out of a hand pump or has been posted as safe to drink, consider it unsafe. Water from all lakes, streams, and rivers must be treated before you drink it. The increasing occurrence of backcountry dysentery caused by *Giardia lamblia* clearly demonstrates the frequency of water pollution in parks and on state land. To ensure your safety, boil water a full minute or run it through a filter whose screen is small enough to remove microscopic organisms along with other impurities.

For some hikers, an even greater fear than bad water is Lyme disease. The bacterium that causes Lyme disease is transmitted to humans through the bite of a deer tick, which is found on all types of vegetation but especially in the woods. The very small deer tick is orange and brown with a black spot near its head. Even more common is the wood tick, which is considerably larger and has white marks near its head but is unlikely to transmit the disease.

The best way to deal with Lyme disease is to avoid the tick. The tick is most active in the spring and early summer but is also present in the fall. Many bug repellents work well against the insect, especially those containing a high percentage of diethyl-toluamide (DEET). Treat shoes, socks, and pant legs as well as skin to repel ticks. Wear long sleeves and long pants, make periodic checks for ticks, and when the outing is over, bathe as soon as possible to wash off any tick you might have come in contact with. A hot shower including a good scrub with a washcloth is probably the best precaution against ticks, which need up to 24 hours to attach.

A diagnosis of Lyme disease is best left to a doctor, but common early symptoms include a ring-shaped rash that can occur 4 to 20 days after the bite. You might also experience fatigue, mild headaches, muscle and joint pain, fever, and swollen glands. Some victims believe they have nothing more than a mild case of flu, while others suffer joint inflammation and other arthritis-like symptoms. Fortunately, the disease is rarely fatal, and if detected early can be treated with antibiotics.

Most important, don't give up hiking or other outdoor activities because of Lyme disease. Some common sense and a few precautions will prevent most encounters with deer ticks.

FEES

A variety of trail fees are charged in Michigan. Most county parks charge a vehicle entry fee, as do the state parks, Sleeping Bear Dunes National Lakeshore, and the Huron and Manistee National Forests. Fee payment is often available in the form of an annual, weekly, or daily pass and can be purchased at a growing number of trailheads, where there are registration stations and fee pipes. A Recreation Passport from the Michigan DNR is required to enter state parks as well as state forest pathways and campgrounds. Passports can be purchased at DNR offices, state park contact stations, or online at the DNR website and Michigan Secretary of State offices when renewing a motor vehicle license plate.

At the few trails where a vehicle pass is not required, there is often a collection pipe for trail users to insert a few dollars. Please pay your fees. Hikers need to join mountain bikers and cross-country skiers in helping to maintain trails through either vehicle fees or donations at a collection pipe. Failure to do so will inevitably result in the loss of foot trails and thus hiking opportunities, something we can ill afford.

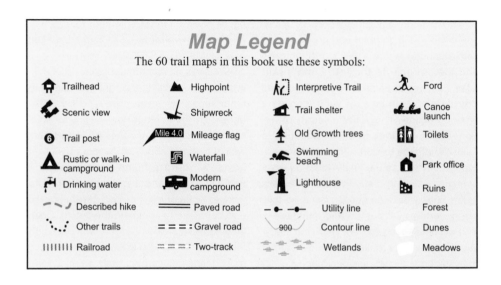

Map Legend

The 60 trail maps in this book use these symbols:

Trailhead	Highpoint	Interpretive Trail	Ford
Scenic view	Shipwreck	Trail shelter	Canoe launch
Trail post	Mile 4.0 Mileage flag	Old Growth trees	Toilets
Rustic or walk-in campground	Waterfall	Swimming beach	Park office
Drinking water	Modern campground	Lighthouse	Ruins
Described hike	Paved road	Utility line	Forest
Other trails	Gravel road	900 Contour line	Dunes
Railroad	Two-track	Wetlands	Meadows

HOW TO USE THIS BOOK

It is not the intention of this guide to give hikers a step-by-step narration of a trail. Some might wonder why it's even necessary to provide walkers with anything more than the location of a trailhead and the length of the path. The answer is simple—time constraints. In this hectic world of raising families and maintaining houses and marriages where both spouses work, we never seem to have enough time to venture outdoors. What little time we do carve out for a hike or a weekend backpacking trip is rare and valuable.

So valuable that it can't be wasted on an ill-planned adventure. That's the reason for this guidebook. I once drove three hours for a hike that turned into an afternoon of walking through clear-cuts and past discarded cars and washing machines—not my idea of a quality trek. If you undertake only a handful of hikes each year, or even a dozen, you want each one to be a good outdoor experience. You want to be spellbound with the scenery, to climb through hills, to find a backcountry

lake to spend the night . . . you don't want to be buzzed by a pack of off-road vehicles.

This book leads you to those treks. It doesn't tell you what's around every bend, but it does cover the highlights of each trail and, in some cases, the low points. It provides facts on the natural or human history of the area for a better appreciation of the land you're walking through. It mentions if there are fish in the lake so you can pack your rod, and notes the campsites along the way so you can plan to spend an evening. Each description lists the length and difficulty of each stretch—most important details. Ill-fated outings usually begin when hikers select a trail too long or too hard for their capabilities.

What makes one trail better than another? Many times your assessment of a trail results from unpredictable circumstances surrounding the hike—good weather, a lucky sighting of a deer or a flock of wild turkeys, or, alternatively, a swarm of mosquitoes that drives you back to the car after only a half mile. But good trails do share many tangible characteristics.

They provide excellent scenery. On many, you climb to a high point and are rewarded with a panorama that's well worth the drive and the struggle to the top. Others skirt lakes that are not encircled by cottages and docks, follow streams, or wind through a wooded hollow. They offer a variety of terrain—hills and ridges to climb, beaches to follow, wetlands to skirt. Often a change in topography makes the hike almost as interesting as reaching a scenic vista. The trails in this book were also chosen because they are generally well posted and maintained. You will thus spend most of your time studying the scenery or looking for wildlife rather than staring at a compass or a map.

Finally, some trails were selected simply for their location. The Penosha Trail in Brighton Recreation Area is an amazing route if for no other reason than that, within 30 minutes of downtown Detroit, there is a place to hike 5 miles in the woods. And that's an important characteristic of a good trail—the ability to escape from the concrete jungle at home. The escape doesn't have to be into a true wilderness; in fact, you'd be hard pressed to find such in the Lower Peninsula. It just has to be a route away from the sights, sounds, and golden arches of our society—if only for an hour or two.

The most important use of this book is for choosing the right hike. At the beginning of each description, you'll find a listing of total distance, hiking time, a difficulty rating, and maps that can be helpful.

Total distance comprises a round-trip hike unless otherwise noted and was measured by a GPS unit. Hiking time, on the other hand, is an estimate; your actual hiking time will depend upon your walking speed. The estimate is based on the fact that reasonably fit hikers cover 2 to 3 miles an hour on level ground and less than 2 mph when moderate uphill walking is involved. The

figure does not include an hour for lunch or an afternoon spent trying to land a bass out of a remote lake.

Rating is even more subjective than hiking time. In general, though, you can consider those treks rated easy to be walks under 3 miles in length on somewhat level ground and along well-maintained trails, where bridges and boardwalks cover wet areas. Moderate hikes usually include some climbing, and their length—from 4 to 7 miles—demands that you carefully plan sufficient time to complete the outing. Challenging treks include not only some rugged terrain but might also involve poorly marked trails. Many challenging trails are also long and require an overnight in the backcountry.

Finally, the question of rating trails: I say why not? We rate movies and cars and books, even washing machines and motels. Why not trails? As a lifelong resident of Michigan, as an avid hiker since my Boy Scout days in Troop 1261, and as an outdoor writer most of my working days, I've hiked hundreds of trails in the Lower Peninsula. What I am presenting here is one man's opinion of the best 60 walks, hikes, and backpacking treks of varying lengths and locations around the state. It's the opinion of a person, you might say, who's been down the trail.

If I were only spending a summer here or were soon moving out of state, here are the five best hikes in Michigan's Lower Peninsula, not to be missed.

1. South Manitou Island. The views from the top of the perched dunes here are breathtaking, while the artifacts from the island's past, from a shipwreck to a historic lighthouse, make this trek one of the most interesting day hikes in the state (Hike 42).

2. Manistee River Trail. This 10.5-mile trail is a scenic, remote, but surprisingly easy hike that skirts the river in the Manistee

National Forest. A new footbridge across the Manistee River allow hikers to combine the trail with a segment of the North Country Trail to form a 23-mile loop and one of the best backpacking adventures in the Lower Peninsula (Hike 45).

3. Highbanks Trail. Located in the Huron National Forest, this point-to-point trail skirts the towering bluffs on the east side of the Au Sable River with the best stretch being the 4-mile segment from its western trailhead at largo Springs to Lumberman's Monument. Along the way you can descend a stairway to gurgling springs, look for eagles at Canoers Monument, and learn about 19th-century loggers at Lumberman's Monument (Hike 12).

4. Jordan River Pathway. Looping through the pristine Jordan valley is this 18-mile pathway that includes scenic ridgetop views, opportunities to fish for brook trout, and backcountry campsites (Hike 57).

5. Chippewa Trail in Negwegon State Park. The park is hard to reach, but the trail winds past the most remote beaches of Lake Huron. The views at the tip of South Point alone are worth the 7-mile walk (Hike 15).

Southeast Michigan

1

Graham Lakes Trail

Place: Bald Mountain Recreation Area

Total Distance: 3.6 miles

Hiking Time: 1 to 2 hours

Rating: Moderate

Highlights: Inland lakes, scenic vistas

Maps: Bald Mountain Recreation Area North Unit Trail Guide from the Michigan DNR, or Graham Lakes Trail map from MichiganTrailMaps.com

Trailhead GPS Coordinates: N 42° 47' 4.07" W 083° 11' 29.16"

In 1983, the Department of Natural Resources staff at Bald Mountain Recreation Area built a loop around Graham Lakes and marked and promoted the new trail for cross-country skiing. Located in hilly northern Oakland County, the lake-studded area seemed a natural for skiers, providing numerous long, downhill runs. To the surprise of the DNR staff, skiers returned the following summer as hikers to discover what the new trail would be like on foot.

What they discovered was one of the most scenic and enjoyable foot trails in southeastern Michigan, and today Graham Lakes Trail, also referred to the Orange Loop, is more popular with hikers spring through fall than with skiers in the winter. There is no actual Bald Mountain here, or anywhere else in the state recreation area, but the trail does ascend a number of ridges and hills, climbing 60 feet at one point, to several scenic overlooks of lakes. Hikers are left feeling physically invigorated at the end. Depending on the time of year, the wildlife encountered ranges from grouse, cottontail rabbits, and a variety of waterfowl, including Canada geese, to deer, which are most often spotted in early spring or September. In spring, patches of wildflowers abound near the wetlands; in the autumn, the ponds are highlighted by the fall colors of hardwood trees. Summer is nice, too, but those stagnant bodies of water are natural hatcheries for mosquitoes, especially late May through June. Also keep in mind that the trails are popular with mountain bikers, with

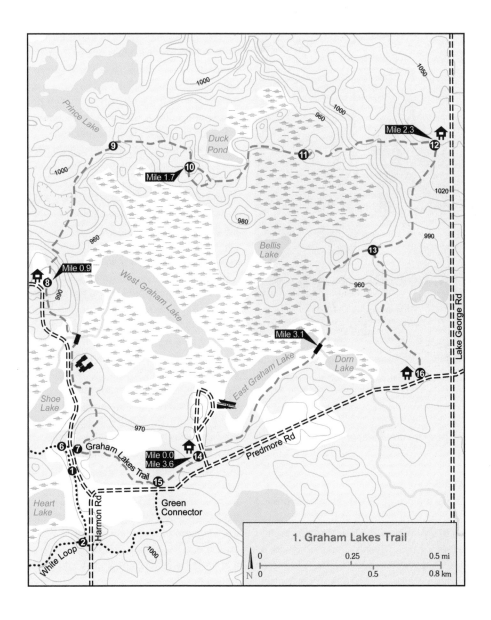

1. Graham Lakes Trail

the activity peaking during the summer and on fall weekends.

The other attraction of the 4,637-acre state recreation area's northern unit is the fishing to be found in the lakes, some of which can only be reached by a belly boat, canoe, or fishing kayak. West Graham Lake is the deepest (at 25 feet) and most productive, but anglers also fish East Graham and Prince Lake targeting species ranging

A hiker crosses a footbridge on the Graham Lakes Trail in Bald Mountain Recreation Area.

from bluegill and other panfish to smallmouth bass.

ACCESS

The northern unit of the recreation area is a 45-minute drive north of Detroit. Located east of Lake Orion, the tract can be reached from M-24 by following Clarkston Road, an especially scenic route where it forms an S-turn to cross Paint Creek. After 2 miles, turn north (left) on Adams Road, which ends at Stoney Creek Road. Head east (right) 100 yards, then turn north (left) on Harmon Road, which leads into the park. There are four trailheads and parking areas to the loop, including one at the end of Harmon Road, another near the corner of Predmore and Lake George Road, and a third farther north on Lake George Road.

This hike is described in a clockwise direction from the trailhead at the East Graham Lake boat ramp, reached by turning right onto Predmore Road from Harmon and heading east for a quarter mile. The park headquarters (248-693-6767) is located in the southern unit and can be reached by departing east from M-24 at Greenshield Road.

TRAIL

At the East Graham Lake boat launch, a large display sign marks post No. 14, where the trail crosses the road to the DNR access site and parking area. The trail is numbered in a clockwise direction. Heading west, you quickly pass post No. 15, marking the junction of the Green Connector, a half-mile spur that crosses Harmon Road to the White Loop. Within a quarter mile you reach post No. 7, where a short spur hops across Harmon Road to reach post No. 6 along the White Loop.

Graham Lakes Trail continues north, where it descends to the remnants of an old two-track to West Graham Lake and climbs the best hill of the day. On the way up, you pass a view of Shoe Lake and then break out at a clearing. Here you'll find a bench, along with a view of West Graham Lake and many of the surrounding ridges you'll walk over on the back side of the loop. You then descend to skirt Harmon Road and at *Mile 0.6* cross an impressive wooden bridge over a stream that flows between Shoe and West Graham Lakes.

The trail swings away from the stream, climbs another hill, and at *Mile 0.9* reaches post No. 8 at the north end of Harmon Road, coming within view of one of the few private homes seen along the way, a rather amazing fact for this rapidly developing region of Oakland County. You leave the post hiking in a northeast direction and enter a pine plantation whose trees are in perfect rows and tower above a bench. From here it's only a quarter mile until you arrive at the end of Prince Lake at *Mile 1.2*. Occasionally you'll see anglers on the water targeting panfish and largemouth bass–the lake has a boat launch on its west end.

Avoid the trails that wander around the lake. From post No. 9, Graham Lakes Trail swings to a more easterly direction and soon passes a view of Duck Lake, a marshy pond surrounded by cattails and deadheads. Post No. 10 is reached at *Mile 1.5* and marks where a skiers' bypass has been built. A bench has been placed here, as the hill serves as an overlook with Duck Pond to the north and the surrounding hills to the west.

The bypass quickly rejoins the main trail. The next quarter mile is mostly downhill past another view of Duck Pond before bottoming out at a marshy area where there may or may not be a sluggish creek. Graham Lakes Trail quickly leaves the wetland at post No. 11 as it steadily climbs a long hill to reach post No. 12 at *Mile 2.3*. The post and map serves as a trailhead for a parking area off Lake George Road. Follow the main trail as it swings south (right) to dip back into the woods and begins a steady route downhill. You descend more than 50 feet by the time post No. 13 pops up, marking a spur from Predmore Road.

You're now less than a mile from the access site. More hills follow until you bottom out at a large wooden bridge over a stream that flows from marshy Dorn Lake, a gathering spot for waterfowl in spring and fall, to East Graham Lake to the north. The bridge makes a nice place to enjoy the wetland scenery. The trail skirts East Graham Lake's east shoreline and at *Mile 3.6* arrives at the parking area where you left your vehicle.

Hikers look for wildlife from a dock on East Graham Lake in Bald Mountain Recreation Area.

2

Springlake Trail

Place: Independence Oaks County Park

Total Distance: 3.1 miles

Hiking Time: 2 hours

Rating: Moderate

Highlights: Nature center, inland lake

Maps: Independence Oaks County Park map from Oakland County Parks & Recreation, or Springlake/Ted Gray Loop map from MichiganTrailMaps.com

Trailhead GPS Coordinates: N 42° 46' 52.91" W 083° 23' 44.33"

Glaciers were good to Oakland County. In the northern portions of one of the state's most populated counties, these ancient rivers of ice scoured the land and left behind ridges, hills, and, most of all, potholes that became a patchwork of inland lakes and ponds. These qualities make for interesting terrain, diverse habitat, and excellent hiking wherever the land has been preserved from urban sprawl.

Independence Oaks County Park is such a place. Established in 1976, it's the largest unit in the Oakland County Parks system at 1,274 acres. The eastern half of the park, where visitors enter, has been developed, with shelters, a boathouse concession, tables, grills, fishing docks, and a swimming area. The western half is a series of rugged ridges and low-lying wetlands that can only be seen from the park's 14-mile network of foot trails. The natural barrier separating the two halves is Crooked Lake, a 68-acre lake with crystal-clear water that is free from the summer buzz of motorboats and Jet Skis.

The route described here is a 3.1-mile hike along most of Springlake Trail to the south end of the park, with a return along the Ted Gray Trail and a portion of the Lakeshore Trail. You begin and end at the park's Lewis E. Wint Nature Center, which is an ideal starting point for many hikers. Because of its terrain, the Independence Oaks supports a wide range of habitat, and hikers pass through upland forests of oak and hickory, pockets of cedar in the bog areas, and maple and beech climax forests surrounding the lake in the floodplains. This diversity of

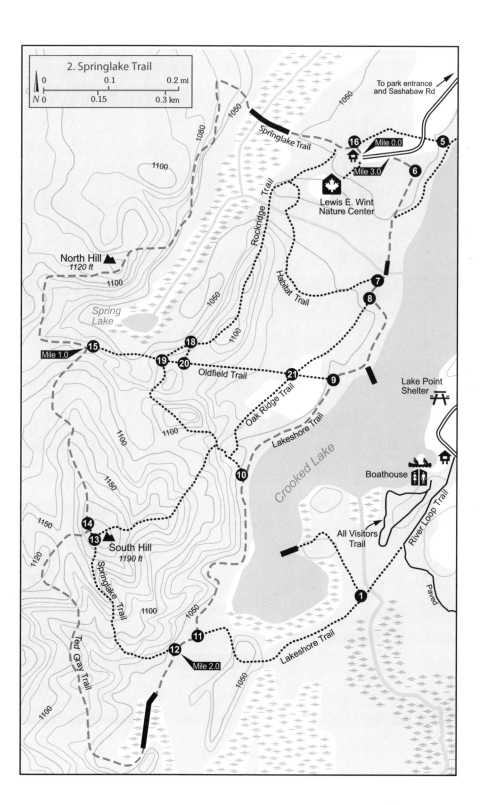

2. Springlake Trail

To park entrance
and Sashabaw Rd

Mile 0.0
Mile 3.0

Springlake Trail

Rockridge Trail

Lewis E. Wint
Nature Center

North Hill ▲
1120 ft

Habitat Trail

Spring
Lake

Mile 1.0

Oldfield Trail

Oak Ridge Trail

Lake Point
Shelter

Lakeshore Trail

Crooked Lake

Boathouse

River Loop Trail

All Visitors
Trail

South Hill
1190 ft

Springlake Trail

Paved

Ted Gray Trail

Mile 2.0

Lakeshore Trail

A hiker follows Ted Gray Trail in Independence Oaks County Park.

habitat and the wildlife it supports is explained through an excellent series of displays within the nature center.

Although the loop is not long, you do end up climbing more than 100 feet along two main ridges, actually old glacial moraines. During the winter, these hills and trails attract cross-country skiers from throughout southeastern Michigan. In the summer, hikers climb the same ridgeline, where they often find a bench and a pleasant view of the park's interior. In this somewhat isolated section of the park, you can sit on a quiet hilltop and not even know that on the other side of the lake there are picnics, volleyball games, and family reunions taking place.

ACCESS

Independence Oaks is located north of the village of Clarkston and can be reached from I-75 by exiting at Sashabaw Road (exit 89). Head north for 2 miles to the posted entrance. After entering the park, the road heads both north and south. To the south the park road ends at Hidden Lakes swimming area and a boathouse that rents out canoes, rowboats, and pedal boats, and sells bait during the summer. Turn north (right) to reach the nature center (248-625-6473), open 10 AM to 5 PM Tuesday through Saturday and noon to 5 PM Sunday and holidays.

The park is open from 8 AM to dusk, and there is a vehicle entry fee for both residents and nonresidents of Oakland County. For more information, contact the park headquarters (248-625-0877; www.destination oakland.com).

TRAIL

A large sign with a park map marks the trail in the nature center parking area, and a few steps away is the posted junction of the Springlake Trail and the Rockridge Trail. Springlake departs to the north (straight)

Two hikers cross a boardwalk in Independence Oaks County Park.

and is a wide path designed to accommodate both hikers and skiers. It begins with a descent into the first marsh of the day, which is crossed on a long boardwalk. Cattails are on both sides of you as the trail crosses the low-lying wet area and then climbs out of it to a ridgeline. You descend briefly, then climb again to the first bench, a half mile from the parking lot. If the leaves aren't too thick, you can view the marsh area, which stretches from Spring Lake to Crooked Lake.

The trail quickly resumes climbing and passes another bench, a few steps off the path and easily missed. This one features a railing since it's perched on the steep side of the ridge, making the view an especially scenic one in mid-October when the fall colors are peaking. Beyond the bench, the trail continues to follow the ridgeline, rising and dropping with its crest, until you reach the posted junction with Oldfield Trail at **Mile 1**. Head down Oldfield a few steps for your only view of Spring Lake. Surrounded by a stand of tamarack, this small pond is a dying lake, slowly being filled in and covered up by the carpet of moss and bog plants that encircle it.

At the junction Springlake Trail curves sharply away from the lake and begins a steady climb to the crest of another ridge, the one that is so clearly seen from Sashabaw Road. You follow the ridgeline for a short spell before topping out at South Hill, elevation 1,190 feet or more than 150 feet above the lake surface. Posted here is the junction with the Ted Gray Trail.

At 0.75 mile, Ted Gray is a bit longer than the last leg of the Springlake Trail but far more interesting. It descends sharply off the ridge, climbs back to almost 1,200 feet, and then drops sharply again in a stretch where more than one skier has lost control and ended up in the trees. It ends in a scenic marsh area crossed by a long boardwalk, where during the fall the surrounding hardwoods will be burning with reds and oranges while the cattails next to you are exploding in a mass of light-brown fluff.

At **Mile 2** Ted Gray returns to Springlake, which quickly merges into the posted Lakeshore Trail. Turning east (right) leads to the east side of Crooked Lake and the boathouse. Head north (left) to return to the nature center by following the shoreline on the west side of the lake. At its south end Crooked Lake forms a small, shallow bay that attracts both waterfowl and anglers in the spring. The lake supports bass and northern pike but is best known for its panfish. This section can be productive, especially in May when the fish are spawning in the shallows, and anglers often tease the fish into striking with rubber spiders or small poppers.

At one point the trail passes a picnic table on a small knoll overlooking the lake, a great place to eat your lunch. At **Mile 2.4** you reach the south end of the Rockridge Trail, an alternative route back to the nature center that includes climbing another ridge. Most hikers elect to continue following scenic Lakeshore Trail that, true to its name, remains in constant view of Crooked Lake.

After passing posts No. 9, 8, and 7 and crossing a footbridge over the outlet stream from Spring Lake, Habitat Trail veers off to left from Lakeshore Trail and climbs to the park road, passing post No. 6 along the way. The park road is reached at **Mile 3**. The nature center parking lot where you began is just to the left.

3

Wilderness Trail

Place: Holly Recreation Area

Total Distance: 5.2 miles

Hiking Time: 3 to 4 hours

Rating: Moderate

Highlights: McGinnis Lake, wetlands, hardwood-forested hills

Maps: Holly Recreation Area Trails map from the Michigan DNR, or Wilderness Trail map from MichiganTrailMaps.com

Trailhead GPS Coordinates: N 42° 49' 50.50" W 083° 30' 54.51"

Calling any trail in Oakland County "Wilderness" is a little presumptuous. Or a lot. Still, this 5.2-mile loop in Holly Recreation Area is a dandy, an oasis in the urban sprawl that someday will turn Dixie Highway between Grand Blanc and Pontiac into nothing but an endless strip mall. This trek is not wilderness by any stretch of the imagination, but it does get you into the woods and away from traffic, pavement, and the developed areas of this state park.

Located on the northern edge of Oakland County, Holly Recreation Area is a 7,817-acre state park that offers a wide variety of terrain on both sides of I-75. Areas east of the highway feature heavily forested hills, second-growth forests, the largest lakes, more wetlands, and open fields that at one time were farmed. In all, Holly has 17 lakes, a handful of creeks, and 30 miles of trails for both hikers and mountain bikers located not much more than 30 minutes from the urban areas between Flint and Pontiac.

The park is actually seven separate units, most of them totally undeveloped and frequented mostly by hunters during the fall seasons. The largest, most developed, and thus most heavily used area is east of I-75 and includes McGinnis Lake north of McGinnis Road, along with Heron, Valley and Wildwood Lakes south of it. Surrounding the lakes are the park's campground, beaches, day-use areas, and rental cabin.

Wilderness Trail lies north of McGinnis Road and loops around McGinnis Lake Campground and its namesake lake. You see the lake but never the campground or

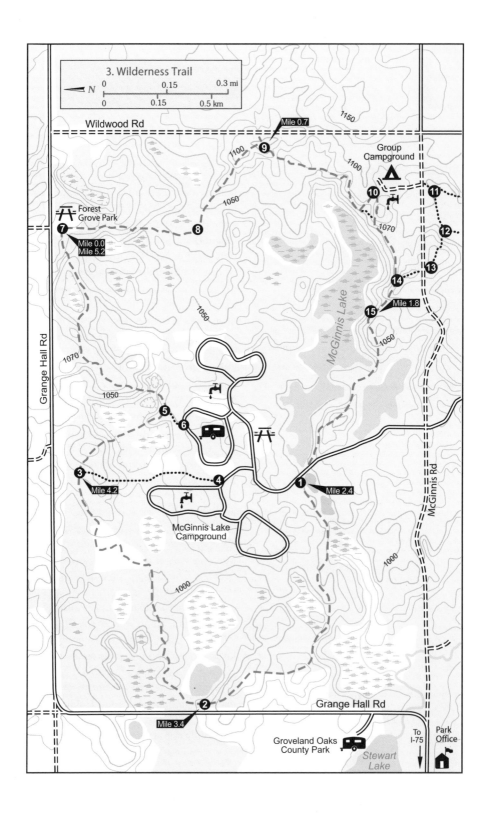

3. Wilderness Trail

N

| 0 | 0.15 | 0.3 mi |

| 0 | 0.15 | 0.5 km |

Wildwood Rd

Mile 0.7

1150

1100

1100

Group
Campground

1050

10

11

Forest
Grove Park

1070

8

12

7

Mile 0.0
Mile 5.2

13

14

McGinnis Lake

Mile 1.8

15

1050

1050

Grange Hall Rd

1070

1050

5

6

3

Mile 4.2

4

1

Mile 2.4

McGinnis Lake
Campground

McGinnis Rd

1000

1000

2

Mile 3.4

Grange Hall Rd

Groveland Oaks
County Park

To
I-75

Park
Office

Stewart
Lake

Two hikers follow the Wilderness Trail in Holly Recreation Area.

Wilderness Trail can be picked up from several places within the recreation area and along several roads that encircle it. This description begins from Forest Grove Park, a Groveland Township park on Grange Hall Road. Depart I-75 at exit 101 and head east onto Grange Hall Road. Just after crossing Dixie Highway, Grange curves to the north (left) and then within a mile curves back to the east (right). Head 1.2 miles east and Groveland Township Hall will be on the right side of the road with the park located behind it. For more information, contact the Holly Recreation Area headquarters (248-634-8811).

TRAIL

Forest Grove Park features parking, play equipment, and a picnic shelter but, unfortunately, no source of drinking water. Located in the back of the township park is post No. 7. The Wilderness Trail is numbered in a clockwise direction. Following it in that direction, you immediately enter the woods along a rolling route through the hilly terrain, a trademark of this trail as much as the numerous marshes and lakes that it weaves past.

You pass three marshes before passing post No. 8 and then make a steady climb to post No. 9, reached at *Mile 0.7*. A short spur heads east (left) to connect the post to Wildwood Road. The main trail heads south (right) and begins the most scenic stretch of the loop. Within a quarter mile you're sidling a ridge high above what looks like a marshy valley below. You then come within sight of McGinnis Lake.

The trail swings east, and at *Mile 1* you pop out at post No. 10, at the edge of the group campground and the hand pump campers use for drinking water. From the

those staying there. The trail stays in the woods, climbing a number of surprisingly large hills and descending past wetlands, ponds, and small lakes. Occasionally you can hear the traffic or even see a house, but this as natural an escape as you're going to find in Oakland County.

Mountain bikers, who have their own trail system in the state park on the west side of I-75, are banned from Wilderness Trail. Hikers will find this trek delightful in April as well as September and mid-October when fall colors peak. In November the views improve with the disappearance of foliage, but in June and July it can get buggy. Just keep moving.

The Wilderness Trail in Holly Recreation Area includes numerous lakes, ponds, wetlands, and marshes.

campground the trail climbs a hill to almost 1,100 feet, where you can look down at what appears to be two lakes—one is the marshy east end of McGinnis Lake—and the ridges that enclose them. It's an incredible view, enjoyed best in April and late October when the foliage is on the ground. A long descent follows, but before you bottom out you arrive at post No. 14, marking the junction with a trail that heads south (left) for Overlook Picnic Area on Wildwood Lake.

This loop heads northeast (right) at the junction and descends another 30 feet before bottoming out at post No. 15 at *Mile 1.8*. Here you can view McGinnis Lake or even follow a short spur north (right) to its marshy shoreline. The main trail continues west (left) and begins with an immediate climb, topping off to views of the open water in the middle of McGinnis Lake. You skirt ridges above the shoreline before finally descending and emerging at the park road to McGinnis Lake Campground. Use the road bridge to cross the dam that created the lake. On the north side or at *Mile 2.4*, you will spot post No. 1, marking where the trail resumes.

The trail immediately reenters the rolling woods, dominated by pine here, skirting a pair of ponds and then a vast cattail marsh, all havens for bird life. Within a half mile from the park road you break out in a grassy meadow and can look down at Stewart Lake and the Groveland Oaks County Park campground on its east side. The trail continues north back into the woods, then swings within view of a house on Van Road. At *Mile 3.4* you arrive at post No. 2, located near the edge of small marshy lake.

The forest is now more hardwood than pine. The next few miles can be stunning in October when the fiery red foliage is framing the muted-brown cattail marshes. The loop swings east beyond post No. 2 and within a half mile moves into a small grassy opening before returning to the woods and reaching post No. 3 at *Mile 4.2*. Here a spur heads south (right) to the modern campground at McGinnis Lake, where there are restrooms and drinking water.

The main trail heads southeast (right), where it begins the longest descent of the day, dropping more than 60 feet to bottom out at a marshy pond. You climb briefly before arriving at post No. 5, where another spur, a considerably shorter one, heads south (right) to the modern campground. The main trail swings northeast and threads its way between two cone-shaped kettles before making a long climb, topping out at 1,080 feet and then skirting a marsh area below.

Shortly after the wetland, you reach Forest Grove Park, returning to post No. 7 at *Mile 5.2*.

4

Haven Hill Natural Area

Place: Highland Recreation Area

Total Distance: 4.8 miles

Hiking Time: 3 to 4 hours

Rating: Moderate

Highlights: Edsel Ford history, hardwood forests, Haven Hill Lake

Maps: Highland Recreation Area Hiking and Ski Trails map from the Michigan DNR, or Haven Hill Blue Trail map from MichiganTrailMaps.com

Trailhead GPS Coordinates: N 42° 38' 5.33" W 083° 33' 4.73"

Looking to escape the pressures of being Henry Ford's only son, and thus sole heir to the Ford Motor Company, Edsel Ford began purchasing hilly property in northwest Oakland County in 1923 and the following year had broken ground on his rural estate. He chose the area because it contained one of the county's highest points, a 1,134-foot-high ridge known as Heaven Hill. Ford renamed it Haven Hill, reflecting the sanctuary that the auto magnate sought.

By 1931 Ford had completed his 6,900-square-foot hilltop lodge and surrounded it with such amenities as a pool, clay tennis courts, a horse-riding stable, a working farm, trails through the woods, and a quarter-mile-long toboggan run with a motorized towrope. Ford and his wife raised their four children at Haven Hill, using the retreat until his death in 1943. Three years later Eleanor Ford sold the estate to the state of Michigan. Eventually Haven Hill became part of the Highland Recreation Area, a 5,903-acre state park unit created in 1972.

The buildings and ruins from the Ford estate lead to Haven Hill being named a state historic site. But the 721-acre tract—which has remained largely undisturbed for the past 75 years—was also designated as a natural area because it contains every principal forest type in southern Michigan, including cedar and tamarack swamps, beech-maple forests, and oak-hickory forests.

In 1976, Haven Hill was registered as a National Natural Landmark by the National Park Service, one of only 12 in Michigan. This combination of history and nature in a

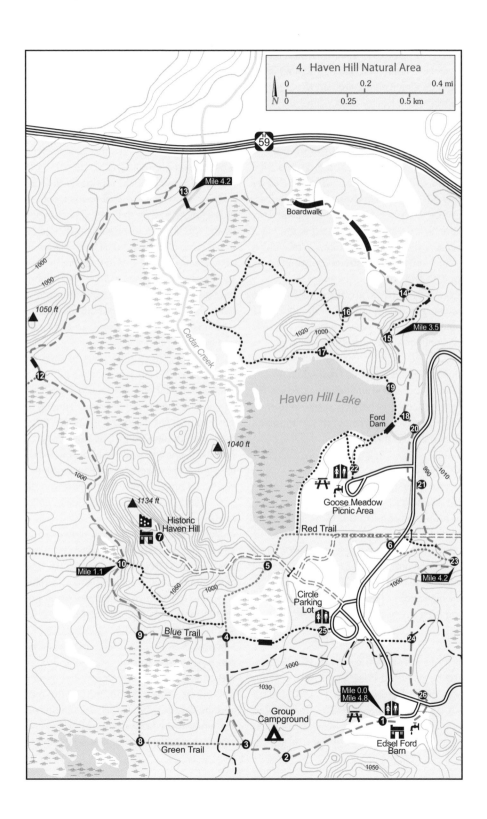

4. Haven Hill Natural Area

0   0.2   0.4 mi
0   0.25   0.5 km

M 59

Mile 4.2
13
Boardwalk

14
16
Mile 3.5
15
17
1050 ft
1000
1000
1020 1000
Cedar Creek
12
Haven Hill Lake
19
18
Ford Dam
20
990 1010
1040 ft
22
21
1134 ft
Goose Meadow Picnic Area
Historic Haven Hill
7
Red Trail
6
1000
10
Mile 1.1
5
23
Mile 4.2
1050 1000
Circle Parking Lot
25
9
Blue Trail
4
24
1000
Group Campground
1030
Mile 0.0
Mile 4.8
26
1
8
Green Trail
3
2
Edsel Ford Barn
1050

setting accessible mostly by trails makes Haven Hill unique and one of the most interesting destinations in southern Michigan for day hikers and history buffs.

The principal trail in the Haven Hill Natural Area is a loop that encircles Haven Hill Lake, with two cutoff spurs that create shorter trails. The entire loop is a 5.2-mile hike marked as the Green Trail. Slightly shorter is the 4.8-mile loop marked as the Blue Trail; the Red Trail is 2.15 miles. The Blue Trail is the hike described here as it is the most scenic and drier than the Green Trail, which is often wet along the stretch between posts No. 3, 8, and 9.

Mountain bikes are banned from the system, and during the winter the loops are popular cross-country ski trails when there is sufficient snow. The drawback is that equestrians share short segments of the system with hikers—and Highland Recreation Area is extremely popular with horseback riders. Be prepared for a few horses on the weekends and a more than a few mounds of droppings in the middle of the trail.

ACCESS

The park drive provides access to the Haven Hill Natural Area. The Edsel Ford Barn parking area is reached from M-59 (Highland Road) 15 miles west of Pontiac. There is a vehicle entry fee at Highland Recreation Area. For more information, contact Highland Recreation Area (248-889-3750; www.michigan.gov/highland) or Friends of Highland Recreation Area (www.friendsofhighlandrec.org).

TRAIL

All three loops at the Haven Hill Natural Area begin at the Edsel Ford Barn parking area. When Ford built the 15,000-square foot barn in the early 1930s, it was one of the largest east of the Mississippi River and could house 1,500 sheep. In 2008,

two-thirds of the building was blown down by high winds, but the rest is being restored through the efforts of the Friends of Highland Recreation Area.

From the parking area, the loop heads west across a field and then dips into the woods near a pair of vault toilets. In less than a half mile the Green Trail peels off at post No. 3, and the Blue Trail swings north (right). At post No. 4 the Blue Trail heads west (left) at the junction while the Red Trail continues north (right). For additional mileage or to see the remains of Edsel Ford's Haven Hill estate, continue on the Red Trail to post No. 5, where you head west and ascend the ridge along a paved service drive that is now closed to vehicles. From post No. 4 it is a 0.6-mile walk up Haven Hill to the impressive Carriage House and the ruins of Ford's lodge.

The Blue Trail heads west to post No. 9, where the Green Trail merges into it and the two loops then swing north (right). The scenery gets interesting here with a long descent to post No. 10, reached at *Mile 1.1*. At this junction the Green Trail departs to the west (left) and the Red Trail continues north (right) around a wetland and small pond. In late fall, if enough foliage is down, you can occasionally see the Carriage House on top of Haven Hill.

Wetlands and wooded hollows follow, and even a bit of seclusion. When you reach post No. 12 at *Mile 1.7*, you are in the heart of the natural area. Wetlands and rolling hills dominate the 1.5-mile stretch between post No. 12 and post No. 14. At *Mile 2.2* you reach post No. 13, where the trail crosses a bridge over Cedar Creek. In the next mile you twice cross long boardwalks through wetlands. There are occasional sounds of traffic from nearby M-59, but for the most part the natural beauty and quiet remoteness you encounter here in one of Michigan's most overdeveloped counties is amazing.

A boardwalk trail through the Haven Hill Natural Area in Highland Recreation Area.

The ruins of Edsel Ford's Haven Hill mansion in Highland Recreation Area.

Post No. 14 is reached at *Mile 3.2* at a junction that can be a bit confusing. The Blue Trail swings to the west (right) here to climb a hill, then turns sharply east at post No. 16 to descend it. Look for trail markers at the four-way junction at post No. 16 to stay on course.

At post No. 15, reached at *Mile 3.5*, you leave the natural area and head south toward Ford Dam. Ford installed the dam in 1926 to convert a small stream and marshy pond into a waterfowl sanctuary he named Haven Hill Lake. The Blue Trail swings east at post No. 18 just before reaching the dam and at post No. 20 crosses the lake's outlet stream. You cross the paved entrance road to Goose Meadow Day-Use Area and then the park road immediately after, marked by post No. 21.

Now on the east side of the park road, post No. 23 is reached at *Mile 4.2* and marks where the Red Trail merges into the main loop. The Blue Trail then heads to the west and then south, crossing the park road once more just before returning to the Edsel Ford Barn, reached at *Mile 4.8*.

5

Penosha Trail

Place: Brighton Recreation Area

Total Distance: 5 miles

Hiking Time: 2.5 to 3 hours

Rating: Moderate

Highlights: Hardwood forest, fall colors

Maps: Bishop Lake Trail System map from the Michigan DNR, or Penosha Trail map from MichiganTrailMaps.com

Trailhead GPS Coordinates: N 42° 30' 2.72" W 083° 50' 6.80"

The actions of both an ice age 25,000 years ago and some unsuccessful farmers in the 1930s resulted in an undeveloped tract in Livingston County where today you can go for a 5-mile walk in the woods to escape the concrete and crowds of southeast Michigan.

The glaciers of the Pleistocene epoch were responsible for Brighton Recreation Area's rolling topography of moraines and ridges, steep-sided kettles, and numerous lakes and ponds. As towns such as Brighton and Howell grew in the 1800s, woodlands were cleared, and farms developed but were never very productive. It was a challenge to make a living by plowing land characterized by glacial drift and wetlands. During the Depression of the 1930s, it became impossible, and farmers began selling out or, in many cases, simply abandoning their property. The state purchased much of Brighton Recreation Area between 1944 and 1949 and continues to add parcels from year to year. The 4,947-acre unit still has a patchwork appearance, though, as private lots break up its continuity.

The largest contiguous section lies on the east side of Chilson Road and is the site of the park's three campgrounds, frontier cabins, and trail system. *Penosha* is the Chippewa word for "long," as opposed to *kawchin,* which means "short" and is the name for the 2-mile loop that shares the same trailhead.

Penosha is not a spectacular walk. For most people this 5-mile trail is a two-and-a-half- to three-hour hike through a hardwood

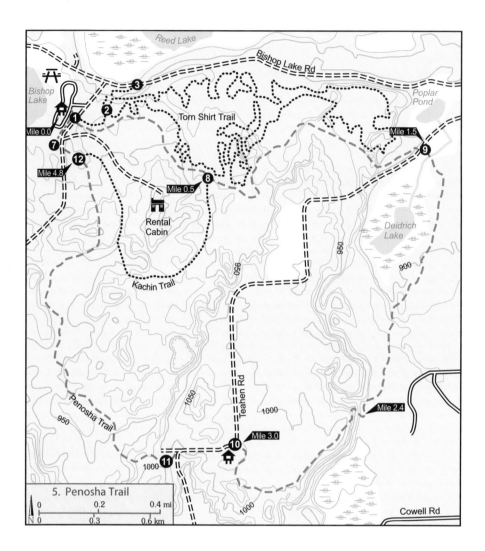

Reed Lake

Bishop Lake Rd

Poplar Pond

Bishop Lake

3

2

1

Mile 0.0

Torn Shirt Trail

Mile 1.5

9

7

12

Mile 4.8

8

Mile 0.5

Rental Cabin

Deidrich Lake

950

900

Kachin Trail

950

Penosha Trail

1050

950

Teahen Rd

1000

Mile 2.4

Mile 3.0

10

11

1000

Cowell Rd

1000

5. Penosha Trail

N
0   0.2   0.4 mi
0   0.3   0.6 km

forest of maple, hickory, and oak. There are many lakes within the park, but the scenery along this walk does not include any of them. Still, the land is interesting and the trees impressive, and together they provide for a pleasant afternoon in the forest with only a few human-made intrusions in view. That includes mountain bikers. Since the late 1990s, they have had their own trail system at Brighton Recreation Area and are prohibited from Penosha.

Wildlife in this area includes white-tailed deer, fox, pheasant, quail, and partridge, but to spot any you have to take to the trail in the early morning or at dusk and maintain a quiet pace. Most Saturday-afternoon outings will flush out little more than a few squirrels or a raccoon.

The trail is well marked by posts with blue dots and maps at all major junctions, making it easy to follow. The numerous ponds and small marshes along the route make it buggy at times in late June and early July. The best seasons to hike are spring and fall. By early April the snow is gone and wildflowers begin to emerge; by May morel mushroom hunters can be seen poking the ground with long sticks. In the fall leaves begin turning between late September and early October, peaking at the end of that month and lingering on well into November. The trail receives its heaviest use during that period, but even on a bright and crisp weekend, you'll see only a handful of other hikers.

ACCESS

From I-96 head south on Grand River Road (exit 145) into Brighton, and from US 23 head west on Lee Road (exit 60) and then north on Rickett Road. Once downtown, turn west on West Main Street, which quickly becomes Brighton Road, and follow it for 3 miles to the posted junction with Chilson Road. The park headquarters is 1.5 miles south on Chilson on the west side of the road. Call the park office (810-229-6566) for a trail map or the stage of fall colors.

Across from the headquarters is Bishop Lake Road, which winds pass Bishop Lake Campground and then 1.1 miles from Chilson Road reaches a day-use area. The facility features picnic tables, modern restrooms, and a fine view of the east half of Bishop Lake. At the back of the parking area is the trailhead to both the park's hiking trails and its mountain bike system.

TRAIL

On the east side of the large parking area of the Bishop Lake Day-Use Area, (not to be confused with the Bishop Lake Campground) is a large display area with a map that serves as the trailhead for both the hiking and mountain biking trails.

Penosha is a loop that is numbered in a clockwise direction. You share the trail with mountain bikers for only a few yards then quickly reach post No. 1, where they head left and you head right. A few more yards and post No. 7 arrives; here the Penosha Trail splits. Head east (right) and you'll immediately arrive at Rolison Trail, the dirt road that heads south to the group campground and rental cabins. Within 100 yards of crossing Rolison Trail, you have escaped into the woods, following a wide path in a rolling topography of predominantly oaks. The trail is

Encountering white-tailed deer is common at Brighton Recreation Area.

marked by blue and yellow dots, because you are also following the Kahchin Trail.

After the first good climb of the day, you bottom out on the other side at post No. 8 at *Mile 0.5*, the junction where Kahchin Trail splits to the south. Just beyond the post Penosha Trail passes what appears to be a long row of boulders. This is the most visible stone fence remaining from the old farms. The fences not only represented property boundaries between farms but were usually convenient places to stack boulders left by the glaciers and removed by the farmers while plowing their fields. The terrain becomes hillier, and at *Mile 0.8* the trail skirts a series of kettles, wooded hollows created by the glacial activity. Some are dry at the bottom; others are marshy and good places to look for wildlife.

At *Mile 1.2* you top off on a ridgeline. An old two-track once headed south along it to a viewing point but is nearly impossible to find now. Penosha Trail continues east, passing through more regenerating fields, semi-open forests with large maples and hickory trees, and kettles on both sides of the path. Eventually, you parallel Teahen Road from above, finally descending to the dirt road via a staircase. On the other side of the road is post No. 9, reached at *Mile 1.5*. You immediately cross a creek that is unbridged and can be muddy in the spring, then pass a unmarked junction. Keep right to enter a more mature forest, and soon you're wondering if you'll spot Deidrich Lake.

You won't. You come close to the east side of this small marshy lake, but the forest is thick here and the leaves prevent you from

spotting it most of the year. For the next mile, the hike remains in the forest and becomes a stroll along the hilly terrain. At one point, you skirt the base of a steep slope. Then at *Mile 2.4* the trail makes a 180-degree turn and ascends to the top of the heavily forested ridge for the most interesting stretch of the day. You steadily climb for a quarter mile and pass the first home of the trek before topping off at 1,035 feet in a grassy field.

You return to wooded hills and make a final climb, topping off at a grassy knoll where you can peer down into the surrounding forest. On a clear October afternoon this is a beautiful place to take a break. Within a few steps, or at *Mile 3*, you arrive at post No. 10, marking a small parking area off Teahen Road. Blue dot posts direct you to head left down Teahen Road. Within a quarter mile a HIKING TRAIL sign directs you to cross a gravel driveway to post No. 11, where you return to a footpath.

You immediately climb a small hill, pass a home, and then follow a fencerow past the back sides of some rather impressive houses. But within a quarter mile of Teahen Road you're back in the woods and away from any signs of civilization.

At *Mile 3.8* you make a long descent that bottoms out between two marshy ponds, the one on the left the largest of the day and filled with croaking of spring peppers in April and May. A long climb follows and tops off with you skirting a large meadow from above and then a smaller one. At *Mile 4.75* you reach post No. 12, where the Kahchin Trail returns, and then immediately re-cross Rolison Trail. The trailhead and day-use parking area are only a couple hundred yards away.

6

River and Blue Trails

Place: Proud Lake Recreation Area

Total Distance: 5.75 miles

Hiking Time: 2 to 3 hours

Rating: Easy

Highlights: Huron River, wetlands, spring wildflowers

Maps: Proud Lake Recreation Area map from the Michigan DNR, or River Trail/Blue Trail map from MichiganTrailMaps.com

Trailhead GPS Coordinates: N 42° 34' 29.49" W 083° 33' 29.24"

Proud Lake is a 4,700-acre state recreation area in the southwest corner of Oakland County whose terrain ranges from rolling dense forests and vast wetlands to a chain of lakes and 3.5 miles of the Huron River. Practically on the doorstep of Milford, Proud Lake draws a good number of hikers along with paddlers, campers, cross-country skiers in the winter when snow is sufficient, and even fly anglers in the spring, who arrive for a special catch-and-release trout season.

The heart of the park, and all its hiking trails, extends from Proud Lake west along the Huron River valley to Wixom Road. The main trailhead is located in the large day-use parking area just down the road from the park headquarters and near the organization campground. But this loop begins at the fishing access site where Wixom Road crosses the Huron River. It includes the River Trail.

Although not often shown on maps, this path is by far the most scenic in the park and is the only one that allows you to hike along the Huron River. The trail winds through extensive wetlands; park staff are constantly working to maintain its many boardwalks and bridges. Check on the trail's status and plan to get your boots wet.

River Trail is an interesting hike any time of the year but particularly in the spring when the Huron River is stocked with full-sized rainbow and brown trout in a program to introduce anglers to fly fishing. Fishing is catch-and-release, flies-only from Wixom Road to Moss Lake in April. Hikers will see not only the graceful casts of fly anglers but the trout as well. At this time of the year the

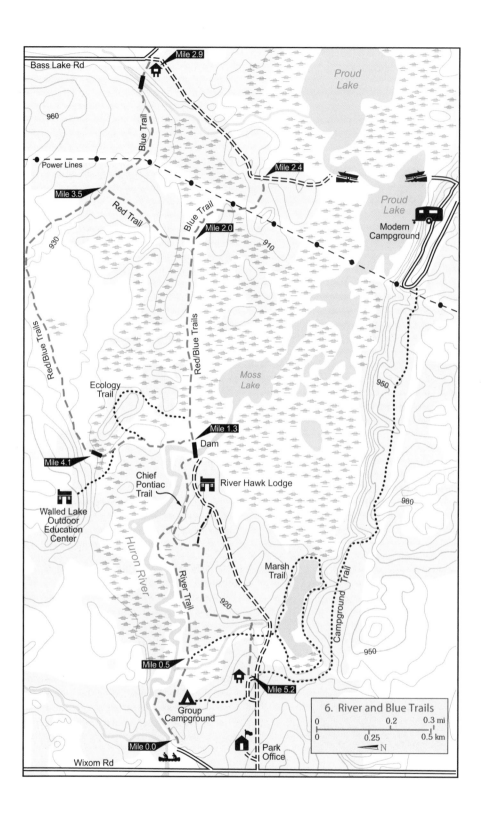

Bass Lake Rd

Mile 2.9

Proud Lake

960

Blue Trail

Power Lines

Mile 2.4

Mile 3.5

Red Trail

Blue Trail

Mile 2.0

930

Proud Lake

910

Modern Campground

Red/Blue Trails

Red/Blue Trails

Moss Lake

950

Ecology Trail

Mile 1.3

Mile 4.1

Dam

Chief Pontiac Trail

River Hawk Lodge

Walled Lake Outdoor Education Center

980

Huron River

Marsh Trail

River Trail

Campground Trail

920

Mile 0.5

950

Mile 5.2

Group Campground

Mile 0.0

Park Office

Wixom Rd

6. River and Blue Trails

0   0.2   0.3 mi
0   0.25   0.5 km
N

Huron River has the clarity of a trout stream in northern Michigan, and it's easy to spot the 10-to-25-inch-long rainbows and browns in the current.

Overall this hike is an easy trek through the vast wetlands and rolling wooded terrain that make up most of this state park. If you begin and end from the main trailhead in the day-use parking lot, the loop is reduced to 4.8 miles.

ACCESS

Proud Lake Recreation Area is just east of Milford or 12 miles southwest of Pontiac. The main entrance is reached from I-96 by heading north on Wixom Road (exit 159) for 6 miles, or from M-59 by heading south on Duck Lake Road for 6.5 miles. Duck Lake Road turns into Wixom Road at Proud Lake Recreation Area; the fishing access site, where this hike starts, is just on the south side of the Huron River off Wixom Road.

A vehicle permit or annual state park pass is required to enter the recreation area. For more information, contact the park office (248-685-2433) or the Friends of Proud Lake (www.friendsofproudlake.org) to find out about organized hikes and interpretive walks.

TRAIL

From the parking lot at the fishing access site, a trail departs east into the woods and begins by hugging the Huron River for a quarter mile. In April the anglers seen here are using flies and wading through the gentle current. Later in the summer they are often casing spinners in the hope of catching smallmouth bass.

Within a quarter mile you arrive at a dock in the Huron River and a shelter where the trail swings inland to a vault toilet and a posted spur trail to the Pines Organization Campground. Continue east (left). At *Mile*

A fly angler in the Huron River at Proud Lake Recreation Area.

0.5 you pass a posted junction to the day-use parking area; stay with the main trail (left). The next stretch is fascinating, a series of bridges and boardwalks through a wooded wetland where in the spring wildflowers are popping up everywhere.

At *Mile 1* River Trail arrives at Chief Pontiac Trail, a wide path marked by a variety of colors (red, blue, green, orange) and featuring a handful of interpretive displays. Continue east (left) and at *Mile 1.2* you'll return to the banks of the Huron River, where you'll find a picnic table and then the Huron River Dam, which forms Moss Lake.

The dam is usually closed off to vehicle traffic and makes for a very scenic spot. A

A belly-boat angler prepares to fish after hiking into a stretch of the Huron River in Proud Lake Recreation Area.

large footbridge arches across the Huron River, and from the middle of it you can see the massive cattail marshes that surround Moss Lake. This is also where the trout are released. Throughout much of April you can see hundreds of them in the pools just below the dam—and usually an angler or two trying to entice them with streamers and nymphs.

On the east side of the bridge you continue east on the Red/Blue Trail. Stay right at the next two junctions; the first is where the loop returns, and the second where the Ecology Trail splits off. Red/Blue Trail moves through more wetlands but stays surprisingly dry and at *Mile 2* arrives at the junction where the Red Trail splits off to the north.

The Blue Trail continues east and is well marked. Within a quarter mile it climbs into an open area to pass underneath a set of power lines. At *Mile 2.4* you arrive at the dirt access road to a boat launch on Proud Lake. Head north (left) on the well-graded road for almost a half mile to a yellow gate near the corner of Bass Lake Road. The gate at *Mile 2.9* marks the spot where the Blue Trail resumes by heading west into the park.

You immediately descend to a footbridge across a stream and then briefly follow a low ridgeline above the wet area the creek creates. At *Mile 3.3* you pass back underneath the power lines and at *Mile 3.5* arrive at the posted junction with the Red Trail. Continue west (right) if you want to avoid backtracking.

The loop immediately crosses another bridge over a stream and then skirts a wetland for a spell. Here the trail winds through an infusion of horsetails, a primitive perennial plant with dark-green hollow segmented stems but no true leaves. Usually found near standing water or wet areas, horsetail stems have sand embedded in their tissue and were often used by early American settlers for scouring pots and pans. This gritty texture gives the plant its common name, scouring rush.

At *Mile 3.9* you arrive at the corner of a fallow field and step over what appears to be an old stone fence. The trail quickly snakes back into the woods and within a quarter mile swings south to cross a wetland area on a long boardwalk. You climb out the other side to a posted junction. If you headed west (right), within a third of a mile you'd climb a ridge to the Walled Lake Outdoor Education Center, a large complex whose rope course and zip line are impressive.

The Red/Blue Trail continues in a southerly direction (left) to quickly pass the posted Ecology Trail and then skirt the Huron River along a boardwalk before arriving back at the dam at *Mile 4.5*. Re-cross the footbridge and backtrack along the Chief Pontiac Trail, this time following it all the way to emerge in the main trailhead parking area at *Mile 5.2*. The easiest way to return to the Wixom Road access site is to hike to the organization campground and then head west on the River Trail for the final half mile of this hike.

7

Crooked Lake Trail

Place: Pinckney Recreation Area

Total Distance: 5.1 miles

Hiking Time: 2.5 to 3 hours

Rating: Moderate

Highlights: Lakes, scenic vista

Maps: Pinckney Recreation Biking and Hiking Trails map from the Michigan DNR, or Crooked Lake Trail map from MichiganTrailMaps.com

Trailhead GPS Coordinates: N 42° 25' 0.35" W 083° 57' 51.36"

The best hiking in southeastern Michigan is in Pinckney Recreation Area, and the Crooked Lake Trail is one reason why. This 5.1-mile loop is a pleasant walk that traverses hardwood forests, marshes, and grassy hillsides. Along the way, you pass three inland lakes, climb to 1,008 feet for a view of Crooked Lake, and plunge down a ridge forested in hardwoods that make this path especially scenic in October.

But the nicest feature of this trail is its proximity to several urban areas, including Jackson, Ann Arbor, and western Detroit. Because of Pinckney Recreation Area, hikers from here don't have to drive all day just to find a scenic trail on state land.

This location also draws a large number of mountain bikers looking for suitable terrain to pursue their activity. In 1990 the park staff instituted regulations that required bikers to follow Crooked Lake in a clockwise direction and hikers walk in a counterclockwise direction.

By following these regulations, at least you have time to react to bikers speeding toward you. If encounters with even conscientious cyclists, who pull over to allow hikers to pass, disturb your walk, find another trail. Crooked Lake and the park's Potawatomi Trail draw more mountain bike activity than any other routes in southeastern Michigan and maybe any other trail in the state. Within 10,201-acre Pinckney Recreation Area is the Losee Lake Trail, a 3.3-mile loop that begins in the Silver Lake Day-Use Area and is for hikers only.

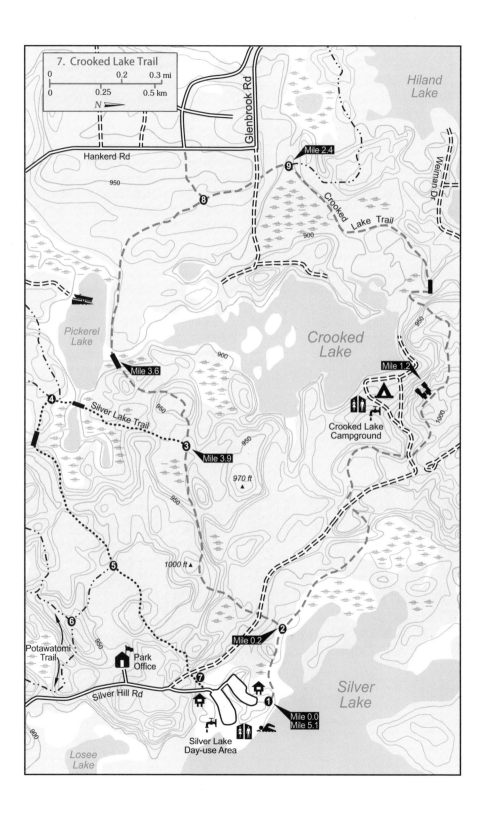

7. Crooked Lake Trail

0   0.2   0.3 mi
0   0.25   0.5 km
N

Glenbrook Rd

Hiland Lake

Mile 2.4

9

8

950

Hankerd Rd

Crooked
Lake Trail

900

Weiman Dr

950

Crooked
Lake

Mile 3.6

Mile 1.2

950

Pickerel
Lake

1000

4

Silver Lake Trail

Crooked Lake
Campground

950

3

Mile 3.9

950

950

970 ft

5

1000 ft

6

2

Mile 0.2

Potawatomi
Trail

950

Park
Office

Silver
Lake

7

Silver Hill Rd

1

Mile 0.0
Mile 5.1

900

Losee
Lake

Silver Lake
Day-use Area

Along with October, when fall colors peak, mid-May is a pleasant time to walk this trail—the ponds and marshes are ringed by wildflowers, and waterfowl can often be sighted on the lakes. These same low-lying areas make the area a little buggy in late June through July, although not excessively bad.

ACCESS

Pinckney Recreation Area is northwest of Ann Arbor and straddles the border between Livingston and Washtenaw Counties. From I-94, depart at exit 159 and head north on M-52 for 6 miles to North Territorial Road, where you turn right (east). The Silver Lake day-use area is reached by turning left (north) on Dexter-Townhall Road, which is reached in 5 miles, and then left at Silver Hill Road where the park entrance is posted. Dexter-Townhall Road can also be reached north of Ann Arbor from US 23 by departing west on North Territorial Road (exit 49) and heading west for 12 miles, or by exiting I-94 at Baker Road (exit 167) and continuing north on Dexter Pinckney Road to North Territorial.

Just before entering the day-use area, you pass the park headquarters (734-426-4913), where you can find information about the park's trails, campgrounds, and other facilities. As at all state parks, a vehicle permit or annual state pass is required to enter the recreation area.

TRAIL

There are two posted trailheads in the day-use area. The upper parking lot trailhead serves hikers for the Crooked Lake, Potawatomi, and Silver Lake Trails. The trail descends to skirt Silver Lake, weaving between low-lying wet areas and young stands

Hikers begin the Crooked Lake Trail in Pinckney Recreation Area.

of trees and then passing the return trail within a quarter mile at post No. 2. You continue straight. Although you can hear boaters and water-skiers on the main body of the lake, the trail is following a narrow inlet of its western shore where in spring and fall a variety of waterfowl can be sighted.

At **Mile 0.5** the trail swings west and begins a long ascent away from the lake to cross Silver Hill Road. On the other side of the road, the trail cuts through an older stand of oak and breaks out on a grassy ridge, where you have a good view of Pinckney Recreation Area's rugged interior. The trail crosses the dirt access road to Crooked Lake Campground, and then climbs to a high point of 1,008 feet. At **Mile 1.2** you'll find a view of Crooked Lake and the surrounding ridges and a bench to sit and enjoy it from. The only intrusion here is a power line that passes through.

From the viewpoint, the trail makes a half-mile descent, passing a mileage post (Mile 9) and a few more glimpses of the lake along the way, and bottoms out at a bridged creek that flows between a small pond to the north and Crooked Lake. Just beyond this creek, you arrive at post No. 9 at **Mile 2.4**. Hikers continuing on the 17.5-mile Potawatomi Trail would head north (right). The Crooked Lake loop swings south (left), crosses another bridge, and then makes a gentle climb to Glenbrook Road, a private drive.

On the other side of the road, the trail remains in the woods as it winds toward the south end of Crooked Lake. At post No. 8 is a spur that heads east (right) to the day-use area on Halfmoon Lake.

Eventually you swing east and skirt a ridge while overlooking Pickerel, the third lake along the way. The structure at the west end is a fishing pier; at the east end is a footbridge along the Silver Lake Trail. You descend the ridge to an even more impressive footbridge across the small river between

Trail runners on the Crooked Lake Trail in the Pinckney Recreation Area.

Pickerel and Crooked Lakes. Reached at **Mile 3.6**, the bridge makes a nice spot to sit and enjoy the view of the two lakes and surrounding ridges.

From the stream, you climb a pair of hills and in a third of a mile come to post No. 3, marking the junction of Silver Lake and Crooked Lake Trails. Continue east (straight), and soon you'll be following a ridge and looking down at marsh ponds on both sides before ascending to a high point of 970 feet. The trail makes a steady descent from here and soon crosses Silver Hill Road for the second time at **Mile 4.8**. On the other side of the road, you pass yet another small pond and return to post No. 2, where the upper parking lot trailhead is reached in a quarter mile by heading south (right).

8

Lakeview and Oak Woods Loop

Place: Waterloo Recreation Area

Total Distance: 3.6 miles

Hiking Time: 2 hours

Highlights: Geology center, scenic overlooks, Mill Lake

Maps: Discovery Center Hiking Trails map from the Michigan DNR, or Lakeview/Oak Woods Loop from MichiganTrailMaps.com

Trailhead GPS Coordinates: N 42° 19' 19.98" W 084° 5' 11.66"

Short trails through diverse terrain and an interesting interpretive center attract hikers from throughout southern Michigan to the Gerald E. Eddy Discovery Center. The center is located in the southeast corner of the Waterloo Recreation Area, a state park lying between Jackson and Ann Arbor. It includes almost 20,000 acres of lakes, wetlands, and some of the most rugged country in this corner of the state.

Originally a nature center that was closed due to state budget constraints, the facility was reopened in 1989 as a tribute to Gerald Eddy, a former chief of the Geological Survey Division. At one time Eddy was also the director of the Department of Conservation, the forerunner to the DNR. The center reflects his career in geology and his dedication to preserving Michigan's natural areas.

The center features two main exhibit rooms, with the first devoted to geology. Displays include a model ice cave where visitors can see themselves standing next to a giant beaver or Jefferson mammoth, or get the latest ice age "weather report." There's a "Fossil Graveyard" featuring lift-a-rock models of fossilized bones and teeth and touch-screen computer games that will teach and test your knowledge of Michigan geology.

The second exhibit room is devoted to the human and natural history of the state recreation area. Displays range from a dugout canoe and a large collection of fluted spear points that Paleo-Indian hunters used in the Waterloo area, to exhibits on the habitats and wildlife that will be encountered while hiking the Discovery Center trails.

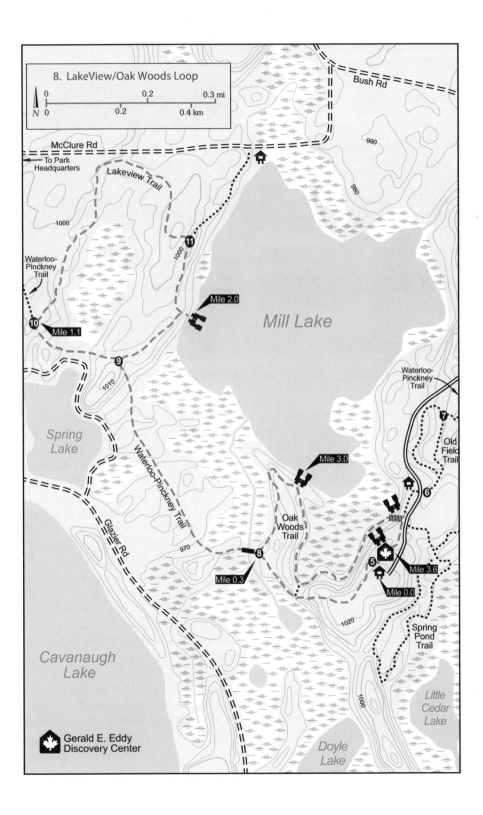

8. LakeView/Oak Woods Loop

N
0   0.2   0.3 mi
0   0.2   0.4 km

Bush Rd

990

990

McClure Rd

To Park
Headquarters

Lakeview Trail

1000

1000

Waterloo-
Pinckney
Trail

Mill Lake

11

Mile 2.0

10

Mile 1.1

9

1010

Spring
Lake

Waterloo-
Pinckney Trail

Waterloo-
Pinckney
Trail

1020

7

Old
Field
Trail

Mile 3.0

6

Oak
Woods
Trail

5

Mile 3.6

8

Mile 0.3

Mile 0.0

Glazier Rd

970

Cavanaugh
Lake

1020

Spring
Pond
Trail

1000

Little
Cedar
Lake

Gerald E. Eddy
Discovery Center

Doyle
Lake

The Gerald E. Eddy Discovery Center at the Waterloo Recreation Area focuses on the geology of Michigan.

An auditorium showing a multi-image program and an observation deck with spotting scopes aimed at Mill Lake round out this interesting interpretive center.

All this new knowledge can be put to good use with a hike along one of the center's six trails. The best outing is to combine the Oak Woods and Lakeview Trails, a 3.6-mile walk that includes several viewing points of Mill Lake. The easy trails combine with a visit to the discovery center make this hike an excellent choice for families with young children.

ACCESS

Located among the rolling hills of Waterloo Recreation Area, the center is between Jackson and Ann Arbor. It is reached from I-94 by departing north onto Pierce Road (exit 157). Brown park signs lead you north along Pierce Road, then west (left) on Bush Road to the entrance of the parking area. From Memorial Day to Labor Day the center (734-475-3170; www.michigan.gov/eddycenter) is open Monday through Saturday 10 AM to 5 PM; Sunday noon to 5 PM. The rest of the year it is closed on Monday. A vehicle permit or annual state pass is required to enter the recreation area and can be purchased at the discovery center.

TRAIL

Pick up the Oak Woods Trail near the interpretive center where it is marked by post No. 5 in upper parking lot. Heading west the trail follows a ridge, a glacial moraine left over from the last ice age. Glaciers swept through here 10,000 years ago, then retreated to leave the rugged hills and ridges found throughout Waterloo Recreation Area as well as lakes such as Mill Lake. Within a quarter mile, a bench has been located at the spot where the oak-hickory forest opens up to views of ponds and lakes.

From this overlook, you are viewing just part of one of the largest concentrations of bogs in southern Michigan, lying south of Mill Lake and the moraine you are following. The open water of the small ponds is slowly being covered up by a bog–a floating layer of plants, mosses, and shrubs, including the carnivorous pitcher plant. The best trail for viewing this environment is the center's Bog Trail, often referred to as a floating trail because it ends as a boardwalk on the delicate layer of plants.

Oak Woods Trail continues in a westerly direction and within a third of a mile from the Discovery Center arrives at post No. 8, marking its junction with the Waterloo-Pinckney Trail. This long-distance route stretches 35 miles from Portage Lake in Waterloo Recreation Area to Silver Lake in Pinckney Recreation Area. Head west (left) and follow it to reach Lakeview Trail.

You immediately use a footbridge to cross a stream. Here the trail becomes a level and pleasant walk through a deciduous forest to post No. 9. Head west (left) at this junction and you'll pass a private cabin on Spring Lake and then arrive at post No. 10 at *Mile 1.1*.

Here the two trails split, the Waterloo-Pinckney Trail heading in a westerly direction (left) and the Lakeview Trail north (right), where it swings near McClure Road and then passes open fields and scrub that was the site of a golf course in the 1920s. In late spring these open areas are covered in wildflowers.

An observation deck overlooking Mill Lake at Waterloo Recreation Area.

Lakeview and Oak Woods Loop

At **Mile 1.8** you arrive at post No. 11, where a spur heads north (left) to the Lakeview Trailhead on McClure Road. The main loop heads south (right) to follow a ridge and within a quarter mile passes a short path that descends to the shoreline of Mill Lake. The main trail continues along the ridge, passing more views of the large lake until it returns to post No. 9 at **Mile 2.2**.

Retrace your steps to post No. 8, but this time head north (left) at the junction and immediately climb a ridge. At **Mile 3** is a bench overlooking Mill Lake, a scenic spot to take a snack break. Oak Woods Trail descends and swings away from the lake, passes a short crossover spur, and at **Mile 3.5** arrives at a long stairway featuring a bench in the middle for one last view of Mill Lake. At the top is the paved path from the lower parking lot. Head right on it and you'll be back at the discovery center in minutes.

Lake Huron

9

Port Crescent Trail

Place: Port Crescent State Park

Total Distance: 2.3 miles

Hiking Time: 1.5 to 2 hours

Rating: Easy

Highlights: Sand dunes, overlooks

Maps: Port Crescent State Park map from the Michigan DNR, or Port Crescent Trail map from MichiganTrailMaps.com

Trailhead GPS Coordinates: N 44° 0' 24.88" W 083° 3' 7.66"

To historians, Port Crescent was a thriving lumbering and fishing town in the mid-1800s. To summer travelers, Port Crescent is a state park with one of the most beautiful beaches on the east side of the state. But to hikers, this preserved tract of windblown dunes, wooded hills, and Saginaw Bay shoreline is the destination for the most scenic and interesting hike in the Thumb region of Michigan.

The sand dunes here and elsewhere along Lake Huron are nowhere near the stature of those along the west side of the state. But in Port Crescent they are high enough to provide sweeping panoramas of the bay, of the miles of shoreline, and of the valley carved by the Pinnebog River. Most people never expect to find such overlooks in the flatland of the Thumb. Hikers take to the trails March through December, relinquishing them only to skiers in the winter. October is unquestionably the best time, since the park is empty of campers and sun worshippers, and the fall colors of the oaks and maples that forest the dunes reach their brilliant peak. If you come in the early morning or at dusk during the fall, you might even spot a deer or two feeding on the acorns along the path.

The trail, a 2.3-mile loop with a 0.3-mile cutoff spur, lies in an area of the park completely surrounded by water, with the Pinnebog River to the west, Saginaw Bay to the north, and the Old Pinnebog River channel everywhere else. The access point used here is from the campground, where a chimney monument and display recount the story

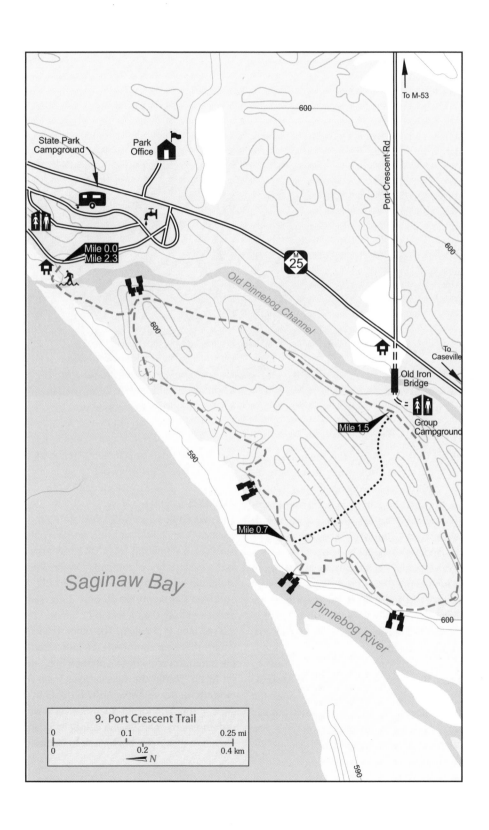

To M-53

Port Crescent Rd

600

600

State Park
Campground

Park
Office

Mile 0.0
Mile 2.3

Old Pinnebog Channel

M 25

600

To
Caseville

Old Iron
Bridge

Mile 1.5

Group
Campground

600

590

Mile 0.7

Saginaw Bay

Pinnebog River

600

590

9. Port Crescent Trail

| 0 | | 0.1 | | | 0.25 mi |

| 0 | | 0.2 | | | 0.4 km |

N

Sand dunes at Port Crescent State Park are among the tallest on the east side of the state.

behind Port Crescent. The town's heyday was in the mid-1800s, when there were almost 700 residents working at Pack Woods Sawmill and two salt mines. The town vanished by the 1930s, with only a portion of the sawmill's 120-foot chimney remaining as a testimony to its industrial past.

What replaced industry was nature, in the form of the 640-acre state park that was dedicated in 1963. Port Crescent features 3 miles of beach—where the sand is almost pure white—the tallest dunes on Lake Huron, a shoreline campground, a day-use area, and the network of trails—often the only place to escape the summer crowds that fill the park. By using the cutoff spur, you can shorten the hike to either a 1.3- or 1.1-mile walk, but you would then miss some of the overlooks. The entire loop is an easy trek with only gentle climbing that can be handled by children as young as five or six years old.

ACCESS

The park (989-738-8663) is located 5 miles west of Port Austin on M-25 and is split in half by the Pinnebog River. The trail area is in the eastern half of the park. One trailhead is the old iron bridge at the corner of M-25 and Port Crescent Road, providing direct access to both the blue loop (1.3 miles) and the red loop (1.1 miles). The other trailhead, where this description starts, is located in the campground, whose entrance is posted on M-25. Begin the hike across from the modern restroom between two beachfront sites. If the campground is not overflowing with too many vehicles and campers for your pleasure, this is the best place to begin the loop. A vehicle permit or annual state pass is required to enter the state park.

TRAIL

From the beautiful beach on Saginaw Bay, you kick off your shoes or boots and scramble through the mouth of the Old Pinnebog River Channel toward the yellow post at the start of some small sand dunes. The yellow spur quickly rises to the first scenic vista and bench, where you get a view of the old river channel, the chimney monument, and the campground below. From here, the blue loop begins, with posts descending south along the old channel or west through a wooded ravine. Turn right (west) to begin the most impressive section of the trail.

The trail passes through a ravine of sorts, forested in hardwoods, and away from the water and sand for a third of a mile. Keep an eye out for blue diamonds on the trees, for the trail takes a sharp turn to the north to reach an overlook of the bay, shoreline, and the open dunes that border it. At *Mile 0.7* you'll reach the junction of the red and blue loops, marked by a large pole and another bench. Head south (left) to return to the yellow spur and reduce the walk to 1.7 miles; but continue west (right) for more views.

Follow the red poles and diamonds, and shortly the trail will emerge at another bench with a panorama of the mouth of the Pinnebog River, the sandy shoreline of Saginaw Bay, and a long line of open and grassy dunes that stretch to the west. This vista is the best in the park, maybe in all of Michigan's Thumb, and even more remarkable considering the flat fields of corn and navy beans you drove through to get here. At your feet is a steep slope of sand leading down to the river, while on the opposite riverbank a handful of anglers are usually trying their luck for perch or panfish. If it's September or October, they are probably fishing for the chinook salmon that spawn upriver.

The trail continues along this sandy bluff above the river until it reaches one final bench at *Mile 1.1*, where you can see much of the Pinnebog River valley and the wetlands that border it. At this point, the trail swings to a southerly direction, then to the east, becoming a walk through woods. Follow the red diamonds carefully, for there are numerous unofficial paths cutting through the open forest of oaks and maples. If it's early or late in the day, hike quietly and be alert; deer are occasionally seen feeding along this stretch.

At *Mile 1.5* you reach the organization campground (vault toilets and a picnic shelter) and then the junction at the old iron bridge, now used only by hikers and skiers to reach the second trailhead and parking area. Entering from the north (let) is the cutoff spur. Continue along the blue loop by dropping down toward the bridge to pick up the trail that skirts the old channel closely. Eventually the trail begins to climb gently again, and within a half mile tops off at the first overlook and bench, where the yellow spur leads back to the campground.

10

Tobico Marsh Trail

Place: Bay City State Recreation Area

Total Distance: 4.8 miles

Hiking Time: 2 to 3 hours

Rating: Easy

Highlights: Wildlife observation towers, birding

Maps: Bay City State Recreation Area map from the Michigan DNR, or Tobico Marsh Map from MichiganTrailMaps.com

Trailhead GPS Coordinates: N 43° 40' 10.57" W 083° 54' 40.18"

Tobico Marsh is an 1,848-acre wildlife refuge that lies within Bay City State Recreation Area and almost within sight of the city itself. Winding through the refuge is an easy 2.7-mile loop that is linked to the park's Saginaw Bay Visitor Center by the Frank N. Andersen Nature Trail, a paved rail-trail. All three make for a pleasant hike any time of the year. But during the fall and spring migrations of waterfowl, the Tobico Marsh Trail is an excellent outing. It begins with an educational visit to an interpretive center and then combines a walk in the woods with birding—the fine art of observing and identifying winged wildlife.

The refuge itself is undeveloped and contains a variety of habitat, from small pockets of cattail marshes and oak and maple climax forests to Tobico Lagoon, a 900-acre body of water and the largest remaining wetland along Saginaw Bay. The entire area is home to deer, beaver, muskrat, and mink, but it's the wide variety of birds, especially waterfowl, that makes this refuge so spectacular. Biologists estimate that in October there are usually 3,000 to 5,000 birds in the marsh; during peak migration from the third week of October to early November, more than 25,000 have been known to gather at one time. In all, more than 200 species of birds have been sighted in the game area.

It is this seemingly endless supply of geese, fish, and other wildlife that has led archaeologists to believe that the area was inhabited by prehistoric tribes, known as Paleo-Indians, several thousand years ago. The marsh was also the frequent site of hunting camps for the Sauk and Chippewa

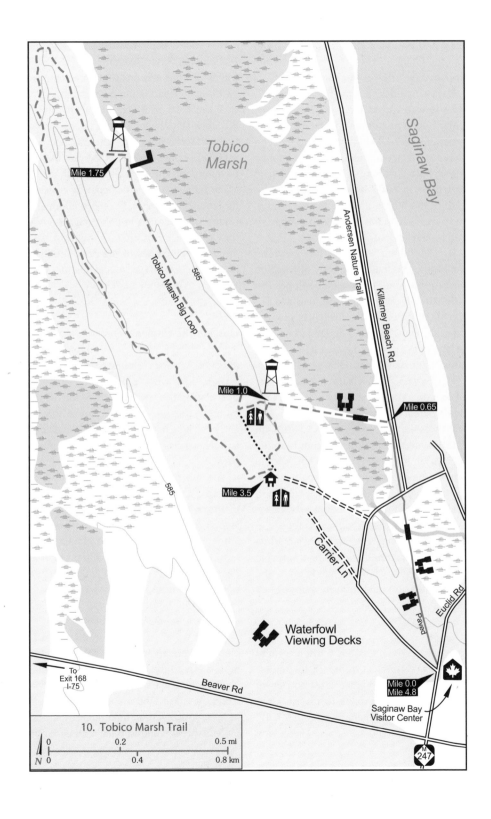

Tobico Marsh

Saginaw Bay

Mile 1.75

Tobico Marsh Big Loop

585

Andersen Nature Trail

Killarney Beach Rd

Mile 1.0

Mile 0.65

585

Mile 3.5

Carrier Ln

Paved

Euclid Rd

Waterfowl
Viewing Decks

To
Exit 168
I-75

Beaver Rd

Mile 0.0
Mile 4.8

Saginaw Bay
Visitor Center

M
247

10. Tobico Marsh Trail

N

0   0.2   0.5 mi

0   0.4   0.8 km

tribes, and the name *Tobico* itself is derived from the Chippewa word *pe-to-be-goong*, which means "little lake by the big lake."

Native Americans remained until 1837, and a few served as local guides for duck hunters even as late as 1925. By 1844 a timber cruiser had already passed through the area, which eventually endured intense logging before six lumber barons purchased the lagoon in 1907. Recognizing the true value of the marsh as a waterfowl refuge, the six men set up the exclusive Tobico Hunt Club for their own private hunts.

By 1956 there were only two surviving members of the club, and they offered the marsh to the state as a wildlife refuge. The $40,000 sale was approved, and the To-bico Marsh State Game Area was created that year. In 1976 the U.S. Department of the Interior designated the area a Registered Natural Landmark for its unique features.

The Saginaw Bay Visitor Center is a required stop for this hike. Originally one of the state's oldest interpretive centers, the center was extensively renovated in 1996 into a 10,000-square-foot facility that features displays on the history and ecology of the marsh, a life-sized diorama of a duck hunter and his layout boat, and an audio-video theater. But the most important exhibits for anybody venturing into Tobico are those devoted to identifying wildlife. They include a collection of mounted birds, a photographic bird list for the area, and a hands-on exhibit that teaches you to recognize waterfowl by their calls.

ACCESS

The state recreation area is 5 miles north of Bay City and reached from I-75 by departing at exit 168 and heading east on Beaver Road. It's almost 5 miles to the park entrance, just past the intersection with M-247. A second trailhead to the Tobico Marsh loop allows you to skip the visitor center and rail-trail portion. From Beaver Road head north (right) for a half mile on M-247 and then west on Killarney Road to the posted entrance.

From Memorial Day to Labor Day the Saginaw Bay Visitor Center is open 10 AM to 6 PM Monday through Saturday, and noon to 6 PM Sunday. The rest of the year the center is closed on Monday; from December 15 to January 15 it is not open at all except for special programs. For more information on the trail, contact the Saginaw Bay Visitor Center (989-667-0717; www.michigan.gov/saginawbayvc) or the park headquarters (989-684-3020). A vehicle entry fee is required to enter the state park.

TRAIL

Outside the Saginaw Bay Visitor Center, marked along Euclid Road, is the start of the Frank N. Andersen Nature Trail, a 1.25-mile point-to-point paved path. This outing begins by following the first half mile of the rail-trail, crossing Killarney Beach Road at **Mile 0.5** and passing a handful of interpretive plaques and two wildlife observation blinds along the way.

Just beyond Killarney Beach Road, the trail splits; reach the heart of Tobico Marsh by heading west (left) on a paved path that is a bit rough in places. This spur skirts the lagoon for a third of a mile and passes two more observation decks, the first being the best one in the park. The huge deck features benches, two spotting scopes, and large plaques that help you identify what's dabbling in the open water in front of you.

This is where you search for wildlife at To-bico. Beavers and muskrats skim its surface on the way to their lodges. Mink and otters have been seen early in the morning hunting along the edge. And in October thousands of birds arrive with puddle ducks; mallards, pintails, green-winged teals, and widgeons

Tobico Marsh is one of the best birding areas on the east side of Michigan's Lower Peninsula.

The Tobico Marsh Trail features observation decks with spotting scopes and viewing towers.

pass through early in the month, followed by diving ducks, mergansers, and geese later on. In a major staging area like Tobico ducks and geese will rest and feed for a few days before moving on, the reason the numbers fluctuate almost daily. Serious birders pack along their own high-powered binoculars, as the majority of the birds are often found in the middle of the lagoon.

At **Mile 1** the asphalt ends and you arrive the first of Tobico's two observation towers. Both towers rise 40 feet into the hardwood trees and were renovated in 2012 thanks to the Friends of Bay City State Recreation Area (www.friendsofpark.org).

A wide dirt path continues west into the woods from the tower to quickly reach a junction with the Tobico Marsh Big Loop Trail. This 2.7-mile loop winds through the wooded interior of Tobico Marsh and is a level and easy ride on a mountain bike and a stunning hike in the fall as you begin by passing through a brilliant canopy of white and red oaks, maples, and poplars.

At **Mile 1.75** you arrive at a second tower while nearby is a 300-foot boardwalk that leads you into an amazing thicket of cattails but little or no view of the marsh's open water. This was the site of the Tobico Hunt Club, which, according to the extant records, never had more than eight members during its existence from 1907 to 1956. The exclusive club was never lacking, however, for it featured cottages with porches and fireplaces, boathouses, blinds scattered throughout the marsh, and a caretaker who lived here year-round with his wife and children. It was Frank N. Andersen, one of only two surviving members of the club, who offered the marsh to the state as a wildlife refuge in 1956.

You begin the back side of the loop just past *Mile 2*, a mostly level trail that winds through the woods and crosses a pair of small wooden bridges. Keep an eye out here for white-tailed deer, gray and red foxes, coyotes, and even gobbling wild turkeys. The Killarney Beach Road trailhead is reached at *Mile 3.5*.

The trail departs from the shelter at the trailhead and quickly comes to a junction. Head east (right) and follow the trail as it crosses three bridges, each spanning an old beach line left behind by a retreating Lake Huron centuries ago. In less than a half mile, you come to the paved path at the south end of the lagoon. The last leg of the hike is to retrace your steps along Andersen Nature Trail to return to the Saginaw Bay Visitor Center, reached at *Mile 4.8*. For more opportunities to look for bird life on the lagoon, continue north on the paved rail-trail and look for sandy paths that head west. Most of them will take you to an open spot to scan the water.

11

Sandy Hook Trail

Place: *Tawas Point State Park*

Total Distance: *1.5 miles*

Hiking Time: *40 to 60 minutes*

Rating: *Easy*

Highlights: *Scenic beaches, birding*

Maps: *Tawas Point State Park map from the Michigan DNR, or Sandy Hook Trail map from MichiganTrailMaps.com*

Trailhead GPS Coordinates:
N 44° 15' 13.59" W 083° 26' 54.32"

Tawas Point State Park in Iosco County is a small unit at only 183 acres, but it contains a big campground:, a modern facility with 193 sites and four cabins spread across three loops. That doesn't leave much room for trails. But the park's lone trail, while short, is a scenic and very interesting hike, especially if you are a birder.

The park preserves the end of Tawas Point, a 2-mile spit that separates Tawas Bay from Lake Huron. The tip of the point is a jagged hook of sandy beaches, wetlands, and small dunes. This unique sand dune ecosystem and its location as a major land-fall for birds migrating across Saginaw Bay make Sandy Hook Trail a popular destination for birders every fall and spring. Birding peaks in mid-May when for three days the park becomes the site of the Tawas Point Birding Festival (tawasbirdfest.com).

During the migrations, the point is said to be "alive with birds." Often spotted along beaches or the small inland ponds are terns and gulls, including Bonaparte's gulls and Caspian terns, along with shorebirds such as red knots, whimbrels, and even the rare piping plover. The ponds also attract loons, flocks of mergansers, and a variety of other waterfowl species. The end of the spit is practically treeless, but warblers, flycatchers, and hummingbirds feed among the willow thickets and shrubs such as sand cherry.

The trail is mainly a sandy path that connects a few stretches of boardwalk along the Tawas Bay and Lake Huron sides of the spit. Its most obvious feature is neither

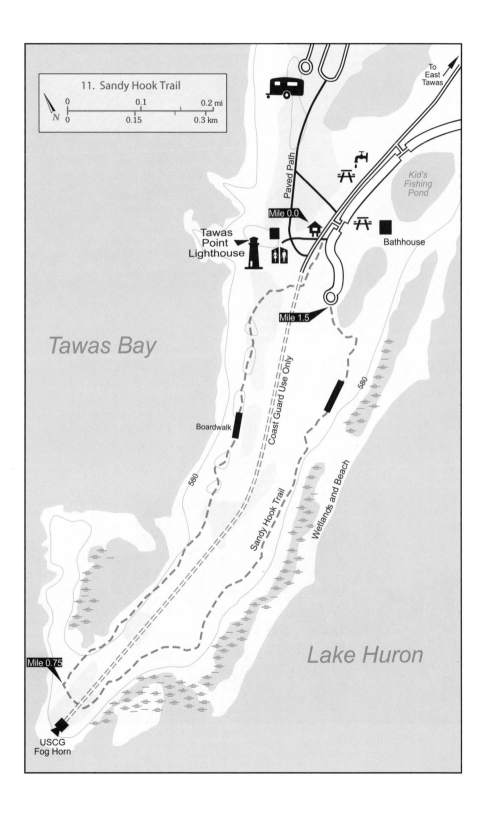

11. Sandy Hook Trail

N

0   0.1   0.2 mi
0   0.15   0.3 km

To
East
Tawas

Paved Path

Kid's
Fishing
Pond

Mile 0.0

Tawas
Point
Lighthouse

Bathhouse

Mile 1.5

Tawas Bay

Coast Guard Use Only

Boardwalk

580

Sandy Hook Trail

Wetlands and Beach

580

Lake Huron

Mile 0.75

USCG
Fog Horn

The Tawas Point Lighthouse.

birds nor beaches but the historic Tawas Point Lighthouse, which you can see from different angles throughout much of the walk. Its 19 posts and interpretive brochure have long since been replaced by a dozen plaques along the trail covering topics such as rare terns, looking for tracks, and the lighthouse.

The trail is closed to mountain bikes, and dogs are prohibited. You can ski it in the winter but its limited mileage and sandy conditions make it unappealing to most Nordic skiers, who would much rather head inland to the Corsair Trails.

ACCESS

The 185-acre park is 3.5 miles from East Tawas or 42 miles from the I-75 and US 23 exit near Standish (exit 188). Follow US 23 northeast of East Tawas and turn east on Tawas Point Road. Signs point the way along Tawas Point Road to the state park entrance at the end. The Sandy Hook Trailhead is located at the west end of the state park's day-use parking area.

Tawas Point State Park features not only the trail and a beautiful swimming beach, but also a bathhouse, picnic shelter, and 193 modern campsites with a handful overlooking Tawas Bay. Reservations are recommended throughout much of the summer, especially weekends.

The park is open year-round, but the Tawas Point Lighthouse and Museum is open Memorial Day through Labor Day from 10 AM to 5 PM daily, and on weekends after Labor Day through mid-October. There is a fee for vehicles entering the park and additional charges for camping overnight or a lighthouse tour. For more information, contact Tawas Point State Park (989-362-5041) or the Tawas Point Lighthouse (989-362-5658).

The Sandy Hook Trail at Tawas Point State Park.

TRAIL

The trailhead is just off the day-use parking area and is posted along the paved path to the Tawas Point Lighthouse. The trail quickly breaks out of the pines and passes the lighthouse complex, which also includes a museum store and restrooms. The original lighthouse was built in 1853 and was located east of here, toward the park headquarters. This one was constructed in 1876, and the cement cribbing at its base is testimony to the 2 feet of water it stood in at the time it was built. The lighthouse is now part of the park; it offers a lighthouse keeper program and lighthouse tours for a small fee.

Beyond the lighthouse, the trail crosses the Coast Guard Service Road (closed to the public) and enters the dune ecosystem to become a soft, sandy path along the crest of a low dune. Within a quarter mile from the parking lot you cross a boardwalk with a bench in the middle and a view of Tawas Bay. To the east you can see the spit extending out and then curving back in its hook. To the northwest is another view of the lighthouse.

A little more than a century ago, most of the point was under water, but the spit of land has been built up by the long shore currents sweeping along the Lake Huron coast. The currents keep sand moving in the shallow water parallel to the shoreline, until Tawas Bay is encountered. Upon reaching the bay, the currents spread out and slow down, depositing the sand in a long, narrow peninsula. The distinctive hook at the end has been formed by advancing waves, which bend and wrap around the end of the point. The most obvious evidence of the spit growing are the older hooks, each of which at one time marked the entrance to the bay. Eventually, geologists say, Tawas Point will extend completely across the bay, turning it into a lake in much the same way Tobico Marsh was formed in Bay City State Recreation Area (see Hike 10).

You hike toward the "hook," skirting a power line at times. At *Mile 0.75* take one last look at Tawas Bay and head south (left) to cross over to the Lake Huron shore. Along the way you re-cross the Coast Guard Service Road near the Fog Signal Building the USCG still maintains. Old park maps show a spur trail beginning here and heading out to the hook, but it's no longer posted. Still, it would not be hard to hike out to the end of the point in this almost treeless area.

The endless blue horizon of Lake Huron provides a vivid contrast with the enclosed Tawas Bay, and the scenery on this side is much more interesting. The grass-covered dunes offer a bit more rolling terrain while the interdunal ponds and wetlands are more extensive and scenic. At times the trail resembles an old two-track but is still very sandy and in the beginning stays close to the service road. At *Mile 1* you swing closer to the beach and have an opportunity to hike out to the edge of Lake Huron without having to kick the shoes off.

At *Mile 1.25* the trail swings left to a viewing deck with a bench. At this point the trail remains above the beach, skirting a low dune and crossing the longest boardwalk of the loop before emerging at the east end of an interdunal pond near the day-use area.

12

Highbanks Trail

Place: Huron National Forest

Total Distance: 4 miles

Hiking Time: 2 hours

Rating: Easy

Highlights: Au Sable River, scenic vistas, Iargo Springs

Maps: Highbanks Trail map from the USDA Forest Service or MichiganTrailMaps.com

Trailhead GPS Coordinates: N 44° 26' 28.47" W 083° 40' 34.38"

Strung along the towering bluffs above the Au Sable River is the Highbanks Trail, a skiing and hiking route that was developed through the Corsair Ski Council and the Huron National Forest. This is a point-to-point trail, and without two vehicles it's almost impossible to avoid backtracking. At times the route also winds close to River Road, and the sound of cars speeding by occasionally breaks up the peaceful tranquility of the wooded path.

But the drawbacks are hardly worth considering when compared with what the Highbanks Trail has to offer: outstanding scenery and views, the possibility of spotting a bald eagle during the spring and summer, and an opportunity to learn about the life of a logger in the 1800s at the Lumberman's Monument. With its mostly level contour along the tops of the bluffs, this trail makes an excellent outing for children. The monuments to the past and the panoramas of the river will keep their minds off tired feet.

The entire trail is a 7-mile hike from Iargo Springs to Sawmill Point, where the Forest Service maintains 17 primitive campsites and a boat launch. Built in 2001, the Sawmill Trailhead allows hikers to turn the trek into an overnight adventure, spending an evening on the banks of the Au Sable River.

This hike describes by far the most scenic portion of the trail, the 3.5-mile walk from Iargo Springs to Lumberman's Monument. This portion can also be turned into an overnight trek by camping at Monument Campground before backtracking to Iargo Springs the next day.

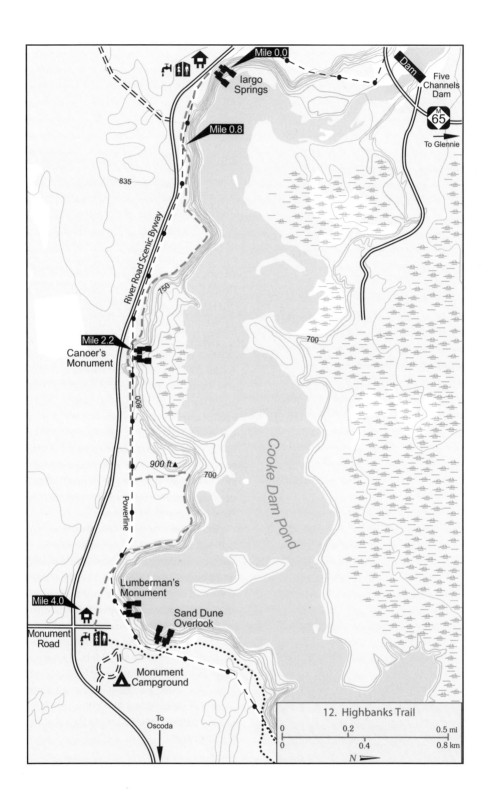

Mile 0.0

Iargo
Springs

Dam

Five
Channels
Dam

M 65

To Glennie

Mile 0.8

835

River Road Scenic Byway

750

700

Mile 2.2
Canoer's
Monument

800

900 ft▲

700

Cooke Dam Pond

Powerline

Lumberman's
Monument

Mile 4.0

Sand Dune
Overlook

Monument
Road

Monument
Campground

To
Oscoda

12. Highbanks Trail

0		0.2		0.5 mi

0		0.4		0.8 km

N

A scenic view of the Au Sable River valley from the Highbanks Trail.

ACCESS

Highbanks Trail is accessed via River Road. The 22-mile paved road roughly parallels the south bank of the Au Sable River and in 2005 was designated a National Scenic Byway. Iargo Springs, the western trailhead for the Highbanks Trail, is located a mile east of M-65 on River Road. The Lumberman's Monument is 3 miles farther east along River Road.

There is a nightly fee for camping at Monument Campground, a rustic facility near Lumberman's Monument, and a Huron-Manistee National Forests vehicle pass is required to hike the trail. For more information, contact the Huron Shores Ranger Station (989-362-8961) in Oscoda or check the Huron-Manistee National Forests website (www.fs.usda.gov/hmnf).

TRAIL

Along with parking, Iargo Springs features vault toilets, picnic shelters, and drinking water. This trek begins with a 300-step, 159-foot descent to the Au Sable River to view the springs. At the bottom of the bluff a quarter mile of boardwalk winds through towering cedars to eight observation decks, half of them perched above the gurgling springs, the rest overlooking the Au Sable.

Iargo is the Chippewa word for "many waters," and it's believed that Native Americans gathered here once for tribal powwows where they would drink the cold, clear water for its medicinal powers. Today Iargo is still a tonic. No matter how many leaf peepers are zipping along River Road, the springs are

Highbanks Trail

always a quiet and tranquil spot that soothes the soul.

From the largo Springs parking lot, Highbanks Trail heads east, where it follows the edge of the bluffs briefly, skirts a gully, and then merges into the power-line corridor. You follow this human-made intrusion for a quarter mile until you come to another panorama of the river at **Mile 0.8** (including descending to the springs), at which point blue diamonds mark where the trail and electrical lines part company. The trail continues to hug the forested edge of the banks for

The Lumberman's Monument along the Highbanks Trail.

another mile, providing you glimpses of the Au Sable River valley between the trees. You break out in the parking lot for Canoer's Monument at **Mile 2.2**. The stone monument, topped by a pair of giant paddles, was originally built as a memorial to Jerry Curley, who died training for the Au Sable River Canoe Marathon. Today it stands in honor of all racers who attempt the annual 150-mile event from Grayling to Oscoda, often cited as the toughest canoe race in the country.

For years this spot was also known as Eagle Nest Overlook because an active nest was located nearby. But the eagles have since rebuilt their nest on the other side of the river. Still, observant hikers, especially those packing along binoculars, will often spot the impressive birds soaring over the river from here.

Beyond the monument, Highbanks Trail again skirts the power lines for a half mile through terrain that is very sandy and rolling. Eventually the trail swings north to return to the edge of the bluff. At **Mile 3** you arrive at one of the best overviews of the Au Sable River in the first half of the hike. Standing on the edge of a high bluff, you gaze down at the Cooke Dam Pond, a simply spectacular sight in the fall.

You stay close to the edge for the next half mile and then break out again at the power lines before passing underneath them. The final half mile is a level stroll through a red pine plantation that takes you to the Lumberman's Monument at **Mile 4**.

The monument itself is a 14-foot bronze statue of a timber cruiser with his compass, a sawyer with his crosscut saw, and a river rat using a peavey to turn a log. The bronze lumbermen have watched over this stretch of the Au Sable since 1932. Surrounding them is a day-use area with picnic tables, restrooms, drinking water, and the

Lumberman's Monument Visitor Center, which is open from 10 AM to 5 PM daily from May until the colors fade away in the third week of October.

The adjacent outdoor exhibit area features replicas of a rollway and logjam while a hands-on peavey display lets you try your skill at being a river rat turning a log. There is also a small video theater where you learn that the lowly logger, viewed by many as a colorful Paul Bunyan–like character, was in reality cheap labor. In the middle of the winter, he made $2 for a 12-hour day spent pulling a saw while cold water and snow sloshed in his boots. Little wonder that by the time most loggers turned 35 they were too worn out or sick to continue logging.

Nearby are observation decks along the edge of the bluffs and a stairway that descends 260 steps to the shores of the Au Sable. Tied up at the bottom of the stairs is a replica of a wanigan: the cook's raft that followed the log drives and kept the river rats well fed. Step aboard and see how one man and his assistants fed an army of lumberjacks.

A side trail leads to nearby Monument Campground, a Forest Service facility with 20 rustic sites in a red pine plantation. Amenities include fire rings, picnic tables, drinking water, and vault toilets.

13

Reid Lake Foot Travel Area

Place: Huron National Forest

Total Distance: 5.25 miles

Hiking Time: 3 to 4 hours, or 2 days

Rating: Easy

Highlights: Backcountry camping, fishing

Maps: Reid Lake Foot Travel Area map from the USDA Forest Service or MichiganTrailMaps.com

Trailhead GPS Coordinates: N 44° 39' 11.73" W 083° 40' 32.83"

Although best known for its cross-country skiing, Reid Lake Foot Travel Area also makes a fine destination for a day hike or even an overnight trip into the woods. Located in the Huron National Forest, the 4,000-acre area is closed to motor vehicles, horses, and mountain bikes and features footpaths that wrap around its namesake lake and Little Trout Lake.

Reid Lake was privately owned until 1966, and some of the surrounding land was still being farmed in the early 1960s, as is evident by the open fields and small orchard. Eventually the Forest Service purchased 3,700 acres, designated it nonmotorized in 1975, and assisted the Youth Conservation Corps in developing a 6-mile trail system around the lake.

In 1991 the Forest Service added Little Trout Lake to increase its acreage to more than 4,000 and in 2002 began expanding the trail system and series of backcountry campsites. Today the foot travel area includes 12 miles of trails, eight backcountry campsites, two charming lakes, and numerous wetlands, marshes, and bogs. It is this mix of marshes intermingled with rolling hills of hardwood forests that attracts and supports an abundance of wildlife.

Trekking is not hard at Reid Lake. The trails are well marked with blue blazes, the junctions are marked with locator maps, and the gently rolling terrain contains few climbs of any significance. Even when trails wind around low-lying wet areas, they are surprisingly dry thanks to the old two-tracks that many follow, as well as a series of new boardwalks.

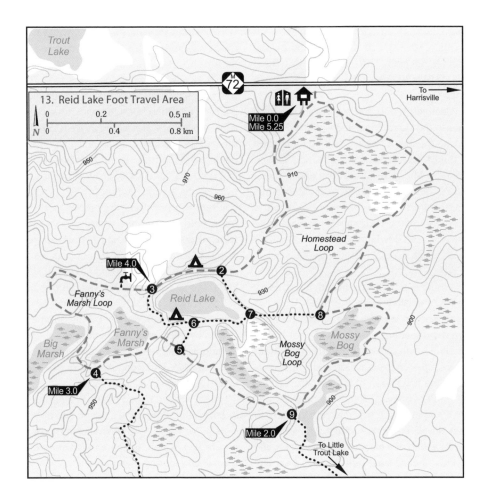

The most scenic area is the northern half of the foot travel area and includes the hike described here, a 5.25-mile loop around Reid Lake. Pack in a tent and a sleeping bag and you can turn this day hike into a pleasant weekend retreat. Half of the backcountry campsites are scattered around Reid Lake, many of them situated on a bluff overlooking the water, and feature wilderness privies and a source of safe drinking water nearby.

Bugs can be heavy at times in June and July while October, as you would expect, is a beautiful month to be hiking in the foot travel area. Just keep in mind that the area is open to hunting, including during firearm deer season from November 15 to November 30. Backcountry camping is permitted anywhere 200 feet off the trails, though I don't know why anybody would want to set up anywhere but on a site.

ACCESS

The foot travel area is reached from Harrisville by heading 19 miles west on M-72 to its posted entrance. From Mio, head east on M-72 for 21 miles to its junction with M-65 near Curran, then continue along M-72 for another 10 miles to the entrance on the south (right) side of the state highway. There is a display board at the parking area with maps.

Camping is free, but you'll need a vehicle pass to the Huron-Manistee National Forests to hike the trail. The pass can be purchased at the M-72 trailhead or at Forest Service offices in Mio (989-826-3252) and Oscoda (989-739-0728). You can also obtain a trail map and additional information from the Huron-Manistee National Forests website (www.fs.usda.gov/hmnf).

TRAIL

This route is a 5.25-mile hike that can easily be accomplished in an afternoon. From the display board in the trailhead parking area, begin by heading east toward post No. 8. The wide trail passes through the perfect rows of a red pine plantation and then breaks out at the first marsh of the day, crossed via a stretch of boardwalk that keeps the boots dry. From here, the trail makes an ascent to post No. 8, reached at *Mile 1.25*. Reid Lake is only a third of a mile to the west (right), but this hike heads east (left) toward post No. 9 along what is known as the Mossy Bog Loop.

In the beginning the trail resembles a former railroad bed before swinging south into a rolling terrain of hardwoods. Eventually you break out at Mossy Bog and tiptoe along a narrow footpath between two open marshes. This is an interesting area in the spring with peepers croaking and wildflowers blooming; it's buggy in the summer, however. The trail ascends away from the bog into a stand of paper birch and just past *Mile 2* arrives at post No. 9. The post marks the junction to Little Trout Lake, reached in 1.1 miles by heading south (left).

This hike continues west (right) and quickly descends off the low ridge to the south end of Beaver Pond, marked by a dam that looks like Grandpa's woodpile. The trail actually crosses in front of the dam on planking and then skirts the rest of the pond itself, a body of water as big as Reid Lake. In the middle is a large lodge, while along the bank are fallen trees with the telltale signs of a beaver's handiwork—gnawed marks and wood chips around stumps.

From the pond, the trail moves into an open field, makes two sharp, 90-degree turns that are well posted, then arrives at post No. 5 at *Mile 2.5*. You can head straight north to reach Reid Lake, just one low ridge away, but to the west (left) is the scenic Fanny's Marsh Loop, a 1.5-mile loop around two more marshes. This segment begins by descending to Fanny's Marsh and skirting its south end before arriving at post No. 4 at *Mile 3*, marking the return trail from Little Trout Lake.

Fanny's Marsh Loop heads in a northerly direction (right) from the junction and climbs over a low ridge. You descend to the east end of Big Marsh, which can be more like a small lake during a wet spring, only to resume climbing again before swinging east.

At *Mile 4* you reach the northwest corner of beautiful Reid Lake and the junction at post No. 3. Just before the junction, you pass a spur to a hand pump for drinking water. If you're not in a hurry to head home, there are four campsites on Reid Lake. The more scenic ones are along the south side of the lake and reached by heading south (right) at post No. 3. These two sites are shady spots that sit on a bluff overlooking the lake and a fishing dock below. Head east (left) at post No. 3 to reach two more sites, which also sit above the lake and feature a wilderness toilet nearby.

A fishing dock at Reid Lake.

A beaver lodge in Reid Lake. There is considerable beaver activity in the Reid Lakes Foot Travel Area.

In all, there are three fishing docks on Reid Lake, one on the south shore and two on the north. At one time Reid was stocked annually with rainbow trout; it may still support a population of the fish. Other species include panfish, especially bluegill, largemouth bass, and some perch. The trout and bass are most often caught by anglers who have hauled in a canoe, but the panfish can easily be landed from the docks on the north side. For either one, anglers usually turn to leaf worms rigged on a small hook and split shot to entice the fish into striking. Add a bobber if you're dock fishing for bluegill.

From the north shore campsite, the trail continues east to quickly reach post No. 2 within a quarter mile. Here you return to the M-72 trailhead by heading north (left). This final leg is a wide path through the woods and, for the most part, a gentle, mile-long descent to the parking lot.

14

Hoist Lakes Foot Travel Area

Place: Huron National Forest

Total Distance: 11 miles

Hiking Time: 6 to 7 hours

Rating: Moderate to challenging

Highlights: Inland lakes, backcountry campsites

Maps: Huron National Forest Hoist Lakes Foot Travel Area map

Trailhead GPS Coordinates:
N 44° 39' 15.68" W 083° 50' 17.38"

Hoist Lakes Foot Travel Area, set up in 1976 to provide a quiet sanctuary from the noise and rumble of our motorized society, offers outdoor opportunities found nowhere else on the east side of the Lower Peninsula. Encompassing 10,600 acres of the Huron National Forest, this foot travel area is large enough to provide backpacking opportunities allowing people to sneak off into the woods for days at a time. With seven small lakes, the area also offers walk-in wilderness fishing adventures for anglers who like having a lake to themselves. And due to its rugged terrain—many hills top 1,200 feet—Hoist Lakes gives you the chance to climb a ridge, sit on its crest, and ponder the panorama at your feet.

Hoist Lakes Foot Travel Area is covered by forests of pine, aspen, and hardwoods that are broken up by small pothole lakes, numerous ponds, marshes, and beaver-flooded streams. There are good opportunities to observe wildlife, with the most famous residents of the area being the ones least encountered: black bears. There are also red foxes, mink, and coyotes, but the wildlife hikers are most likely to spot are wild turkeys, ruffed grouse, white-tailed deer, beavers, porcupines, and a variety of waterfowl and birds.

Winding through the backcountry are 20 miles of footpaths in four loops that are accessed from either the West Trailhead on County Road F-32 or the East Trailhead on M-65, just south of M-72. From the West Trailhead most hikers follow a 6.4-mile loop past Byron and No-Name Lakes, backtracking the final 1.7 miles from post No. 9. From

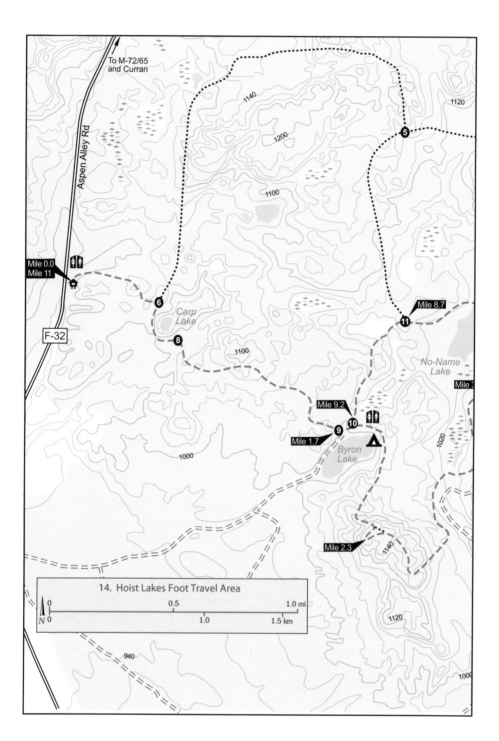

To M-72/65
and Curran

Aspen Alley Rd

1140

1200

1120

1100

⑤

Mile 0.0
Mile 11

F-32

⑥

Carp
Lake

⑧

1100

Mile 8.7

⑪

No-Name
Lake

Mile 3

1000

Mile 9.2

⑩

⑨

Mile 1.7

Byron
Lake

1020

1000

1120

Mile 2.3

1140

14. Hoist Lakes Foot Travel Area

N

0   0.5   1.0 mi

0   1.0   1.5 km

940

1120

1000

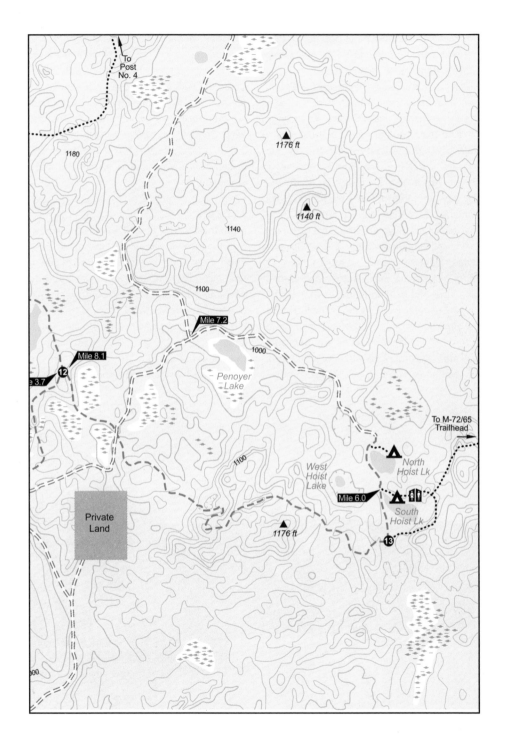

To Post No. 4

1180

1176 ft

1140 ft

1140

1100

Mile 7.2

Mile 8.1

1000

e 3.7

12

Penoyer Lake

To M-72/65 Trailhead

North Hoist Lk

1100

West Hoist Lake

Mile 6.0

South Hoist Lk

Private Land

1176 ft

13

000

the East Trailhead the most popular trek is a 5.2-mile loop to South and North Hoist Lakes.

This description is an 11-mile loop that begins at the West Trailhead and offers the best scenery within the tract, including six of the seven named inland lakes. With backpacking gear, you can turn this route into an easy overnight adventure. On the day you arrive, the trek to the walk-in campsites on Byron Lake is only 1.7 miles; on the following day, shouldering only a day pack, you can enjoy an 8-mile loop to the Hoist Lakes that ends back at your Byron Lake campsite.

Hoist Lakes is also a well-known cross-country ski area, so trails tend to be wide, well posted with locator maps at most junctions, and easy to follow even though a handful of old two-tracks cross the tract. Forest Service regulations prohibit camping or campfires within 200 feet of an open body of water, swamp, or foot trail except at designated sites. Horses, motorized vehicles, including boats with outboard motors, and mountain bikes are not permitted in the area.

The inland lakes feature not only some beautiful walk-in campsites but also back-country fishing opportunities. North Hoist Lake supports a panfish and bass fishery while South Hoist Lake is a designated trout lake that is regularly stocked with rainbows. Anglers fish Byron Lake for smallmouth bass and perch.

ACCESS

The Hoist Lakes Foot Travel Area is east of Mio, 22 miles west of Harrisville, or a good three-hour drive from Detroit. If you're heading north, depart I-75 at exit 202 and continue north on M-33 for 36 miles. In Mio continue north M-72/M-33 for 5 miles and then go east on M-72 for 15.9 miles. Head south on M-65/M-72 for 0.75 mile; just past the hamlet of Curran turn right on County Road F-32 (also labeled Aspen Alley Road)

A belly-boat angler changes his fly while fishing Byron Lake.

Lake Huron

and head south for 5.5 miles to the posted trailhead on the right.

A Huron-Manistee vehicle pass is required to hike Hoist Lakes. You can purchase a weekly or annual pass at the Huron Shores Ranger Station (989-739-0728) in Oscoda, at the Mio Ranger Station (989-826-3252), or from a fee pipe at the trailheads.

TRAIL

The parking area for the west trailhead contains a vault toilet and a large display board with maps and a fee pipe. From here, the trail departs into a rolling forest of mixed pines and hardwoods. In less than a half mile you climb over a small hill and gently descend to the first junction, post No. 6. Head south (right) for Byron Lake.

You immediately reach Carp Lake. The trail skirts this small, roundish lake from above and then swings east to arrive at post No. 8 at *Mile 0.65*. Many older maps show a source of water here, but the hand pump is long gone.

You continue east, with the trail passing through a stand of predominantly maple that is magnificent in the fall, to climb a ridge and top out in paper birch. From here you begin a long but gradual descent back into hardwoods, finally bottoming out at post No. 9, reached at *Mile 1.7* near the north end of Byron Lake.

One of the largest lakes in the area, Byron has panfish, perch, and a population of smallmouth bass but is tough to fish from the shoreline. Since it's not an easy portage for hauling in a canoe, some anglers attempt to fish the lake in waders, while others hike in with a belly boat or float tube strapped to their backs.

An unmarked path follows the west bank, while the main trail climbs away from the north end of the lake to quickly arrive at post No. 10. To the north (left) the trail heads for post No. 11; to the east (right) the path is marked with a CAMPSITES sign and quickly leads to three official campsites, many unofficial ones, and two wilderness privies. One campsite is on the bluff above the lake and along with a fire ring and a bench features a long stairway down to the water. This is one of the best spots to pitch a tent in the entire Lower Peninsula, a place where you can spend an evening gazing out on Byron Lake and the forested ridges behind it.

The trail continues to follow the ridge along the east shore, passing views of Byron Lake below. Eventually you descend past an old two-track, climb away from the lake, descend again, and then begin climbing once more. This time it's a long haul up, but at *Mile 2.3* you top off at 1,140 feet. Here a short spur leads right to the edge of the ridge. At one time this spot was a clearing with a 180-degree view of the rugged terrain leading to the Au Sable River. But Mother Nature has since taken over—now trees full of foliage block the view from late spring to late fall.

The main trail skirts the top of the hill as it makes a sharp turn, then begins a half-mile descent off it. You bottom out at a clearing, where you skirt a marsh with a pond, a good place to search for beavers and other wildlife. You then follow a level route to post No. 12, reached at *Mile 3.7*. The post marks a junction where the trail to the north (left) heads for No-Name Lake, while the trail to the east (right) leads to post No. 13 and the Hoist Lakes. Head east.

You pass through another wetland area and in less than a half mile cross a grassy two-track with the trail clearly marked on the other side. You climb a low hill and then begin climbing again to start one of the more scenic stretches of this loop. After topping off on the crest of the ridge, you follow it for the next half mile, passing giant red pines and reaching 1,160 feet where you are able to peer down into ravines below for deer.

A belly-boat angler sets up his equipment at a Byron Lake campsite.

You make a long descent off the ridge and reach post No. 13 at **Mile 5.8.**

Head north (left) at the junction to immediately break out to a view of South Hoist Lake. You pass a trail to the South Hoist Lake campsite at **Mile 6** and then begin skirting North Hoist Lake, quickly reaching the spur to the campsite on its north side. Both campsites are located on low bluffs above the water with views of the entire lake. Nice spots to pitch a tent.

South Hoist is the largest of the three Hoist Lakes and has a maximum depth of 24 feet, the reason it is stocked with rainbow trout. Most anglers fishing for the rainbows will use small garden worms and work the deep portions in the middle of the lake. North Hoist Lake has a depth of only 10 feet and is strictly a warmwater fishery for bluegills and other species of sunfish. Also nearby is West Hoist Lake, a small marshy body of water not seen from the main trail.

From the junction to the North Hoist Lake campsite, an old two-track continues north and gives you a route to back to Byron Lake without having to backtrack

the segment between posts No. 12 and No. 13. The two-track is not marked but is very distinguishable and easy to follow. The wide grassy lane in the woods swings to the northeast and within a mile skirts the north end of scenic Penoyer Lake. At **Mile 7.2** it merges into the two-track crossed earlier. Head south (left) and in a half mile look for the blue diamonds where the trail crosses two-track. Head east (right) on the trail to return to post No. 12 at **Mile 8.1**.

This time at the junction head north (right) toward No-Name Lake, descending near the marshy end of the shallow lake in a quarter mile and reaching post No. 11 at **Mile 8.7**. At this junction, the trail to the north (right) reaches post No. 5 in 0.75 mile and then the west trailhead, via post No. 6, in 3.3 miles.

Head south (left) instead and within a half mile you'll return to post No. 10 and the Byron Lake walk-in sites, reached at **Mile 9.2**. If you're spending a second night at this lovely lake, your day is done. If not, then all that remains is to backtrack the first leg of this trek, a 1.7-mile walk to the trailhead on County Road F-32.

15

Chippewa Trail

Place: Negwegon State Park

Total Distance: 7 miles

Hiking Time: 3 to 4 hours

Rating: Moderate

Highlights: Lake Huron beaches, shoreline views

Maps: Negwegon State Park map from the Michigan DNR, or Chippewa Trail map from MichiganTrailMaps.com

Trailhead GPS Coordinates: N 44° 51' 18.21" W 083° 19' 27.34"

They have erected signs along US 23 and Black River Road, and the crew from the Alcona Country Road Commission has been grading Sand Hill Trail. Now finding and driving to Negwegon State Park is easy.

Too bad.

In the past just getting to the state park was half the adventure. Back then Sand Hill Trail, the only access to Negwegon, was a sandy, deeply rutted county road that in effect made the Lake Huron park the most remote in the Lower Peninsula. After an agonizing 2.5-mile drive along Sand Hill Trail, when most first-time visitors were sure they were going to lose their muffler if not some other part of their vehicle, they were stunned to arrive at a huge park sign and a wide, graveled entrance drive in the middle of nowhere.

From the parking area at the end, they headed into the woods and within 50 yards emerged at a crescent-moon bay framed in by a sandy shoreline and the turquoise waters of Lake Huron and unmarred by beach blankets and beer coolers. It was such an amazing scene at the end of such a scary drive that the bay was as far as most people would get in this 3,738-acre park.

Too bad.

Beyond the beautiful sandy beaches and 6.5 miles of undeveloped shoreline, Negwegon is a mixture of lowland areas and small ridges with pockets of wetlands and meadows mixed in with stands of mature pine forests, hardwoods, and aspen. An abundance of wildlife, from bald eagles and wild turkeys to white-tailed deer and black bears, thrive in the area.

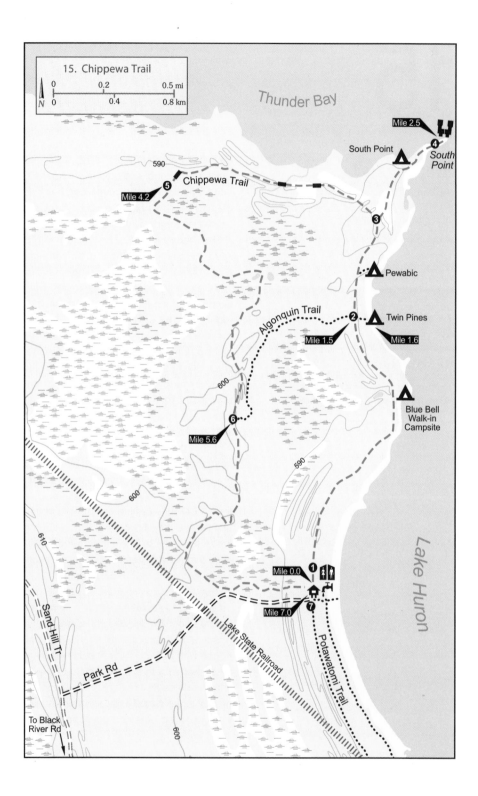

15. Chippewa Trail

0   0.2   0.5 mi
0   0.4   0.8 km

N

Thunder Bay

Mile 2.5

South Point

4

South Point

590

Chippewa Trail

Mile 4.2

5

3

Pewabic

Algonquin Trail

2 Twin Pines

Mile 1.5

Mile 1.6

600

Blue Bell
Walk-in
Campsite

590

6

Mile 5.6

600

Lake Huron

610

600

Mile 0.0 **1**

Sand Hill Tr.

Lake State Railroad

7

Mile 7.0

Park Rd

Potawatomi Trail

To Black
River Rd

600

Acquired in 1962, Negwegon was re-named from Alpena State Park in 1970 to honor a chief of the Ojibway tribe who was loyal to the U.S. side during the War of 1812. Besides the gravel entrance drive and parking area, the only development Negwegon has ever experienced is the construction of a 10-mile trail system that was laid out and posted in the early 1990s by the Michigan Civilian Conservation Corps. In 2009 it was enhanced with the addition of four backcountry campsites.

The trail system at Negwegon is divided into three loops, with posted trailheads located in the parking area. Heading south is the Potawatomi Trail, a 3.3-mile loop that hugs Lake Huron before swinging inland for its return. Departing to the north is the Chippewa Trail, a 7-mile loop past all four backcountry campsites and the spectacular views at the end of South Point, making it one of the finest treks on the sunrise side of the state. A crossover spur labeled Algonquin Trail shortens the loop to 3.7 miles but begins the return before you reach South Point.

The hikes to the sites range from a mile to 2.2 miles, and the only amenities they feature are a picnic table, fire ring, wilderness toilet, and bear pole. But all are on the Lake Huron shoreline, rewarding campers who spend the energy to hike in with quiet evenings and spectacular sunrises.

Scenic campsites and close-to-home backpacking opportunities; that's worth a drive on Sand Hill Trail.

A backcountry campsite at Negwegon State Park.

A backpacker taking in the view from South Point in Negwegon State Park.

ACCESS

From Harrisville head northwest on US 23 for 13 miles and then east on Black River Road (right). Head north (left) on Sand Hill Trail, where the park is signposted; you'll reach the entrance in 2.5 miles.

A vehicle permit or annual state park pass is required to enter Negwegon, and there is a nightly fee for the campsites. The sites can be reserved in advance through Harrisville State Park (989-724-5126). Additional information about Negwegon is available through the website of the Friends of Negwegon (www.fonsp.org).

TRAIL

Numbered posts are laid out in a counter-clockwise direction on the Chippewa Trail.

The first half of the loop follows an old two-track that in the 1800s was Stage Coach Road, the main route between Alpena and Harrisville. The park can be wet in the spring or after heavy rains, but a series of board-walks keeps you out of the deepest water.

At *Mile 0.7* you catch a glimpse of Lake Huron for the first time through the trees. At *Mile 1* you arrive at the posted spur to Blue Bell Campsite. Surrounded by pines, the campsite overlooks Lake Huron and is marked along the shoreline as well for kay-akers needing a place to pull out and spend the night. In another half mile you reach post No. 2, marking the Algonquin crossover spur to the west and the side trail to Twin Pines Campsite to the east. The hike remains level and easy, and you quickly reach the spur to the Pewabic Campsite.

Post No. 3 is at *Mile 2*, on the edge of a large meadow, marking the side trail to South Point. The open field is where stagecoach passengers once took a well-deserved break from their jarring journey. Today it's where hikers depart the main loop for the most spectacular views in the park.

The rocky tip of the small peninsula is reached in a half mile and provides an almost 360-degree view of Lake Huron. To the north are Bird Island and Scarecrow Island, a protected nesting area that is part of the Michigan Islands Wilderness Area, while across Thunder Bay you spot the water towers of Alpena. To the south is Negwegon's jagged shoreline.

With just a turn of the head, you can gaze over miles of shoreline, acres of water.

On the way to the rocky tip you pass South Point Campsite, a 2.2-mile hike from the trailhead. This is the most scenic spot by far to pitch a tent: It's located a low bluff overlooking the waters of Thunder Bay and the two islands just offshore. It's tranquil when the weather is nice, gusty when it isn't, as there is little protection from winds out of the north or south.

Many hikers never make it farther than South Point, but to complete the loop return to post No. 3. The Chippewa Trail swings to the west and provides an occasional glimpse of Thunder Bay while crossing a series of high arching bridges over streams and wetlands.

Post No. 5 is reached at *Mile 4.2*. Here the trail swings south and winds through the interior of the park on its return to the trailhead. This stretch, particularly between posts No. 5 and No. 6, is only lightly posted at best and can be wet at times. It offers the best opportunities, however, to spot wildlife.

Post No. 6, reached at *Mile 5.6*, marks the junction with the Algonquin Trail that heads to the east (left). Chippewa Trail continues south (right). Eventually the trail swings east and emerges at the trailhead parking area at *Mile 7*. Time for a swim on a beach you can call your own.

Heartland

16

Bishop's Bog Preserve Trail

Place: Portage South-Central Greenway
Total Distance: 4.6 miles round-trip
Hiking Time: 2 hours
Rating: Easy
Highlights: Floating trail through extensive bogs and wetlands
Maps: Portage South-Central Greenway map from the Portage Parks and Recreation Department, or Bishop's Bog Trail from MichiganTrailMaps.com
Trailhead GPS Coordinates: N 42° 9' 57.29" W 085° 35' 57.39"

The signs at South Westnedge Park say STAY ON TRAIL AT ALL TIMES, but most people wouldn't dare wander off it. Bishop's Bog Preserve Trail is aptly named. It passes through the heart of a bog that's so wet in the spring that the floating trail has the wiggle of a water bed; every step results in small eruptions between the plastic planking that will soak your boots.

But wet socks and damp toes are a small price to pay for this quick and unusual escape from the city. Within five minutes you can go from Kalamazoo and I-94 to the middle of a 140-acre bog featuring stunted black spruce, tamarack trees, and a variety of wildlife.

The 1.2-mile, point-to-point trail is part of the Portage South-Central Greenway, a series of five parks that total 483 acres and are linked together by 6 miles of trail, a fourth of it floating on bogs and marshes. The parks included in this hike are West Lake Nature Preserve, South Westnedge Park, Bishop's Bog Preserve, and Schrier Park. Only once, while hiking from park to park, do you have to cross a road. It's an amazing oasis in the urban sprawl of Michigan's 11th-largest city.

The centerpiece of the greenway is Bishop's Bog. The "relict bog" is a holdover from the last ice age and harbors a number of climatically cool-region plants extremely rare for this part of the state. With its extensive mat of sphagnum moss, tamarack trees, and blueberry bushes, the bog is something botanists would expect to find 300 miles to north. Yet five minutes south of Kalamazoo,

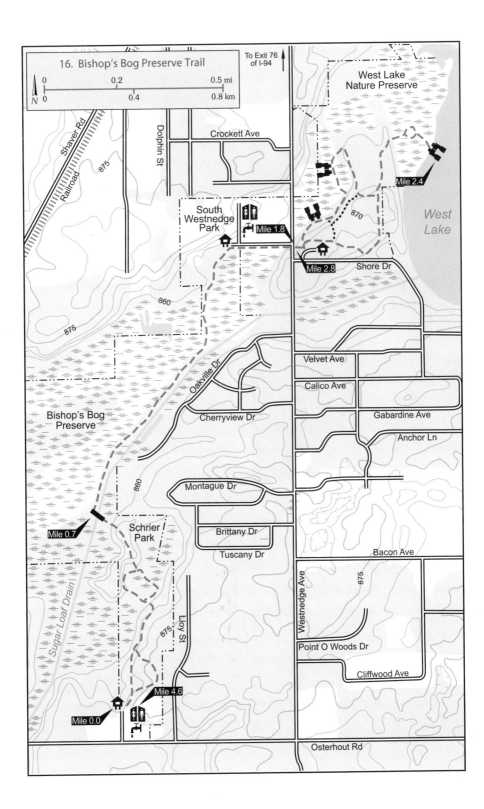

16. Bishop's Bog Preserve Trail

To Exit 76 of I-94

West Lake Nature Preserve

West Lake

Mile 2.4

Crockett Ave

Dolphin St

Shaver Rd

Railroad

875

South Westnedge Park

Mile 1.8

Mile 2.8

Shore Dr

870

860

875

Velvet Ave

Calico Ave

Oakville Dr

Cherryview Dr

Gabardine Ave

Anchor Ln

Bishop's Bog Preserve

Montague Dr

860

Mile 0.7

Schrier Park

Brittany Dr

Tuscany Dr

Bacon Ave

Westnedge Ave

875

Sugar Loaf Drain

875

Lloy St

Mile 4.6

Point O Woods Dr

Cliffwood Ave

Mile 0.0

Osterhout Rd

A hiker on the Bishop's Bog Preserve Trail.

4.6 miles. For a shorter day, you can just as easily turn around in South Westnedge Park and hike only Bishop's Bog Preserve Trail for a return outing of 3 miles.

ACCESS

To reach Schrier Park, depart I-94 at exit 76 and head south on Westnedge Avenue. Along the way you will pass the Portage City Offices, where you can pick up or download a trail map from the Portage Department of Parks and Recreation (269-329-4522; www.portagemi.gov). You'll also pass the entrance to South Westnedge Park. West Lake Nature Preserve is reached by heading east on South Shore Drive. Within 5.3 miles turn west on Osterhout Road; you'll reach the entrance to Schrier Park within a half mile.

TRAIL

Schrier Park is a 56-acre unit that anchors the south end of the Portage South-Central Greenway and features restrooms, drinking water, picnic tables, and a pavilion. From the parking lot a paved trail leads through the open day-use area and into the woods. By staying to the left at every intersection, you'll quickly find yourself on a path in a hardwood forest of red maple, white oak, a few hickories, and wild cherry. At **Mile 0.7** the trail uses a footbridge to cross Sugar Loaf Drain.

there it is—for all practical purposes a slice of the Upper Peninsula.

In 1987 the Michigan Nature Conservancy registered the area as the "largest remaining relict bog in southern Michigan." That year the Portage Parks and Recreation Department began piecing together the greenway. Bishop's Bog Preserve Trail, the final link of the trail system, was completed in 1997.

The hike described here is a combination of trails in all the parks. It begins in Schrier Park and makes for an interesting walk of

On the other side you enter Bishop's Bog, a 152-acre preserve in which the ancient relict bog was left untouched and today is home to several rare plant species, including the orange fringed orchid and stemless pink lady's slipper. The trail through the bog becomes a bouncing boardwalk of plastic planking. This intriguing floating trail lasts for almost a mile as it passes through the middle of the sensitive wetland. The trail is handicapped-accessible, and every 200 feet there is a turnaround for wheelchairs.

Every 1,000 feet there is a bench where you can sit and search the surrounding mat for carnivorous sundew and pitcher plants or lowbush cranberries.

At the north end of the bog the trail enters South Westnedge Park and becomes an asphalt path that swings sharply east and at *Mile 1.8* reaches South Westnedge Avenue. On the other side you enter West Lake Nature Preserve, the north end of the greenway. The 110-acre park is an upland hardwood forest bordered on three sides by either an extensive bog or the marshy shore of West Lake. Winding through the preserve are 2 miles of paths with the outside loop set up as a mile-long interpretive trail. There are 18 stops that correspond to a pamphlet that's available at the trailhead or can be downloaded in advance from the Portage Department of Parks and Recreation website (www.portagemi.gov).

The interpretive trail is numbered in a clockwise direction and includes a pair of short spurs in the first half mile that extend to observation decks floating on a bog. If it's winter you can often see in the snow the prints of the rabbits and pheasants that use the brushy marsh for cover. Eventually the trail swings into the woods and then at reaches a junction at post No. 10.

Here a spur leads to almost a quarter mile of bouncing boardwalk through a rare stand of tamarack and across the open bog that borders the lake's northwest corner. At the end of the spur is a third floating deck, reached at *Mile 2.4*, which allows you to scan the water for whatever wildlife there might be. During the spring and fall migrations there could easily be more than 100 waterfowl bobbing within 75 yards of the deck.

From the spur the trail heads south, and signs will direct you back to the pavilion, where you pick up the asphalt path that heads west. You quickly cross South Westnedge Avenue and within a quarter mile reach the posted north end of Bishop's Bog Trail in South Westnedge Park.

The remainder of the hike is a return through Bishop's Bog Preserve. When you reach Sugar Loaf Drain at *Mile 3.9*, stay to the left at every intersection to enjoy the rest of Schrier's interpretive loops. At *Mile 4.6* you'll return to the day-use area and parking lot where the outing began.

17

Hall Lake Trail

Place: Yankee Springs Recreation Area

Total Distance: 3.4 miles

Hiking Time: 2 hours

Rating: Easy to moderate

Highlights: Unusual geological formations

Maps: Yankee Springs Recreation Area map from the Michigan DNR, or Hall Lake Trail map from MichiganTrail Maps.com

Trailhead GPS Coordinates: N 42° 36' 48.25" W 085° 29' 25.12"

The rugged terrain, inland lakes, interesting bogs, and unusual depressions known as Devil's Soup Bowls provide Yankee Springs Recreation Area with ideal hiking qualities. Its location, almost centered among the urban areas of Grand Rapids, Kalamazoo, and Battle Creek, makes it a popular park with everybody.

In the past the park's network of trails were used for so many different recreational functions that the paths proliferated with directional arrows and colored diamonds. At times, it was confusing to know which way to go—a junction might feature signs for snowmobilers, skiers, hikers, and even an old post indicating a nonexistent bridle path. All this is to be expected whenever a park draws more than 700,000 visitors annually, making it one of the five most popular units in the state park system.

In the early 1990s, however, new trails were cut in an effort to separate user groups, particularly hikers and mountain bikers. Off-road cyclists now have their own 12-mile system with a staging area located at Deep Lake on the east side of the park. A new segment of the Chief Noonday Trail was built to remove it from the mountain bike area and eventually was designated as part of the North Country Trail. Additions to the bridle trails have been restricted at the south end of the park.

Such careful planning has greatly improved the situation at Yankee Springs. Still, I try to avoid the park on weekends from July to mid-August when the majority of the visitors arrive. Springtime, especially from

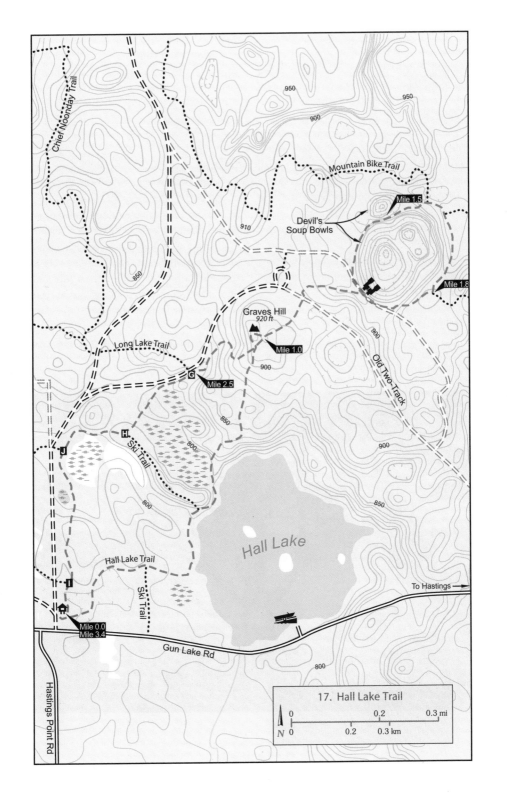

Mile 1.5

Devil's
Soup Bowls

Mile 1.8

Mountain Bike Trail

Chief Noonday Trail

950

950

900

910

850

Graves Hill
920 ft

Mile 1.0

Long Lake Trail

900

900

Old Two-Track

G

Mile 2.5

900

850

H

Ski Trail

800

900

J

850

800

Hall Lake

To Hastings →

Hall Lake Trail

Ski Trail

Mile 0.0
Mile 3.4

Gun Lake Rd

800

Hastings Point Rd

17. Hall Lake Trail

N

0   0.2   0.3 mi

0   0.2   0.3 km

mid-April to early May, is best for viewing wildflowers and reemerging plants. Since the nearly 5,200-acre park is well forested with more than 70 species of native trees, mid-October to early November is also an excellent time to wander through its woods.

Yankee Springs has more than 16 miles of designated hiking trails, but few of the routes are loops. One of the few that is, Hall Lake Trail, is also one of the more scenic walks in the park when combined with the connector to the Devil's Soup Bowls for a 3.4-mile outing. There is no longer an overlook from Graves Hill—foliage now blocks out all views except in late fall and winter—but the Soup Bowls are interesting, and the hike along Hall Lake is scenic.

Although there is a bit of climbing to Graves Hill and around the Soup Bowls, the trails are wide, well posted, and easily hikable in running shoes. There are lots of wildflowers and trees to identify, but don't expect to encounter much wildlife in mid-summer. With almost a million visitors a year to this park, you can bet that the residents of the woods remain well hidden during the day.

ACCESS

The state park unit is a 30-minute drive from either Grand Rapids or Kalamazoo off US 131. From the highway, depart at exit 61, follow County Road A-42 east for 7 miles to its junction with Gun Lake Road, and turn right. From the east, head west on M-37 from Hastings for 2 miles, then turn onto Gun Lake Road (also A-42 at this point) to reach the park in 10 miles.

The trailhead for Hall Lake Trail is marked across from the entrance of Long Lake

Hall Lake seen at the beginning of Hall Lake Trail.

Yankee Springs Recreation Area is laced with many trails and signposts. A posted junction along Hall Lake Trail.

Outdoor Center, posted along Gun Lake Road 2 miles from County Road A-42 or 1.5 miles beyond the park headquarters (269-795-9081). There is parking for three or four cars at the trailhead but no other facilities or drinking water.

Yankee Springs has several campgrounds, including a modern facility on Gun Lake. Because the 200-site campground is filled throughout much of the summer, it's considerably easier to obtain a site in the park's Deep Lake Campground, a rustic facility of 120 sites. A state park vehicle permit or daily pass is required to hike or camp at Yankee Springs.

TRAIL

With a trailhead located across from the entrance of Long Lake Outdoor Center, Hall Lake Trail is a 2-mile loop to Graves Hill. This description includes the extra 1.4 miles to Devil's Soup Bowls and begins with an immediate junction with the return loop. By heading up the right-hand fork, you pass the posted junction with a winter ski trail in a quarter mile and arrive at a view of Hall Lake at *Mile 0.4*. The trail here is wide and easy to follow as it crosses a bridge and then skirts the lake for the next quarter mile, providing good views of the islands in the middle and any anglers who might be fishing for bass or bluegill.

At the northwest corner of the lake, the trail begins to climb gradually and then leaves the watery view for a sharper ascent to the high point. Just before *Mile 1* you reach a junction with a bypass around Graves Hill and the return loop that's posted as the route to Long Lake and Chief Noonday Trails. Head straight; in less than 100 yards you'll be standing on Graves Hill, but most likely not seeing much. The high point with an elevation of 920 feet used to provide a view of the wooded interior of the state recreation area and a portion of Gun Lake. But now, other than late fall and winter, foliage obscures the view even when you stand of one of several large rocks strategically placed at the top.

A trail leads northeast off the high point and is posted as the route to Devil's Soup Bowl. You quickly cross an old two-track featuring the orange markers of a snowmobile trail and at *Mile 1.3* arrive at the first Soup Bowl; a wooden fence keeps hikers from peering too far over the edge. The bowls are very steep, glacially carved depressions known as kettles. Despite the foliage, you can still peer down into the main one and, if you have the energy, descend almost 100 feet into it.

Follow the trail in a clockwise direction around the large soup bowl. At *Mile 1.5* you'll find yourself tiptoeing a narrow ridge with the large bowl to the right and the small one to the left. With a simple twist of your head you can look into both of them. The steep climb that follows tops off at a junction posted as the Deep Lake Trail and the mountain bike trail. Head right and right again in less than 100 yards while keeping an eye out for off-road cyclists—Yankee Springs is a popular mountain bike area.

At *Mile 1.8* the mountain bike trail departs to the left while you continue skirting the large soup bowl. At *Mile 2* you'll return at the fenced overlook. Backtrack to Graves Hill and follow the return loop marked for Long Lake Trail. It's a steady descent off the glacial moraine that bottoms out at *Mile 2.5* near the park road. Here Long Lake Trail heads west for the interior of the recreation area. Hall Lake Trail is the left-hand fork that continues to the southwest, skirting several wetlands and passing three junctions with ski trails, each marked by a letter.

At *Mile 3.4* you emerge at the trailhead and small parking area across from the Long Lake Outdoor Center.

18

Green Trail

Place: Lake Lansing Park–North

Total Distance: 3.3 miles

Hiking Time: 1 to 2 hours

Rating: Easy

Highlights: Interpretive displays, wetlands

Maps: Lake Lansing Park–North Trail Guide from Ingham County Parks, or Green Trail map from MichiganTrailMaps.com

Trailhead GPS Coordinates: N 42° 45' 56.30" W 084° 23' 42.72"

Lake Lansing Park–North is a misnomer. The Ingham County Parks Department does maintain two smaller units on the lake: Lake Lansing Park–South and the Lake Lansing Boat Launch, but this one isn't anywhere near the water.

The 410-acre preserve is across the street from the popular lake and features day-use facilities, picnic areas, shelters, and volleyball and baseball fields. But the vast majority of the park is a natural setting, an intriguing mix of pine, mature oak, and maple woodlands, and extensive wetlands and marshes, accessed by a 5-mile system of footpaths and boardwalks. This system is well marked with color posts and location maps, making it easy to hike. Best of all, the trails can provide a quiet escape despite being on the fringe of that political beehive known as Lansing.

The heart of the system is the Green Trail, a 3.3-mile loop that winds between woods and wetlands and in doing so crosses a dozen boardwalks, some surprisingly long. Other spurs allow you to lengthen or shorten the walk. The Blue Trail is the longest loop at 3.8 miles; the Red is the shortest at 1 mile.

To shorten this outing–especially if you're hiking with children–follow the first half of the Green Trail then use the Yellow Cutoff. This 2.4-mile loop is marked by a series of well-designed interpretive plaques, thanks to the Michigan Non-Game Wildlife Fund. Titled HABITAT: A PLACE CALLED HOME, the plaques carefully explain which species live where in the various habitats you pass through.

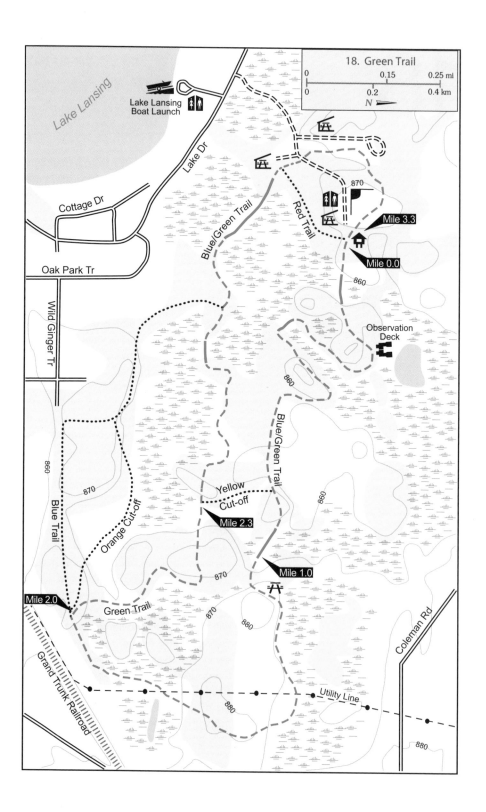

18. Green Trail

0   0.15   0.25 mi
0   0.2   0.4 km
N

Lake Lansing

Lake Lansing
Boat Launch

Lake Dr

Cottage Dr

Oak Park Tr

Wild Ginger Tr

Blue/Green Trail

Red Trail

870

Mile 3.3

Mile 0.0

860

Observation
Deck

860

Blue Trail

870

860

Orange Cut-off

Blue/Green Trail

Yellow
Cut-off

Mile 2.3

Mile 1.0

Mile 2.0

Green Trail

870

870

880

860

Coleman Rd

Grand Trunk Railroad

880

Utility Line

880

A bench along a wetland boardwalk at Lake Lansing Park–North.

The trail system is groomed for skiing in the winter. Rental equipment is available at the main picnic shelters, which double as warming huts. In the summer the trails cater solely to hikers; mountain bikes are not allowed in the park.

ACCESS

From I-96, depart at exit 110 and head north into Okemos. Turn east on Grand River Avenue and then turn north at the first light onto Marsh Road. Follow Marsh Road through Haslett and turn east on North Lake Drive, where the park is posted in 1.5 miles.

For more information, contact the Ingham County Parks Department (517-676-2233; http://pk.ingham.org).

TRAIL

There are two trailheads in the park. The main trailhead is near Sandhill Shelter, a picnic area that includes restrooms, a playground, and a softball field on the north side of the parking lot. From the east end of the parking lot a short trail leads to the large trailhead display, featuring a map and mileage. It also marks the junction with the Red Trail, a 1-mile loop that stays almost entirely in the developed area of the park.

From Sandhill Shelter, the trail immediately descends to the first stretch of wetlands of the day and crosses it on a boardwalk that features a bench in the middle. At the other end you return to the forest and climb a low ridge to an observation deck perched on the edge with an interpretive plaque nearby. The deck allows you to view a pond in the middle of a sea of cattails; if it's near dusk there could be a whitetail or two nearby.

At *Mile 0.3* from the trailhead you arrive at your third boardwalk and wetland as well as another interpretive plaque. But this one is not on the trail; rather, it's in the marsh, surrounded by cattails. Another low rise

A father and son pause to study the wetland at Lake Lansing North County Park.

follows. Here the trail swings south to reach the posted junction with the Yellow Cutoff at *Mile 0.9*. Just beyond it is another boardwalk and the *Mile 1* marker.

You pass a covered picnic table that was an Eagle Scout project at *Mile 1.2* and in another quarter mile break out in a utility line corridor. The trail passes underneath it, loops through a pine forest, and then passes underneath the utility line again at *Mile 1.7* in the most unappealing segment of the loop.

You're now heading back toward the developed entrance of the park. Just before the post marking *Mile 2* is the junction where the Green Trail splits north from the Blue Trail. You begin skirting a large marsh and then pass through an impressive stand of spruce–pines so large and old they form an almost impenetrable canopy against the sky. There is little sunlight in this grove and thus little undergrowth on the forest floor, which make the dark trunks stand out even more.

You emerge from the spruce at an old two-track that the trail follows west to arrive at the second junction with the Yellow Cutoff, at *Mile 2.3*. The trail continues west, winding along the edge of hardwoods while skirting yet another marsh.

Eventually a boardwalk leads you across the marsh and to the junction with the return of Blue Trail. The most impressive stretch is just ahead, the longest boardwalk in the park across its largest marsh. Cattails are all around you, and if you're not in a hurry there's a bench where you can sit and ponder this amazing scene. At the other end of the wooden walkway you arrive at Oak Knoll Shelter and a picnic area.

At this point the Green/Blue Trails cross the entrance road and swing through the developed portions of the park, passing the volleyball court and skirting the softball field before returning to the trailhead. A far more interesting and shorter route is to follow the Red Trail here: It skirts the wetland you just crossed before ending at the trailhead. Or you can simply follow the park road back to your vehicle at Sandhill Shelter.

19

Ledges Trail

Place: Fitzgerald County Park	
Total Distance: 2.4 miles round-trip	
Hiking Time: 1 to 2 hours	
Rating: Easy	
Highlights: Ancient rock cliffs, Grand River	
Maps: Fitzgerald Park brochure from Eaton County Parks, or Ledges Trail Map from MichiganTrailMaps.com	
Trailhead GPS Coordinates: N 42° 45' 34.90" W 084° 45' 39.34"	

The ancient sedimentary outcroppings that tower above the Grand River are the only place in the Lower Peninsula—other than climbing walls—where somebody can lace up a pair of rock shoes and dip their fingers into a chalk bag. That's on the north side, where at the City of Grand Ledges' Oak Park climbers set ropes and tackle routes with names like Rocket Man and Second Thoughts.

Hikers head to the south side where the mile-long Ledges Trail skirts the base of the cliffs, linking Fitzgerald County Park with Island Park. Except for the initial descent to the river, this point-to-point path is a level and easy stroll that provides both a close view of this unique geological formation and a good vantage point from which to watch those daredevil climbers across the river.

The ledges have attracted people throughout history, beginning with Chief Okemos, a legendary Indian who led his tribe to the river of the "Big Rocks" each spring to hunt and tap trees for maple syrup. Later the area was known as Robbers Caves, since the many caves at the base of the ledges were supposedly used by thieves to stable stolen horses while they awaited sale. Other legends tell of fugitive slaves using the caves as part of the Underground Railroad in their flight to freedom in Canada.

By 1894 the beauty of the ledges had attracted a religious group, which established the Grand Ledge Spiritualist Camp Association. Within Fitzgerald Park, they constructed a large pavilion and organized a camp that brought thousands here at the turn of the

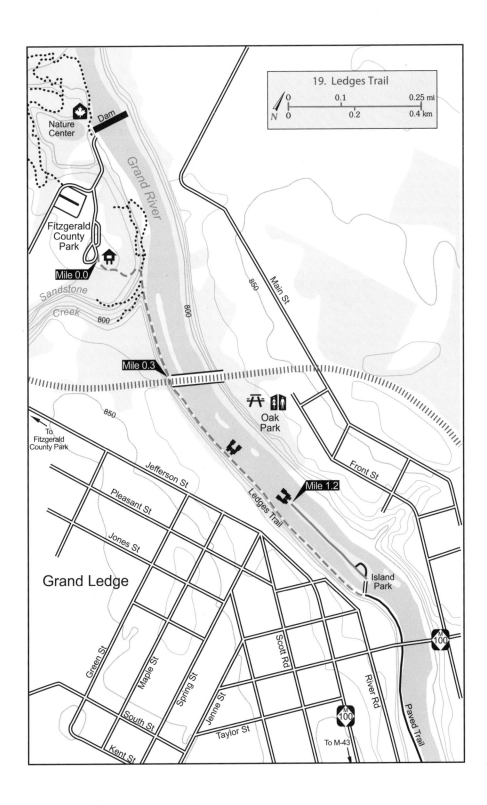

19. Ledges Trail

0   0.1   0.25 mi
0   0.2   0.4 km

N

Nature
Center

Dam

Grand River

Fitzgerald
County
Park

Mile 0.0

Sandstone

Creek

800

850

Main St

800

Mile 0.3

Oak
Park

To
Fitzgerald
County Park

850

Jefferson St

Pleasant St

Jones St

Front St

Mile 1.2

Ledges Trail

Grand Ledge

Island
Park

Green St

Maple St

Spring St

Jenne St

Scott Rd

River Rd

M-100

M-100

South St

Taylor St

Kent St

To M-43

Paved Trail

century for "summer encampments." The pavilion that the spiritualists originally used for séances was later used for a factory, roller-skating rink, and basketball court, successively. Today it's the big red barn in the park and serves as the home of the Over the Ledge Theater Company.

This round-trip, 2.4-mile outing, which includes hiking the length of Island Park, was made for kids, combining an easy walk past interesting scenery with a chance of seeing rock climbers in action. The first third of the trail lies in Fitzgerald County Park and

A hiker following the Ledges Trail.

has been developed as interpretive path with a corresponding brochure that can downloaded from the Eaton County Parks website.

The 78-acre county park borders the Grand River and features six picnic sites, 3 miles of trails, a fish ladder, and a small nature center that is open May through October 1 to 5 PM on Wednesday, Saturday, and Sunday.

ACCESS

From I-96, depart at exit 93-A and head west on M-43 for 6 miles. Turn right on Jefferson Street; the entrance to Fitzgerald County Park will be a half mile farther on the left. The park is open year-round from 8 AM to dusk; a motor vehicle entry fee is required from April through October. For more information, contact the Eaton County Parks and Recreation Department (517-627-7351; www.eaton county.org/departments/parks-department).

TRAIL

The trailhead for the Ledges Trail is just east of the large red barn that is now the Ledges Playhouse. The trail immediately descends to the Grand River via a long stairway, passing two interpretive posts along the way. At the junction at the bottom, head east (right) to cross Sandstone Creek and reach the first set of ledges on the other side.

The impressive rock cliffs were formed 270 million years ago when most of Michigan was covered by water that carried and deposited sediments (sand, silt, and clay) in layers along riverbanks and beaches. After time and pressure compacted the layers into rock, the Grand River sculpted the cliffs through years of erosion.

On both sides of Sand Creek are several short side trails: River Bottom and Baneberry Trails on the west side, Sandstone Creek Trail on the east. The Ledges Trail continues

Rock climbers on the Grand Ledges, which can be seen while hiking the Ledges Trail.

east, skirting the Grand River. At **Mile 0.3** it reaches post No. 8 at the boundary of Fitzgerald Park, located underneath a railroad trestle built in 1888 by the Detroit, Grand Rapids, & Western Railroad. The remainder of the trail crosses private property, but only a couple of houses pop into view above you. Most of the time you are secluded among hemlock pines with the Grand River on one side of you and the sandstone cliffs on the other.

At **Mile 0.5** you reach the spot where it's possible to see the steepest ledges in the area on the north bank of the river. These 70-foot-tall cliffs are where rock climbers congregate. A pair of binoculars will assist in watching the climbers, though by June the heavy foliage on both sides of the river blocks a good portion of the view.

The trail ends at Island Park, where an old iron bridge crosses the river to the second island of what used to be the Seven Islands Resorts, a popular vacation spot at the turn of the century. Today the long, narrow island has benches, picnic tables, small docks along the shoreline, and a paved trail down the middle of it. The western tip of the island, reached at **Mile 1.2**, is an ideal spot to enjoy an extended break before beginning the return to Fitzgerald Park.

If there are climbers on the ledges, you can also watch them in Oak Park on the north side of the Grand River, reached from M-100 by heading west on Front Street.

20

Maple River

Place: Maple River State Game Area
Total Distance: 2.3 miles
Hiking Time: 1 to 2 hours
Rating: Easy
Highlights: Wetlands, birding opportunities
Maps: Maple River State Game Area map from the Michigan DNR, or MichiganTrailMaps.com
Trailhead GPS Coordinates: N 43° 8' 48.22" W 084° 33' 45.46"

The Maple River State Game Area is mid-Michigan's largest contiguous wetland complex, an extensive area of floodplains, lowlands, and marshes along the Maple River that begins in Gratiot County and spills into Clinton County. The 9,252-acre game area is divided into two sections, with the West Unit containing most of the acreage but no established trails other than short access trails for handicapped hunters.

Hiking opportunities are available in the East Unit, however. Straddling US 27, the East Unit features pools and diked-in ponds that serve as the water basin for the Maple River and attract migrating birds. Hiking along dikes is easy, and the spectacular congregations of birds among the cattails in the warm glow of a late-afternoon sun make this trail system scenic and interesting for families and anybody who enjoys birding.

There are more than 5 miles of trails in the state game area, but the dikes in Unit A and Unit B are the most popular for hiking and birding. This hike is in Unit B, a 2.3-mile loop on the east side of US 27 that includes passing a photo blind and an observation tower.

Wildlife can be viewed practically year-round in the game area. Spring viewing from March through May is excellent: Thousands of ducks, geese, and swans use the wetlands as a stopover on their migration to northern breeding grounds. Throughout the summer herons are a common sight in the area while the observant or those who pack along binoculars might spot bald eagles or ospreys perched on dead snags.

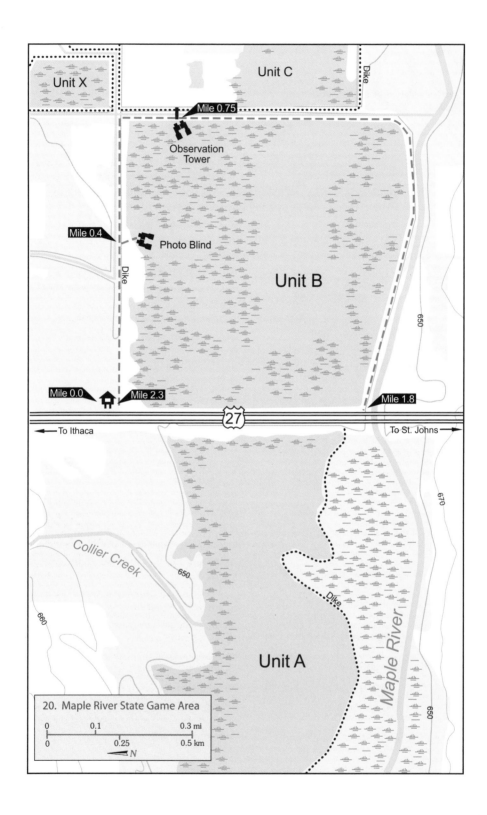

Unit X

Unit C

Dike

Mile 0.75

Observation
Tower

Mile 0.4

Photo Blind

Dike

Unit B

650

Mile 0.0   Mile 2.3

Mile 1.8

27

To Ithaca

To St. Johns

Collier Creek

650

670

660

Dike

Unit A

Maple River

650

20. Maple River State Game Area

0   0.1   0.3 mi
0   0.25   0.5 km
N

ACCESS

From St. John's, head north on US 27 for 8.5 miles. The Unit B trailhead is a gated two-track and parking lot on the north side of the state game area, reached just after the highway crosses the floodplains. There are no entry or vehicle fees for hiking the state game area.

Both units are open to hunting and bright colors or even blaze orange should be worn during the fall, especially during the October duck season. For the DNR map of Maple River State Game Area, go to www.michigan .gov/dnr and click on "Press Releases, Maps & Publications" on the left-hand side of the page. For more information, call the Rose Lake DNR Operations Service Center (517-373-9358) in East Lansing.

TRAIL

The trailhead for Unit B is reached just after you cross the Maple River floodplain and comes up quickly. Use caution when you slow down—US 27 can be a busy highway at times. Other than the small parking lot and a display sign, there are no facilities at the trailhead.

In the parking lot a gate marks the dike that heads due east, straight as an arrow. At one time this portion of the dike was a two-track of crushed slag, but gradually most of the gravel is being hidden by grass.

At *Mile 0.4* you reach a long boardwalk that extends into the cattails. At the other end is a barrier-free blind, a three-sided shelter that keeps hunters comfortable during the fall and camera lenses dry the rest of the

The photobraphy blind at Maple River State Game Area.

Marsh and wetlands at Maple River State Game Area.

year. There is open water south of the blind, providing hikers the opportunity to quietly watch great blue herons, bitterns, and other birds fishing.

The dike continues east with the cattail marsh to the right and a low-lying woods to the left. Eventually you swing south and at **Mile 0.75** arrive at the observation tower. The wooden structure rises 20 feet above the marsh to provide a different vantage of the winged wildlife than does the blind. Also at the tower is a bridge that leads to Unit C and a dike on the opposite side of the canal.

It's possible to hike around Unit C and end up back at this bridge with the additional loop turning your outing into a 4-mile trek.

The Unit B dike continues south and then swings sharply west, where you find yourself hiking a causeway between the extensive marsh and the Maple River. At **Mile 1.8** you arrive at US 27. It's a half mile along US 27 back to the trailhead and your vehicle. The highway has a very wide shoulder and is scenic as it cuts through the heart of the floodplain. But use caution; it can be busy at times.

21

Birch Grove Trail

Place: Manistee National Forest

Total Distance: 9.8 miles

Hiking Time: 5 to 6 hours

Rating: Moderate

Highlights: Loda Lake Wildflower Sanctuary, historic schoolhouse

Maps: Birch Grove Trail map from the North Country Trail Association or MichiganTrailMaps.com

Trailhead GPS Coordinates: N 43° 36' 52.73" W 085° 48' 52.28"

It's been around for more than 130 years and has served as a place of learning, a national headquarters, comfortable lodging for sore-footed backpackers, a hostel for travelers from around the world. It has also been the answer to a trivia question: Where is the halfway point of the North Country Trail, the country's longest footpath that someday will extend from North Dakota to New York?

The Birch Grove Schoolhouse.

The classic, one-room schoolhouse was built in the late 1870s in what was then Park City, a logging town on the north shores of Diamond Lake. When the loggers left, Park City became a ghost city, so local farmers moved the building in 1906 to its present location 7 miles northwest of White Cloud. Here it served rural students for more than 70 years. Then a century after it was built the empty, in-the-middle-of-nowhere schoolhouse was given a new lease on life when it was donated to the fledging North Country Trail Association, an organization trying to build a trail across seven states.

Even though in 1979 most of the North Country Trail was a vision, not a path, organizers hung a sign outside that said HEAD WEST AND YOU'LL REACH LAKE SAKAKAWEA, NORTH DAKOTA IN 1,633 MILES. HEAD EAST AND YOU'LL ARRIVE AT CROWN POINT, NEW YORK IN 1,603 MILES. The trail is now projected to end up being at more than 4,600 miles, but the sign is still there.

Right from the beginning the historic schoolhouse was also a place of lodging for volunteers building the trail, backpackers following large chunks of the NCT, and

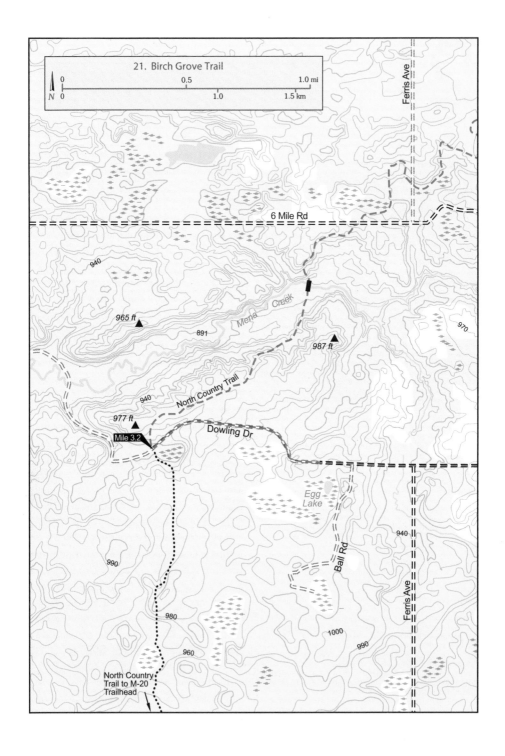

21. Birch Grove Trail

0   0.5   1.0 mi
0   1.0   1.5 km

N

Ferris Ave

6 Mile Rd

940

965 ft ▲

Merla Creek

891

987 ft ▲

970

North Country Trail

940

977 ft ▲

Mile 3.2

Dowling Dr

Egg Lake

Ball Rd

Ferris Ave

940

990

980

1000

990

960

North Country
Trail to M-20
Trailhead

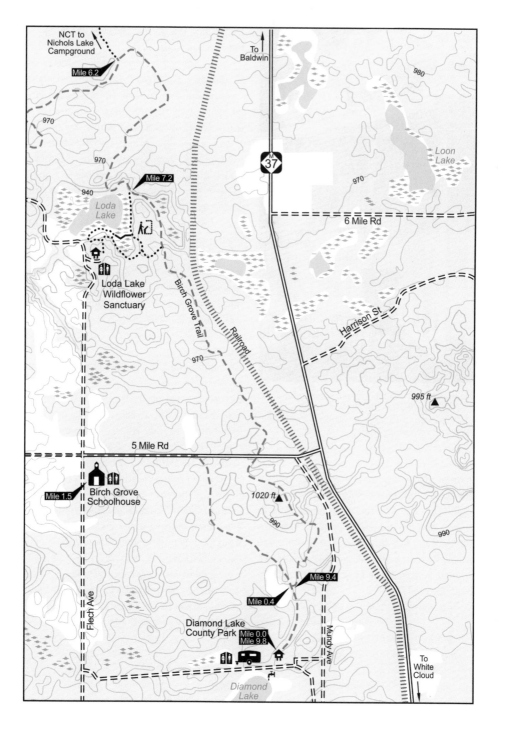

NCT to
Nichols Lake
Campground

Mile 6.2

970

970

970

To
Baldwin

980

Loon
Lake

M 37

970

6 Mile Rd

940

Mile 7.2

Loda
Lake

Loda Lake
Wildflower
Sanctuary

Birch Grove Trail

Railroad

970

Harrison St

995 ft ▲

5 Mile Rd

Birch Grove
Schoolhouse

Mile 1.5

1020 ft ▲

990

990

Mile 9.4

Mile 0.4

Diamond Lake
County Park

Mile 0.0
Mile 9.8

Mundy Ave

Flech Ave

Diamond
Lake

To
White
Cloud

The Birch Grove Schoolhouse once served as the headquarters for the North Country Trail Association and today is lodging for those hiking the Brich Grove Trail.

travelers from around the world as part of the American Youth Hostel system. The NCTA has since moved its headquarters to Lowell, and the schoolhouse is no longer a hostel. But it still serves as a pleasant place to stay for hikers and backpackers walking a 9.8-mile loop composed of the NCT and the Birch Grove Trail.

The loop was completed in 2007 when the Birch Grove Trail was pieced together, a 6.4-mile route of forest roads, old railroad grades, and footpaths diverting from the NCT in Newaygo County. The new trail connected to the national trail not only its namesake schoolhouse but also Diamond Lake County Park and Loda Lake Wildflower

Sanctuary, the only wildflower sanctuary in the national forest system.

This description begins at Diamond Lake. Originally a company retreat for Steelcase Corporation employees, the 156-acre Newaygo County park features a 60-site modern campground along with a swimming beach, a picnic area, and a boat launch with boat rentals. Both the Birch Grove Schoolhouse and Diamond Lake are best situated to be used as a base for hikers who can then undertake the loop as a day hike. Backpackers, however, can set up camp along the North Country Trail.

There are several ways to shorten the hike, including beginning at the schoolhouse and using 5-Mile Road to bypass the segments south of it to Diamond Lake. This would be a 7.8-mile trek.

ACCESS

Diamond Lake County Park is 6 miles north of White Cloud and is reached from M-37 by turning west on 5-Mile Road. You immediately cross a set of railroad tracks and then turn left on Mundy Road. The park is entrance is a mile south at 3351 Mundy Road. To reach the Birch Grove Schoolhouse, continue past Mundy Road for a mile on 5-Mile Road and then turn right on Felch Avenue.

For more information on the Birch Grove Trail or to reserve a campsite at Diamond Lake County Park, contact Newaygo County Parks and Recreation (231-652-9298; www.countyofnewaygo.com/Parks). For accommodations at the Birch Grove Schoolhouse or a map of the loop, see the West Michigan Chapter of the North Country Trail Association website (www.northcountrytrail .org/wmi).

TRAIL

Within Diamond Lake County Park, the trailhead for the Birch Grove Trail is located on the road that heads north to the service area. The trail is well posted, and there is limited parking. You head north into the woods along an old railroad grade and at **Mile 0.4** reach a junction with the return segment from the NCT and Loda Lake Wildflower Sanctuary. Head northwest (left).

The trail winds past an open area and then makes a gradual ascent before breaking out at 5-Mile Road, reached at **Mile 1**. Head west (left) and follow the paved road. At **Mile 1.5** the pavement ends at the junction with Felch Avenue. Just to the south (left) is the Birch Grove Schoolhouse; less than a mile to the north (right) is the entrance to Loda Lake Wildflower Sanctuary.

The Birch Grove Trail continues west along 5-Mile Road, now a graded dirt road lined by farm fields. In less than a half mile you pass the junction with Ferris Avenue before the road begins ascending, topping off on a ridge where it swings north (right) to become a sandy, badly rutted two-track labeled Dowling Drive on some maps. You follow the two-track for 0.8 mile and then arrive where the NCT crosses it at **Mile 3.2**.

The NCT swings northeast and follows a ridge through an area that is crisscrossed with off-road-vehicle (ORV) trails. Stay on course by keeping an eye out for the blue diamonds that are used to identify the NCT. Within a mile the trail begins a long descent off the ridge, bottoming out at Mena Creek, which you cross on a footbridge. On the north side a sharp climb awaits you before you descend to reach 6-Mile Road at **Mile 4.7**.

Follow 6-Mile Road briefly to the east (right) before picking up the NCT where it descends to a marsh and winds around it to the northeast, crossing Ferris Avenue within a half mile. The trail then continues as a high, dry ribbon along rolling wooded slopes, descending occasionally to one swampy area after another. At **Mile 6.2** you arrive at the posted junction with Birch Grove Trail. The NCT heads north (left) here; you head in an easterly direction (right) to follow an old railroad grade.

Birch Grove Trail swings to the south, skirts an old bog, and then reaches the north end of Loda Lake and at **Mile 7.2** a junction with the sanctuary's trail system. Head left here for the most direct route back to Diamond Lake. Or go right to enjoy the wildflowers or even a bench overlooking Loda Lake.

Originally part of a 1,000-acre private reserve, much of the land around Loda Lake was farmed before the USDA Forest Service purchased it and invited the Federated Garden Clubs of Michigan in 1938 to help them create a sanctuary for native plants. Today the sanctuary is a noted destination for botanists, who are attracted to the wide variety of habitats found in such a small area. The sanctuary's 1.5-mile trail winds through oak-maple woodlands, alongside a stream and floodplain, through old pine plantations, and on a boardwalk through a shrub swamp and emergent wetland. Lining the trail are 39 posts that correspond to an interpretive guide, with each identifying a plant or wildflower.

Without dipping into the sanctuary, you reach the junction with Birch Grove Trail within a quarter mile. Head south (left) and soon you'll be following that old railroad grade again. At **Mile 8.6** you cross paved 5-Mile Road and continue south to climb to a high point of 1,020 feet. Birch Grove Trail descends sharply to bottom out at a marsh and then swings southeast and arrives at the junction to Diamond Lake County Park at **Mile 9.4**. Retrace the first half mile of this hike to return to your vehicle.

22

Pine Valleys Pathway

Place: Pere Marquette State Forest

Total Distance: 4.1 miles

Hiking Time: 3 to 4 hours

Rating: Moderate

Highlights: Inland lakes, backcountry campsites

Maps: Pine Valleys Pathway map from the Michigan DNR or MichiganTrail Maps.com

Trailhead GPS Coordinates: N 44° 5' 18.25" W 085° 49' 32.25"

Lake County's Lost Lake isn't really lost, just well hidden in Pere Marquette State Forest by a shoreline of high bluffs.

Travelers zipping along nearby MI 37 may be oblivious to this small but scenic body of water, but for hikers who make an effort to locate the trailhead, the lake is easy to find and well worth the effort expended to reach it.

The water of Lost Lake is clear, and the shoreline is sprinkled with fallen trees and other structures, making this an attractive destination for any walk-in angler. All but one corner of the lake has a shoreline of steep bluffs, and in that corner the DNR's Forest Management Division has built a five-site backcountry campground where the door of every tent has a scenic view of the water.

Built in the mid-1970s, Pine Valleys Pathway is actually a network of three loops, with the northern and southern loops passing near or through numerous clear-cut areas. The most pleasant hike is the 4.1-mile middle loop, which travels the bluffs above Lost Lake before heading back.

Keep in mind that 7-Mile Road continues as a dirt road beyond the trailhead and runs near the trail at certain points. For this reason, no doubt, off-road-vehicle (ORV) destruction is very noticeable in places, particularly along the southern loop. The pathway also draws an occasional mountain biker or horseback rider from the camp on Stewart Lake. If you walk this trail in the middle of the summer, however, you'll probably have the path as well as the lakeside campground to yourself.

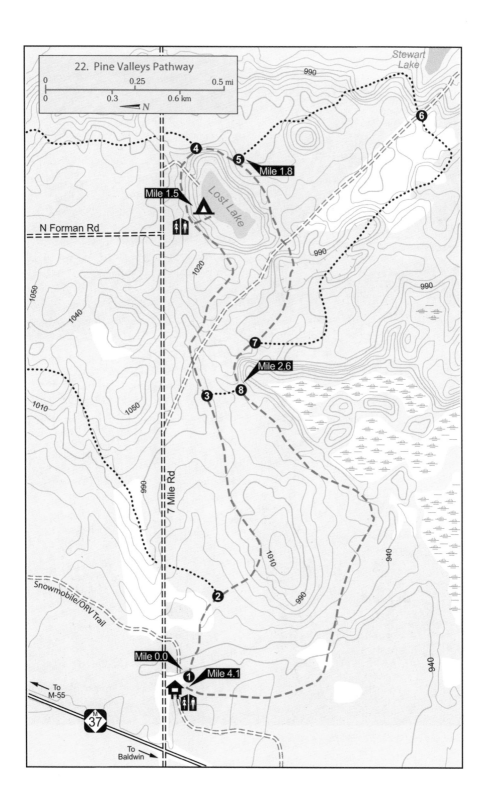

22. Pine Valleys Pathway

Stewart Lake

990

6

4

5 Mile 1.8

Mile 1.5

Lost Lake

N Forman Rd

990

990

1020

990

1050

1040

7

Mile 2.6

1010

1050

3 **8**

990

940

1010

990

940

Snowmobile/ORV Trail

7 Mile Rd

2

Mile 0.0

To M-55

1 Mile 4.1

M 37

To Baldwin

0   0.25   0.5 mi
0   0.3   0.6 km
N

Lost Lake along the Pine Valleys Pathway.

ACCESS

The pathway is in the northern portion of Lake County, 13 miles north of Baldwin or a 30-minute drive west of Cadillac. From MI 55, head south for 9 miles along M-37, then turn east onto 7-Mile Road, which is posted for the park. The dirt road passes a few homes and then comes to a large, grassy parking area on its south (right) side. The trailhead is posted here by the locator map.

If you're coming from the south, keep in mind that the DNR Baldwin field office (231-745-4651) is located just north of town right along M-37 and can provide maps and other information about the pathway.

TRAIL

Pine Valleys Pathway is marked with a series of numbered posts laid out in a clockwise direction. Half hidden in the back of the parking area, marking what is usually an overgrown path, is post No. 1. Head east (left) to reach post No. 2 in 0.2 mile. This is the junction where the northern loop splits off to the north (left).

The middle loop continues to the east (right) and becomes a wider trail to handle skiers in the winter. The hike also becomes more hilly as you gain elevation on the way to post No. 3, reached at *Mile 0.8*. This post marks a short crossover spur south to post No. 8 along the return trail. At this point, the middle loop follows an old vehicle track before veering to the right to cross the dirt road to Stewart Lake. The pathway is clearly posted on both sides.

Beyond the dirt road, the pathway swings to the southeast. At *Mile 1.4* you climb a bluff for your first view of Lost Lake. The trail skirts the bluff high above the lake briefly before arriving at a pair of vault toilets. From here a path descends to the five lakeshore sites. The vault toilets are the campground's

only amenities—the hand pump that once existed here has been removed. Pack in water or filter what you use from the lake.

Despite the lack of luxuries or even toilet paper in the outhouses (pack that in, too), Lost Lake is a wonderful spot to pitch a tent. The small lake is less than 1,000 feet in length but enclosed by 60-foot-high bluffs forested in a variety of hardwoods. Even when there is a wind, the lake is usually quiet and still, its lightly rippled surface often reflecting those shoreline colors. In the morning you'll want to linger at Lost Lake, watching the sunrise spread across its surface while savoring a second cup of coffee.

Go ahead and linger. The return trip to your car is a walk of only 2.6 miles.

Resuming along the top of the shoreline bluffs, the pathway continues to skirt Lost Lake with many unofficial paths leading down to the water made by either hungry beavers or anglers. You soon skirt 7-Mile Road, seen through the trees, and in less than a quarter mile arrive at post No. 4, where the northern loop reenters. The trail continues to traverse the lakeside bluffs and, at *Mile 1.8* from the campground, arrives at post No. 5.

The fork heading south (left) is the start of the southern loop, which leads to Stewart Lake, a small body of water with cottages and a church camp on it that is reached in 0.6 mile. The southern loop then returns to the middle loop at post No. 7, though you have to stomach some clear-cuts.

To remain on the middle loop, head west (right) from post No. 5. It immediately begins a nearly half-mile descent, bottoming out at the dirt road to Stewart Lake. From there, it remains a forested walk, reaching the locator map at post No. 7, at *Mile 2.4* or a mile from the campground.

Post No. 8, one hill and 0.2 mile away, is quickly reached, and then the trail swings

A camper at Lost Lake along the Pine Valleys Pathway.

southwest to arrive at what appears to be a flooded pond. Actually, it's an arm of Little Syers Lake that has been heavily dammed up by beavers and now attracts a variety of wildlife, especially birds and waterfowl. The trail swings away from the lake on an old logging track that arrives at a wildlife project. The grassy clearing is a planting of ryegrass for the benefit of deer (and thus hunters), which feed in such open areas. The trail never crosses the clearing but rather skirts the edge of it.

Keep an eye out for trail markers as the pathway crosses three logging roads and cuts through a second ryegrass clearing during the next half mile. Eventually the trail swings near M-37, where at times it's possible to hear the traffic rumble by, then returns to post No. 1 in the trailhead parking area, reached at *Mile 4.1* or 1.5 miles from post No. 8.

23

Silver Creek Pathway

Place: Pere Marquette State Forest

Total Distance: 4 miles

Hiking Time: 2 to 3 hours

Rating: Moderate

Highlights: Pine River, state forest campgrounds

Maps: Silver Creek Pathway map from the Michigan DNR or MichiganTrail Maps.com

Trailhead GPS Coordinates: N 44° 7' 6.38" W 085° 41' 8.69"

Silver Creek Pathway has been a work in progress, an evolving trail that is now considered well worth the wait by visitors to this corner of Lake County. What began as a short path for campers in the 1970s is now a 4-mile loop that extends between two state forest campgrounds and follows both sides of the scenic Pine River. The key to the trail's development was the installation of a pair of bridges that allow hikers and others to cross the river and return to the trailhead.

The first arrived in 1985 when the Department of Natural Resources purchased what was then the Baxter Bridge, a one-lane, iron-trestle structure the Michigan Department of Transportation was replacing across the Manistee River. The 80-foot-long bridge was moved south to the Pine River and renamed the Lincoln Bridge.

In 1988 the DNR used a donated bridge to span the Pine a second time, this one at Silver Creek State Forest Campground. With the bridges in place, the pathway was then extended, first north along the east bank of the Pine to Lincoln Hills State Forest Campground and then several years later along the west bank back to Silver Creek Bridge.

The result is a delightful loop that skirts both sides of the Pine. The blue-ribbon trout stream winds 3.5 miles between the two campgrounds and is considered by paddlers as the fastest river in the Lower Peninsula. In the summer hikers skirt high bluffs, watching anglers in the morning and evening and canoeists and kayakers bobbing through the swift current in between. At one point

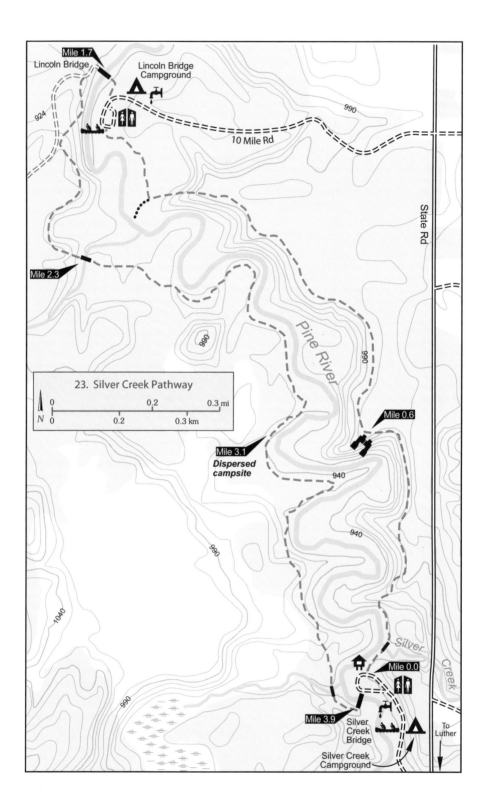

23. Silver Creek Pathway

Mile 1.7
Lincoln Bridge
Lincoln Bridge Campground

924

990

10 Mile Rd

State Rd

Mile 2.3

Pine River

990

990

N

0   0.2   0.3 mi
0   0.2   0.3 km

Mile 0.6

Mile 3.1
Dispersed campsite

940

940

990

1040

990

Silver

Mile 0.0

Creek

Mile 3.9
Silver Creek Bridge

Silver Creek Campground

To Luther

along the west side, you are within view of the Pine for almost a mile, making the Silver Creek Pathway one of the finest river trails in Michigan.

The main trailhead is located in Silver Creek State Forest Campground, an excellent place for a weekend stay to hike and fish for rainbow trout. The more adventurous can bring a backpack and follow the west side of the loop to a handful of great spots for a backcountry campsite overlooking the river.

The trail is open to hikers and mountain bikers. At the north end it comes close to the Lincoln Hills ATV Trail, a 35-mile system that also utilizes the Lincoln Bridge, making the Lincoln Bridge Campground a popular base camp for off-road-vehicle (ORV) drivers. But overall the motorized activity is kept at bay and the groups are well separated.

ACCESS
Silver Creek State Forest Campground is reached from US 131 by exiting onto Luther Highway and heading west for Luther, the small town on the banks of the Little Manistee River. At Luther head north on State Road for 5.5 miles; look for the posted entrance of the campground. There are no vehicle entry fees but there is a nightly camping fee at Silver Creek and Lincoln Bridge State Forest Campgrounds. The best place for information is the DNR Cadillac office (231-775-9727).

TRAIL
One trailhead for the pathway in Silver Creek State Forest Campground is located next to site No. 10 and is well posted with a display map. Heading north, you immediately arrive at the confluence of the Silver Creek with the Pine River, a deep hole that's accented with a thick rope swing over it. If the day's hot, there's no better way to end this trek than by taking a turn on the rope swing. Eeeha!

The trail uses footbridges to cross Silver Creek and then a smaller stream before climbing a steep riverbank to its first edge-of-the-bluff view of the Pine. Continuing along the bank, you pass a spur at *Mile 0.3* that heads east (right), the start of a short loop that is poorly marked and hard to follow. Stay on the main trail to skirt the bluff to a great overlook at *Mile 0.6*. The view includes two bends in the river, any anglers casting for trout, and a ridge several miles away.

Hikers use the Lincoln Bridge to cross the Pine River along the Silver Creek Pathway.

In the next mile you dip twice onto an ORV trail and then make a rapid descent to a T-junction. Head right to emerge at the Lincoln Bridge Canoe Landing at **Mile 1.6**. There are toilets, water, campsites, and picnic tables either at the launch site or the nearby State Forest campground.

Also nearby is the Lincoln Bridge. This classic trestle bridge is set in a wooded ravine and from the middle you can view the Pine upstream and downstream or look below for trout. On the other side is a two-track that is posted as the Irons Snowmobile Trail, an ORV trail and the hiking trail. Truly, a multi-use trail. Within 100 yards the pathway veers south (left) away from the two-track to enter the woods and leave the other motorized trails behind.

The west side of the loop features fewer bluffs and less climbing. After swinging away from the river and intersecting a pair of two tracks, you descend to a foot bridge across a small stream at **Mile 2.3**. Within a third of a mile from the bridge you return to the banks of the Pine and begin the highlight of the loop.

For almost a mile the pathway skirts the river, sometimes right along it, other times just above it. The water is so clear and the current so swift that you can see trout facing upstream, waiting for some morsel of nourishment. At **Mile 3.1**, or less than a mile from the Silver Creek Bridge, is an ideal place to set up a dispersed campsite, a place where you can pitch your tent in a grove of large cedars overlooking the river.

In another quarter mile the trail takes a sharp turn to the west (right) along with the river, climbs the river bluff and then skirts the bluff for a short distance. Keep a sharp eye for trail markers at **Mile 3.7** where the pathway crosses an old two-track in a red pine plantation as this area can be confusing. Shortly after that another foot bridge over a feeder stream is crossed and the Pine with the Silver Creek Bridge arching over it pops into in view. Silver Creek State Forest Campground is just on the other side.

24

Lost Twin Lakes Pathway

Place: Au Sable State Forest

Total Distance: 3.4 miles

Hiking Time: 2 hours

Rating: Moderate

Highlights: Old-growth pines, sinkholes

Maps: Lost Twin Lakes Pathway map from the Michigan DNR or MichiganTrailMaps.com

Trailhead GPS Coordinates: N 44° 12' 52.98" W 084° 42' 7.97"

Lost Twin Lakes is a 3.4-mile loop built in the mid-1980s. It remained a soggy, lightly used pathway until 1999, when members of Boy Scout Troop 944 turned the trail into an Eagle Scout project and constructed a series of bridges and boardwalks over the wettest parts.

Thanks to the Scouts, the trail is a much drier hike now, but it still remains relatively obscure. Much of that is due to its remote location. Part of the Au Sable State Forest, the trailhead is south of Houghton Lake along Reserve Road (County Road 400), a winding dirt road with few signs. This is especially true when you get that sinking feeling you might not know where you are.

Lost Twin Lakes is worth searching for, however. The main attractions are the century-old white pines scattered along the trail, giant trees that survived waves of loggers in the late 1800s, then somehow survived the devastating forest fires that followed the logging. The pathway also features an interesting topography that includes ridges, sinkholes, wetlands, swamps, and those small namesake lakes that gives it a wonderful North Woods ambience.

There are no facilities at the trailhead other than parking and a posted trail map. Bring drinking water; from May through July bug repellent is a requirement in every day pack.

Like all state forest pathways, Lost Twin Lakes is open to Nordic skiing and snowshoeing as well as mountain biking. But the trail isn't groomed in the winter, and off-road cyclists usually bypass it, choosing instead

24. Lost Twin Lakes Pathway

East Branch

Mile 1.5

Wolf Creek

1180 ft

1150

1130

1150

1130

Mile 2.1

1140

1180 ft

To M-55

1150

Mile 0.3

Mile 0.0

Mile 3.1

Mile 2.7

Lost Twin
Lakes

1180

1150

Old Growth Pines

Reserve Rd

trails with more mileage that are easier to access from I-75 or US 131.

This pathway is for people who like to walk in the woods.

ACCESS

From I-75, depart at exit 227 and head west on M-55 for 11 miles. Turn south on Reserve Road (County Road 400) and follow it 6.4 miles. A state park annual or daily pass is required to hike the pathway. For more information, call the Roscommon DNR Office (989-275-5151).

TRAIL

Within a third of a mile of departing the trailhead parking lot, you pass the first giant pines of the trek and arrive at the trail's only junction. It's easy to envision the railroad grade that passed through here during the turn-of-the-century logging era.

As you follow the loop in a counterclockwise direction, you'll reach the first Boy Scout–built bridge at **Mile 0.5**. Originally the Scouts built the structure with a roof–a covered bridge for hikers, you might say–but in 2011 a tree fell on the center of it. The unusual roof was beyond salvageable and had to be removed. The rest of the bridge remains, however, and still keeps your boots dry.

Beyond the bridge, the pathway begins climbing and for most of the east half of the loop follows the crest of an ancient glacial moraine. This narrow, forested ridge is bordered on both sides by wetlands; from its crest you're rewarded with glimpses and vistas of marshland and patches of open water. On its slope are a scattering of old-growth pines. The first are seen in less than a mile from the trailhead. You'll find a more impressive set at **Mile 1.3** after the trail reaches a high point of 1,180 feet.

At the north end of the ridge, just before the loop swings sharply south for its return,

A timber cruiser from the Michigan DNR admires an old-growth pine along the Lost Twin Lakes Pathway.

are a series of sinkholes, conical depressions that are the result of underground streams dissolving the limestone bedrock. The sinkholes aren't visible from the pathway, but by leaving the trail to the west you can quickly spot them. They're not as deep or as classic as the ones seen along Sinkholes Pathway (see Hike 55) in the Mackinaw State Forest, but there is no doubt what these steep-sided funnels are when you see them.

Also at the north end of the ridge is a short spur that leads to the East Branch of Wolf Creek, a scenic setting and a place to linger if the mosquitoes aren't out in full force.

A hiker passes through a pair of giant pines that guard the Lost Twin Lakes Pathway.

Heading south now, the pathway levels out but remains fairly dry. At **Mile 2** giant white pines begin appearing, and after the trail swings sharply east you pass between two towering pines standing guard on both sides of the pathway. These are the largest trees along the trail; some could be 150 years old, if not older.

The pathway arrives at a wavy bridge at **Mile 2.7**, and the creek that it crosses connects Lost Twin Lakes. They're easy to miss if you're staring up at the crowns of giant pines, but the main one to the south is more easily viewed than its twin to the north. Both lakes are tiny, the larger only 2 acres, and shallow, making them ideal havens for wildlife, especially if you're here at dawn or dusk.

In less than a half mile you return to the junction and backtrack the first segment to return to the parking area at **Mile 3.4**.

Lake Michigan

25

Mt. Randal Trail

Place: Warren Dunes State Park

Total Distance: 4 miles

Hiking Time: 2 to 3 hours

Rating: Moderate

Highlights: Sand dunes, beach walking

Maps: Warren Dunes State Park map from the Michigan DNR, or Mt. Randal Trail map from MichiganTrailMaps.com

Trailhead GPS Coordinates: N 41° 54' 14.50" W 086° 35' 49.90"

Occasionally somebody comes to Warren Dunes State Park to hang glide; others arrive to study the plant succession; and many come to lie on the beach or play in the Lake Michigan surf. Ultimately, though, there's one main attraction drawing people to this corner of the state—sand. The 2 miles of Lake Michigan beach and the windblown dunes that tower 230 feet above the water attract a variety of visitors, from thrill seekers and sunbathers to university botany classes and even hikers.

This 1,952-acre park offers hikers a 4-mile loop that includes a bit of everything: a stroll along Lake Michigan, stretches through forests, knee-bending climbs up mountains of sand. You'll even get a good look at how life gets started. It's possible during this hike to stand on a small ridge of sand looking at nothing but bare beach and water to the west, at the first clumps of well-scattered grasses at your feet, at the next stages of succession to the east—shrubs emerging from grasses, poplars, and other short-lived trees replacing shrubs—and finally the well-shaded canopy of an oak and hickory forest covering the ridge of a dune. Life, from sand to trees, in one sweeping view.

Others are intrigued by the geology of the area and come to identify the different types of dunes: parallel dunes, blowouts, and parabolic dunes (parallel dunes that have been carved by a series of windblown indentations).

Even if you have little interest in ecology or geology, Warren Dunes is simply a pleasant place to take a hike . . . most of the

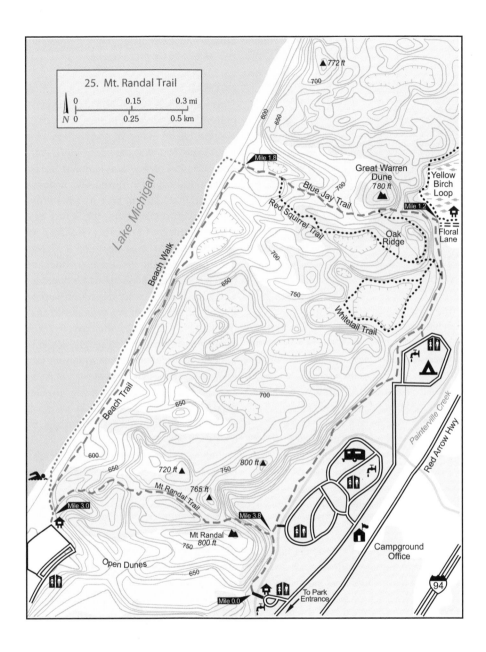

25. Mt. Randal Trail

year. Because of its location close to several major urban areas, including Chicago, Warren Dunes traditionally receives the second-highest number of visitors of any state park. Almost 1.5 million people pass through its entrance gate each year, with the vast majority being out-of-staters arriving from June to September. If you hike to sneak away from crowds and other signs of humanity, Warren Dunes is not the place to go on the Fourth of July.

Puccoon is a wildflower that grows in open dune areas like those found in Warren Dunes State Park.

The best time to venture into the park is when the wildflowers bloom in April, or in mid- to late October when the leaves of the hardwood forests are torched with brilliant oranges and reds. Arrive in midweek during these off-season months and the crowds will be gone, the campground practically empty; often you'll be the only one on a stretch of beach.

If you are planning to arrive during the summer, the best days are Monday and Tuesday, the lull between the weekend crowds. By Wednesday the campground is filling up again, and Saturday there often are so many people at Warren Dunes that parking is almost impossible. If this is the case, avoid the main entrance and begin the loop off Floral Lane. Better yet, head north and explore Grand Mere State Park (see Hike 27), saving this hike for another day.

The walk described here is a combination of several trails in the park, including the scenic Mt. Randal Trail. Boots are not necessary for the hike; it can easily be done in running shoes. Keep in mind that a portion of the route over open sand is not marked and that there are quite a few dunes to climb during the outing. Children under the age of six and

others with weak knees might require more time than what is listed above.

ACCESS

The state park is just off I-94, 15 miles north of the Michigan-Indiana border. From the interstate, depart at exit 16 and head south on Red Arrow Highway. In a little more than a half mile, you pass Floral Lane, at the end of which is a parking area and a posted trailhead that you can start at if the park is crowded. The main entrance is 1.5 miles farther south on Red Arrow Highway. The south end of the park contains a 182-site campground in the woods away from Lake Michigan and a 36-site rustic campground. There are also day-use areas featuring picnic grounds, swimming areas, and three bathhouses along Lake Michigan. From the contact station, head north (right) along the park drive, passing the headquarters (stop here to pick up a map) and arriving at a small parking area and main trailhead just before entering the main campground in the woods. Within the parking area are vault toilets, picnic tables, and a water pump.

From more information on Warren Dunes, contact the park headquarters (269-426-4013).

TRAIL

From the back of the parking area the Nature Trail crosses Painterville Creek and then heads north (right), reaching the junction with Mt. Randal Trail within a quarter mile. Along the way you'll pass unofficial trails that head up Mt. Randal, the migrating dune that rises 220 feet above the lake and is literally pouring sand down between the trees, determined to bury the trail someday.

'Mt. Randal Trail heads west (left) and skirts the sand dune before ending at the day-use beach. Continue north (right). Nearby, a footbridge crosses the creek to the campground, while the main trail passes through a low-lying area. This area once held a pond, which was drained off by farmers in the early 1900s. Even though the interdunal ponds are gone, in the spring this stretch can still be wet and muddy.

You'll see more reminders of unsuccessful farming efforts just to the north when the trail passes a small, grassy meadow. The farmer's failure has turned out to be the hiker's gain 70 years later, though. Unable to grow a crop in the sandy soil, farm families let their 8-acre plots revert to the state rather than pay a $25 tax on land. That allowed Edward Warren, a merchant and conservationist from Three Oaks, to purchase the duneland for next to nothing, preserving it from future development.

Painterville Creek swings out of sight, along with the campers on its east side. At *Mile 0.8* you come to an old farmhouse foundation and what appears to be the end of a road. The rustic campground is nearby, as is the junction of the White Tail and Red Squirrel Trails. The Nature Trail continues along the former road, pavement popping up now and then, and at *Mile 1.2* reaches Floral Lane, where there is a trail map.

To the north is the Yellow Birch Loop. Head west (left) on Blue Jay Trail to continue this hike and venture onto Great Warren Dune. The trek to Lake Michigan begins in the woods but quickly climbs to the edge of a 200-foot open dune. A path leads to the top, but the trail actually skirts it along its south side. For the first time on the hike, you leave the forest and view the park's interior, a section dedicated by the state as the Great Warren Dune Natural Area. The panorama includes dunes all around you, some forested, others covered with grass, and a few just bare sand. On the horizon is Lake Michigan, and straight ahead is the sandy avenue that makes up the trail.

Numerous paths, including one posted as Oak Ridge Trail, depart in every direction where hikers have wandered off to explore the park's backcountry. It's hard to get turned around, however. Just keep heading west and at *Mile 1.8* you will reach a low, sandy bluff above the beach. The first thing most people notice is the wind. What seems like a gentle breeze in the forest can be gale-like by the Great Lake.

Here you have a choice. The Beach Trail follows the undulating bluff above the shoreline, dipping and climbing around blowouts. Halfway back to the day-use area you cut

A signpost junction points out sandy trails in Warren Dunes State Park.

across two fascinating blowouts that beckon you to climb their sandy slopes for a better view of the area. This is very interesting terrain, but the hiking is harder and at times the trail is not well marked.

The alternative, the one favored by most visitors, is to simply drop to the shoreline and follow Lake Michigan south to the day-use parking area. It's a 1.2-mile trek along the beach to the third parking lot of the day-use area, reached at *Mile 3*.

From the northwest corner of the parking lot in the day-use area, a FOOT TRAILS sign can be seen on the edge of a wooded dune. This marks the Mt. Randal Trail and begins with an immediate climb into the hickory-oak forest. In early spring and late fall, you never lose sight of Lake Michigan in the first half mile, and you can usually hear the surf any time of year.

The trail tops off at a spot many believe to be Mt. Randal, comes within view of the back side of a blowout that was crossed earlier, and at *Mile 3.6* arrives at a boot-print marker. The sign directs you down a log staircase; more boots keep you descending into a steep trench between Mt. Randal and the next dune. Just when you think the trail is going to head into a low-lying wet area, it skirts Mt. Randal and breaks out near the footbridge to the park's campground. Backtrack south (right) along the trail to return to the parking area and trailhead.

26

Warren Woods

Place: Warren Woods Natural Area	
Total Distance: 2 miles	
Hiking Time: 1 hour	
Rating: Easy	
Highlights: Beech-maple climax forest beech trees, birding	
Maps: Warren Woods Natural Area map from the Michigan DNR or MichiganTrailMaps.com	
Trailhead GPS Coordinates: N 41° 49' 54.04" W 086° 37' 29.86"	

The story of Edward K. Warren, conservationist and visionary, is almost as intriguing as the stand of primeval beech and maple trees enjoyed today along this 2-mile loop through the Warren Woods Natural Area. In the 1870s Warren was a partner of a general store in Three Oaks, Michigan, barely making a living. When he decided to purchase a 200-acre tract of virgin forest around the Galien River, townspeople wondered about his sanity.

He purchased Warren Woods in 1879, only seven years after the country's first park, Yellowstone National Park, was established. The conservationist knew that this particular woodland represented one of the last surviving stands of virgin beech and maple in the state. Everything else had been logged. He held on to the area, despite financial problems that in 1883 forced him to beg from his neighbors to clothe his family.

But things have a way of coming around. Eventually, Warren developed a process that substituted turkey-wing feathers for the increasingly scarce whalebone in women's corsets. He set up the Warren Featherbone Company and made a fortune at the turn of the century. He promptly used much of his profits to buy duneland along Lake Michigan, which bankrupt farmers were letting go to the state for back taxes of less than $25. While others shook their heads at him, Warren deeply believed that someday "these lands would be of great value to thousands of people as a place of recreation."

The vision of this general-store merchant was incredible. Today the dunes that were

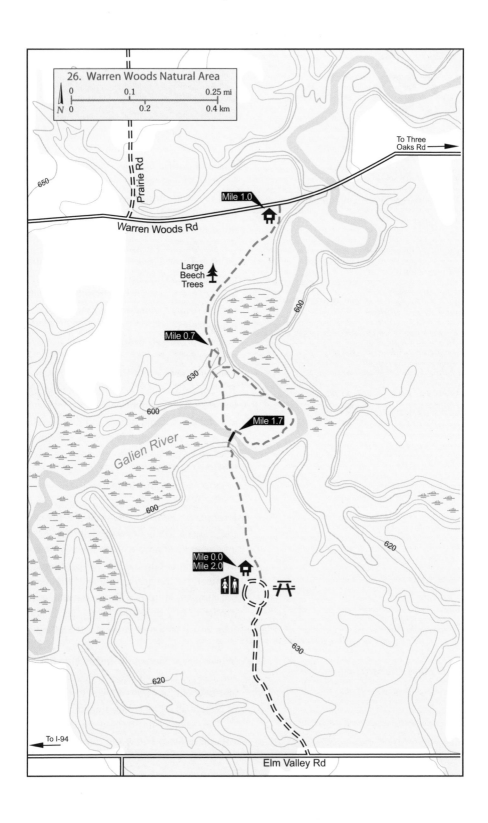

26. Warren Woods Natural Area

N

0   0.1   0.25 mi
0   0.2   0.4 km

650

Prairie Rd

To Three
Oaks Rd →

Mile 1.0

Warren Woods Rd

Large
Beech
Trees

600

Mile 0.7

630

600

Mile 1.7

Galien River

600

620

Mile 0.0
Mile 2.0

630

620

630

To I-94 ←

Elm Valley Rd

The fall colors are spectacular at the Warren Woods Natural Area, known for its beech-maple climax forest.

The natural area is open daily from 8 AM to dusk year-round, but the best time to come is late September through mid-November when the leaves take on their autumn colors. Birders arrive in the spring, however, to look for warblers and other songbirds, while skiers enjoy the trails during the winter when there is sufficient snow. The trail is easy to follow and makes an ideal family outing. But beware: The Galien is a sluggish river, and during the summer mosquitoes can terrorize young hikers. Bring plenty of protection for insects then.

ACCESS

The natural area can be reached from I-94 by departing at Union Pier (exit 6) and heading east on Union Pier Road, which quickly becomes Elm Valley Road, for 2.5 miles to an unmarked entrance that resembles a dirt road. There is also a posted trailhead on Warren Woods Road, 7 miles east of Warren Dunes State Park, but the southern entrance is the best place to begin the hike. From Elm Valley Road, it's a quarter-mile drive to a parking area with vault toilets, tables, and a large display map.

To enter Warren Woods you need either a daily vehicle entry permit or an annual state park pass. To purchase a pass or for more information, contact Warren Dunes State Park (269-426-4013).

TRAIL

From the Elm Valley Road parking area, the trail begins as a wide, wood-chip path just east of the display map. It skirts a wooded ridge, and in a third of a mile you come to a pair of benches that sit on a bluff overlooking the Galien River and a wooden bridge across it. Steps descend to the bridge, and on the other side the trail splits.

Head west (left), so that the blue DNR pathway triangles face you. The trail follows

worthless in the early 1900s are part of Michigan's Gold Coast. The only thing he misjudged was the number of people who would enjoy his dunes. Thousands? More than 1.5 million visitors a year arrive at Warren Dunes State Park from across the country (see Hike 25).

That state park also manages the Warren Woods Natural Area. Located 7 miles inland, this wooded tract is a conspicuous contrast with the rest of the unit on Lake Michigan: no towering dunes, but also no crowds, no overflowing parking lots, and no filled-to-capacity campgrounds. Amazingly, the natural area can be a quiet spot even at the height of the summer season when rangers are turning away visitors at the state park.

the bank of the river for a short spell, then ascends a bluff for an overview of the water. These stretches along the river are where birders look for warblers and thrushes. During the spring migration, the birds move through the woods and often can be seen in the sycamores along the banks. This area is one of the best in Michigan to see a yellow-throated warbler, a small, gray bird with a distinct yellow bib. Other birds regularly spotted in the area include pileated wood-peckers during the summer and redheaded woodpeckers in fall and winter.

A half mile from the start, the trail takes a sharp swing north and enters for the first time the rare stand of virgin hardwoods. If the size of the trees doesn't overwhelm you, consider that as far as historians can verify, this portion of Warren Woods has never been deliberately disturbed by people. Warren purchased it in 1879 because it had not been logged, and since then the area has not experienced selective or any other type of cutting. When the huge trees fall, the deadwood is not even removed by state park officials.

At *Mile 0.7* you arrive at the junction with the return trail to the bridge. But don't skip the quarter mile to the trailhead at Warren Woods Road, for here is where the largest trees are seen. It's mind boggling that at one time all of southern Michigan was covered by a forest like this. Most trees are so large that two people can't link their arms around them. Sadly, some people feel compelled to carve their initials into these virgin beeches and maples.

The return trail is a level walk that follows a ridge from the junction and in a quarter mile comes to a view of the Galien River, which most of the year, especially in the summer, is a slow-moving and muddy waterway. Eventually the trail descends the low bluff and hugs the riverbank for a third of a mile before arriving at the bridge at *Mile 1.7*, which you cross to return to the parking area.

27

Baldtop

Place: Grand Mere State Park

Total Distance: 2 miles

Hiking Time: 2 hours

Rating: Moderate

Highlights: Scenic vistas, sand dunes, Lake Michigan beach

Maps: Grand Mere State Park map from the Michigan DNR or Michigan TrailMaps.com

Trailhead GPS Coordinates: N 42° 0' 14.61" W 086° 32' 33.84"

Since Grand Mere State Park was established in 1973, the vast majority of users have been either locals strolling along Lake Michigan or educational groups and college botany classes intrigued by the area's many rare and endangered plants. Hikers in this 985-acre tract of woods, towering dunes, and wide, sandy shorelines have been few. And it's no wonder. For years the only park signs were on the beach, not near the I-94 exit, while the trails were unmarked and the maps published by the state's Department of Natural Resources misleading.

In 1990 the main entrance drive and parking area of the state park were paved and a half-mile, handicapped-accessible trail was built around the South Lake. A paved nature trail with 10 interpretive posts was added, along with a picnic shelter, and slowly hikers began to discover this treasure of dune ecology.

The unique land formations and flora that attract naturalists to the park are the reasons Grand Mere was designated a National Natural Landmark. The glaciers that scooped out the Great Lakes 10,000 years ago also carved out a number of smaller depressions along the western edge of the state, which evolved into interdunal lakes, ponds, and wetlands. At one time Grand Mere contained five such lakes, which were protected ecologically by a line of windblown sand dunes between them and Lake Michigan. Now there remain only three, a result of aquatic succession. Today Grand Mere is a textbook example of the various stages of succession. Beginning at North Lake, you can see how

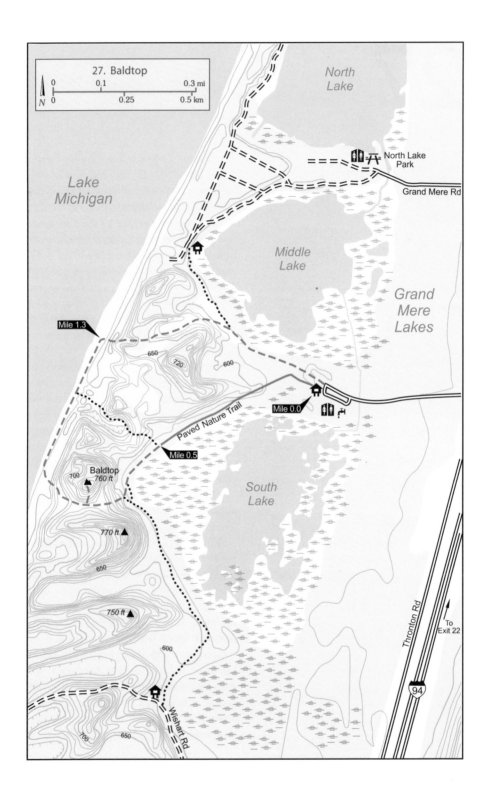

27. Baldtop

North Lake

Lake Michigan

Grand Mere Rd

North Lake Park

Middle Lake

Grand Mere Lakes

Mile 1.3

650
720
600

Paved Nature Trail

Mile 0.0

Mile 0.5

Baldtop
760 ft

700

770 ft ▲

South Lake

750 ft ▲

650

600

Thronton Rd

To Exit 22

94

Wishart Rd

700   650

Catching some rays on the beach at Grand Mere State Park.

each lake is progressively disappearing, with open water turning into marsh and, eventually, woodland, the fate of the former two lakes.

Dunes not only protect the lakes and wetlands surrounding them but also create a cooler environment for plants that are not found elsewhere in southern Michigan. Hemlock and white pine give Grand Mere the traces of a boreal forest normally seen only in northern Michigan, while the profusion of wildflowers includes the rare starflower.

The park also attracts a number of birders, for it lies on a major migration flyway. Almost 250 species of birds have been sighted here. During the spring and fall you can see large numbers of hawks migrating on the east winds, along with common loons, cormorants, and a variety of waterfowl and herons.

Even for those not into rare plants, aquatic succession, or birds, Grand Mere makes an excellent destination for a hike. The route described here, a 2-mile hike around the park's tallest dune, often called Baldtop, is not only a natural loop, it's the most scenic walk in the park. Though short, it can be a workout because of the steep climb to Baldtop's excellent views and stretches through the soft sand of open dunes. The beach is wide and somewhat private, even though you can view cottages at each end. The only drawback is the presence of insects, especially deerflies from mid-July through mid-August. Given the natural wetlands, such pests are expectable, but at times the deerflies are as ferocious as any I have encountered in Michigan. The only blessing is that they diminish in number the closer you are to Lake Michigan.

ACCESS

The park is south of St. Joseph. From I-94, head west on John Beers Road (exit 22), immediately coming to the junction of Thornton and Grand Mere Roads. Three roads lead into the park, but the official entrance that was paved in 1990 is off Thornton Drive, a half mile south of Grand Mere Road. You

The view from the top of Baldtop in Grand Mere State Park.

can also access the trail by continuing west on Grand Mere Road, where a trail sign and parking for a half-dozen cars lie at its end. The third access point is the end of Wishart Road, reached by following Thornton south and Willow Road west (right).

Camping is not allowed in the park, and a daily vehicle permit or annual state park pass is required to enter it. Grand Mere is managed by Warren Dunes State Park (269-426-4013).

TRAIL

It's a half mile from Thornton Road to the park's parking lot, where you also find a pair of vault toilets and a picnic shelter. The trailhead is near the shelter, and the hike begins along a paved, handicapped-accessible trail. You skirt South Lake, though it's almost impossible to see it through the trees, and within a third of a mile pass the side of an open dune. At *Mile 0.5* you reach the end of the paved nature trail at a V-junction. A sandy trail heads west (right) into the dunes for Lake Michigan. Continue southwest (left) to quickly come to another junction and your first glimpse of South Lake.

This time choose the route to the right. The path to the southeast (left) continues west of the lake and in 1 mile reaches the end of Wishart Road at the park border. Actually, this trail used to be Wishart Road, which curved around South Lake and ended at what is now the park entrance drive.

The right path at the junction makes a steep climb and heads west toward Baldtop. You climb the wooded base of a dune but soon break out in a sandy pass, with Baldtop to the north and a wooded dune to the south. Visible straight ahead is Lake Michigan. True to its name, Baldtop is free of trees at its 760-foot peak. The top is a 100-foot climb from here and a heart-pounding effort for most people. But from the high perch of the open dune you can see all of South Lake, including the vast wetland area that surrounds it. To the west is the wide beach along Lake Michigan, and to the south is the distinct dome of Cook Nuclear Power Plant.

Descend back to the sandy pass and follow it west, the easiest and most common route to Lake Michigan. You head downhill to the wide beach. The west side of Baldtop is a huge blowout: From the beach it looks like half the dune was scooped out by a giant kid with a sand bucket and shovel.

Reached at *Mile 1*, the beach is wide—40 yards or more depending on the current level of Lake Michigan—and the water is shallow. You can hike south to view the towering wooded bluffs that border the shoreline, but in a third of a mile you'll come to state land border signs. Head north from Baldtop, and at *Mile 1.3* you'll hike around the dune's forested north side and arrive at another blowout area, though not nearly as impressive. A GRAND MERE PARK sign has been posted here.

Hike inland and climb to the edge of the dune, where you'll see South Lake again to the southeast while due east is the wooded fringe of the open area with trails wandering through the trees. By heading northeast, you can pick up a wide path through the beach grass that climbs around a distinct wooded dune and then enters more open sand on the other side.

From here you can view all of Middle Lake, which has considerably more open water than South Lake. These two lakes show how someday both will fill in and become woodland.

Hike down to the lake and find the sandy path skirting it through the low brush and grass. By heading east (right) you will return to the parking area, passing some great blackberry patches along the way. If you head north here, you'll end up at the Grand Mere Road trailhead.

28

Livingston Trail Loop

Place: Saugatuck Dunes State Park	
Total Distance: 3.4 miles	
Hiking Time: 2 to 3 hours	
Rating: Moderate	
Highlights: Sand dunes, Lake Michigan beach, scenic vistas	
Maps: Saugatuck Dunes State Park map from the Michigan DNR, or Livingston Trail Loop map from MichiganTrail Maps.com	
Trailhead GPS Coordinates: N 42° 42' 1.90" W 086° 11' 45.26"	

What began as a place for religious contemplation later became a minimum-security prison and eventually the least developed state park along the golden coast of Lake Michigan. What a strange journey it has been for Saugatuck Dunes State Park! In the end, though, hikers and cross-country skiers have been blessed with a track of dunes that are as natural and pristine as any along the west side of the state.

The 1,000-acre state park was a trade-off after the St. Augustinian Order sold the land and its 30-year-old seminary to the state in 1971. Environmentalists and locals howled in protest when it was revealed that the buildings were going to be converted into a 400-bed correctional facility. Crime won out, but to calm its citizens, the governor's office declared all but 50 acres of the tract Michigan's newest state park. For years hikers passed by barbed wire and bullhorns on their way to sand dunes and shoreline.

Eventually the prison was removed, and the patch of open field that it occupied is now Shore Acres Township Park. Saugatuck Dunes State Park remained as undeveloped and remote as ever.

There's no campground at Saugatuck Dunes, nor any other facilities beyond vault toilets and picnic tables. There's also no quick way to reach Lake Michigan, for the nearest stretch of beach is almost 1 mile from the parking area. With the majority of park users being skiers who arrive from December through February, you have Saugatuck's most charming aspect: beaches without crowds and trails that still possess a

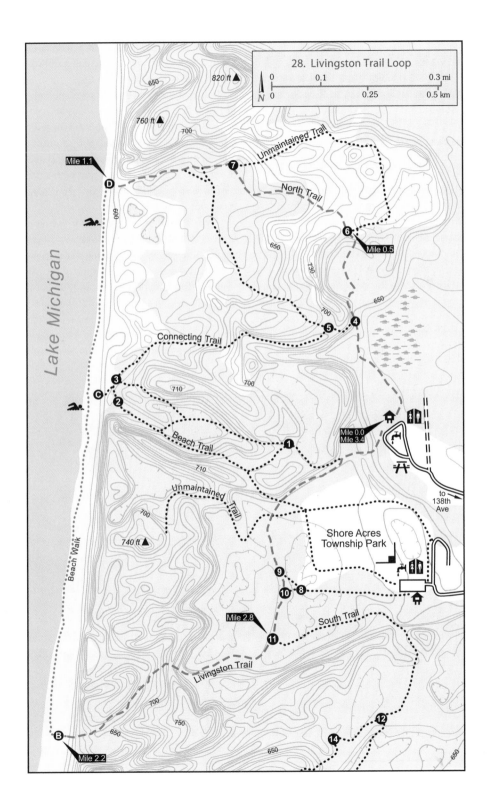

28. Livingston Trail Loop

N

0   0.1   0.3 mi

0   0.25   0.5 km

820 ft ▲

760 ft ▲

700

650

Unmaintained Trail

Mile 1.1
D

7

North Trail

600

6
Mile 0.5

650

730

Lake Michigan

650

Connecting Trail

5   4

700

3

710   700

C

2

Beach Trail

1

Mile 0.0
Mile 3.4

710

to
138th
Ave

Unmaintained Trail

700

740 ft ▲

Shore Acres
Township Park

9

10 8

Beach Walk

Mile 2.8

11

South Trail

Livingston Trail

700

750

650

12

14

B

650

650

Mile 2.2

little solitude even at the height of the summer season.

The park's major attractions are its 2.5 miles of shoreline, most of it wide, sandy beaches, and a 300-acre natural area featuring coastal dunes more than 200 feet tall. The park's terrain varies from steep slopes to rolling hills and is home to three endangered plant species.

The Saugatuck's 14-mile network of footpaths is divided into three basic loops referred to on park maps as North Trail, Beach Trail, and South Trail. All are wide paths and well marked, with location maps at almost every junction. South Trail is a 5.5-mile loop that extends into the designated natural area in the bottom half of the park and offers skiers and hikers the most level terrain. The Beach Trail is a 2.5-mile trek and the most popular stretch during the summer, since

Lake Michigan lies less than 1 mile away, along a route that looks more like a dirt road than a trail in the woods.

The loop described here is a combination of the North Trail, a beach walk, and a return via Livingston Trail. The 3.4-mile outing offers hikers a pleasant mix of open dunes, stands of pine and hardwoods, impressive overviews of Lake Michigan from high, sandy bluffs, and a stroll down an uncluttered beach for more than a mile.

A midday hike on a summer weekend results in encounters only with the kind of wildlife that wears bathing suits and carries in beach towels and suntan lotion. If you take to the paths early in the morning or during the early evening, though, it's possible to spot a variety of woodland animals including white-tailed deer, woodchucks, chipmunks, rabbits, and raccoons.

Hikers on the beach at Saugatuck Dunes State Park.

Experienced birders find the park rich in species, including the common tern (which is not such a common sight in Michigan anymore). You're more likely to spot brown thrashers, grosbeaks, pileated woodpeckers, tufted titmouses, and even great horned owls and turkey vultures.

ACCESS

The park is reached from I-196, just north of the town of Saugatuck. Depart at exit 41 and go west on Blue Star Memorial Highway. You immediately turn right onto 64th Street, just west of the overpass. Head north for 1 mile and turn west (left) onto 138th Avenue, where a sign points the way to the state park. Follow 138th Avenue to the park entrance and day-use area, which includes the parking area, tables, grills, vault toilets, a shelter, and a display board.

Generally, the contact station at the park's entrance is closed, but a box on the outside is usually stocked with park maps. For more information on this unit, contact Van Buren State Park (269-637-2788).

TRAIL

The trailhead for the Center and South Trails is easy to spot from the south end of the parking area. The trailhead for the North Trails is a little more obscured and begins at the north end of the parking lot. The trail quickly enters the woods and appears as the typical wide path built to accommodate skiers in the winter. The beginning section travels beside a wooded dune ridge to the west and a marsh on the right. The birds should be plentiful around the marsh, as will be wildflowers in spring and early summer when it's possible to spot pink lady's slipper orchids at times.

Within a quarter mile the trail climbs away from the marsh and arrives at post No. 4. Head north (right) at the junction; the wide trail will continue to skirt the base of the wooded dune and then pass a NOT A MARKED TRAIL! sign just before arriving at post No. 6 at *Mile 0.5*. Both junctions to the right lead to what is occasionally referred to as the Outer Loop of the North Trail, a hard-to-follow segment in open sand. Stay left and soon you'll be in the rolling topography normally associated with dune country. Within a third of a mile you arrive at post No. 7, marking the west end of the Outer Loop.

The main trail continues west (left), passing two unmarked trails to the south that complete the North Trail loop, and then climbs a forested dune, topping off to a scenic view of Lake Michigan. You descend along a sandy path and at *Mile 1.1* arrive at post D, half buried in sand and often easily missed. The four posts that mark where trails depart from the beach are labeled in letters, as opposed to the numbers used at junctions.

You head south along the beach and will soon discover that the sand is harder and easier to hike the closer you are to the water. At *Mile 1.5* you pass post C, marking the access to Beach Trail. This one is easy to spot as there are three benches on the bluff above it and, generally, more people enjoying this stretch of beach. Continuing south, you come to the west end of Livingston Trail at *Mile 2.2*; this is marked with a signpost on the edge of the forest where the trail leaves the open dunes to disappear into the trees.

From the beach you climb the shoreline dune and then descend along a ravine between two forested dunes, where the scenery changes dramatically. In almost no time at all you have moved from the endless views of Lake Michigan to a tight cut in a thick forest. Livingston Trail descends off this dune and bottoms out in a stand of impressive beeches and maples that are stunning in the fall. At *Mile 2.8* you arrive at post No. 9,

The open dunes of Saugatuck Dunes State Park.

marking the junction between the Livingston Trail and South Trail. Head north (left).

The final leg is the return to the trailhead and can be a bit confusing due to all the trails, many of them unmarked remnants of old two-tracks, that you pass. Within a few hundred yards you pass post No. 10 and post No. 9—marking trails heading east to Shore Acres Township Park—and then parallel segments of the township park's mountain bike single-track. If that wasn't enough, you then pass the junctions with a pair of old two-tracks, the first posted with a NOT A MARKED TRAIL! sign.

The main trail, however, is the widest and most easily distinguished. At *Mile 3.2* it arrives at the junction with the Beach Trail, which is clearly posted. Head east (right); it's less than a quarter mile back to the trailhead parking lot.

29

Homestead Trail

Place: P. J. Hoffmaster State Park

Total Distance: 2.7 miles

Hiking Time: 1 to 2 hours

Rating: Moderate

Highlights: Lake Michigan overlook, sand dunes

Maps: P. J. Hoffmaster State Park map from the Michigan DNR, or Homestead Trail map from MichiganTrailMaps.com

Trailhead GPS Coordinates: N 43° 7' 29.93" W 086° 15' 53.58"

Sand dunes, contrary to most people's first impressions, are more than just big hills of sand that are fun to run down. The dunes found along the Lake Michigan shoreline are actually part of a complex ecosystem that is made up of many different zones, including beaches, wetlands, climax forests, and lastly open dunes where plants struggle to gain a foothold against shifting sands and a scarcity of nutrients. Dunes are also one of nature's most beautiful formations, delicate works of art where gentle breezes carve windswept sculptures from the sands of the Great Lakes.

In Michigan we are blessed with a shoreline that showcases 275,000 acres of sand dune formations, the largest display of freshwater dunes in the world. They stretch from the tip of the state's thumb off Saginaw Bay to the giant perched dunes above Lake Superior and include the country's most famous dunes, the Sleeping Bear Dunes, off Lake Michigan. Perhaps the best place to learn about these truly remarkable formations is at P. J. Hoffmaster State Park, where you can combine a visit to Gillette Nature Center, Michigan's Sand Dune Interpretive Center, with a hike through the various life zones of a dune along the Homestead Trail.

The Gillette Nature Center was built in 1976 as a bicentennial project to serve as an interpretive center to the state's most noted natural treasure. The two-story center is literally overshadowed by a huge, windblown dune that can be viewed from a glass wall on the west side of the lobby. The center features a hall titled *Michigan Coastal Sand*

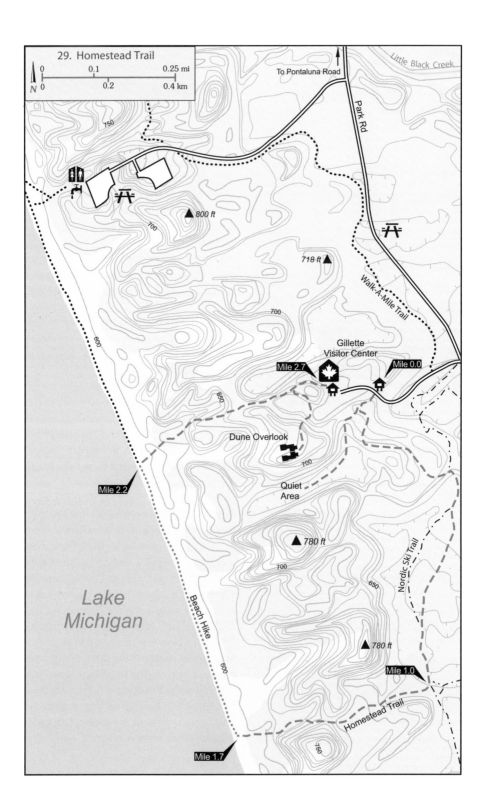

29. Homestead Trail

N

| 0 | | 0.1 | | 0.25 mi |
| 0 | 0.2 | | 0.4 km |

To Pontaluna Road

Little Black Creek

Park Rd

750

800 ft

718 ft

Walk-A-Mile Trail

700

700

800

Gillette
Visitor Center

Mile 2.7

Mile 0.0

650

Dune Overlook

Quiet
Area

700

Mile 2.2

780 ft

700

Lake
Michigan

650

Nordic Ski Trail

780 ft

Mile 1.0

600

Beach Hike

Homestead Trail

Mile 1.7

750

Dunes Like Nowhere Else on Earth in which dioramas depict the four dune habitats, including models of the animals, plants, and trees, with the sounds of waves and birds in the background. Nearby is an animation station that shows how sand dunes are formed.

There is also an 82-seat theater that uses a nine-projector, multi-image slide show to explain further the dunes' delicate nature and the reason the state has moved to protect them from overdevelopment. Finally, check out the three-dimensional relief map to see the type of terrain you'll be covering in the next two to three hours. The Homestead Trail circuit may look rugged, but the climbs are moderate and the route can be handled by children as young as five or six if you schedule in an extended swim or lunch break on the Lake Michigan beach.

Most of the trail passes through a designated Natural Area and includes possible side trips to a Quiet Area, the park's most remote corner. You also climb up a long stairway to magnificent views from the Dune Overlook Platform. Summer is an ideal time for this hike, when you can stop for a swim in the Great Lake, but it's also the park's busiest season. Many like to come here in spring or fall when the crowds are gone and there's nothing on the beaches but sand, driftwood, and a boot print or two.

ACCESS

The 1,043-acre park is located just south of Muskegon and can be reached from I-96 by departing at Fruitport (exit 4). Head south on 148th Avenue and immediately turn west (right) onto Pontaluna Road for 6 miles, until it dead-ends at the park entrance. From US 31, depart onto Pontaluna Road, halfway between Muskegon and Grand Haven, and head west for 3 miles.

Gillette Nature Center (231-798-3573; www.michigan.gov/gillettevc) is open from Memorial Day to Labor Day from 10 AM to 5 PM Monday through Saturday and noon to 5 PM Sunday. There are reduced hours the rest of the year. There is no fee to visit the interpretive center, but there is a vehicle fee to enter the park. For more information on campground reservations or fees, call the park headquarters (231-798-3711).

TRAIL

The circuit should be walked in a clockwise direction. Therefore, you start by heading south from the trailhead off the parking area and end at the trailhead behind the interpretive center. Those who hike it in the other direction often miss where the trail leaves the

A swimmer studies the Lake Michigan surf at Hoffmaster State Park.

The open dune country of Hoffmaster State Park.

beach. The parking lot trailhead is posted HOMESTEAD TRAIL / QUIET AREA, and the trail begins by climbing a wooded dune and then reaching a bench and the marked junction to the Quiet Area. This special area, reached by following the one-way, quarter-mile spur to its end, is a deep ravine surrounded by steep wooded dunes that form a quiet escape for hikers. Even on the park's busiest weekends, you can sit here and enjoy some peace of mind.

The main trail continues south to descend through woods and pass a posted junction with a trail that veers off north to a picnic area and shelter. Orange boot prints lead you along the Homestead Trail as it passes through a stand of young trees and then a large, grassy meadow. After crossing the meadow, you reenter the woods and at *Mile 1* (mileage includes visiting the Quiet Area) reach a well-posted, four-way junction. Here the hiking trail merges with a ski run.

Head east (right) along the Homestead Trail and enter the park's Natural Area along a wide path that also accommodates skiers in the winter. The trail begins with a gentle climb as it skirts the base of a dune forested in oak and maple. The trees found here and elsewhere away from the beach stabilize the dunes and protect them from wind erosion—sometimes. In less than a quarter mile of the four-way junction, you pass a spot where the dune has begun migrating across the trail.

At *Mile 1.7* you break out onto the Lake Michigan beach. If it's summer, this spot can seem a striking contrast to the first half of the hike, spent in the cool, shaded dune forest. If it's a blistering 90 degrees, you won't be able to run fast enough into Lake Michigan.

For the next half mile, you follow the beach north along a natural path formed between the waves rolling in from the west and the sandy bluffs that box you in on the east. Occasionally you pass a blowout, a

U-shaped depression of loose sand, but most of the time the beach meets an eroding bluff lined at the edge by trees, many of them tumbling toward the lake. After a good storm, the beach can be an impressive sight, with whitecapped waves pounding the shoreline and washing up everything from helpless fish, a spare tire, or somebody's tennis shoe to a plank with rusty bolts in it and whole trunks of trees.

At *Mile 2.2* a NATURE CENTER sign mounted in a small hill of sand directs you back inland, where you quickly come to a boardwalk. The planked trail leads you into foredunes, and soon you ascend to a large interpretive sign. The display marks an excellent spot to compare the different zone communities of dunes. You've just departed the beach zone, an area of seasonal and even daily extremes that has few permanent residents, sunbathers included. You are now in the foredunes, areas of loose sand that are battered by wind and hikers and held in place only by clinging vegetation such as dune grass, sand cherry, and riverbank grape. But the sign is near a trough, a depression between dunes. These low-lying areas result in interdunal wetlands—shallow ponds and pools that in wet periods support a variety of insects, shorebirds, and other plants. Finally, you are about to climb into a zone of backdunes, and the display points out that these dunes are secured by oaks, maples, and towering white pines. Unless marred by fire or so-called development, the backdune is the climax of this chain of succession and the symbol of a stable area.

From the interpretive sign, you begin a quick climb up a sandy path that turns into another stretch of boardwalk. When it tops out, you'll be in a well-shaded area, looking at a forested gully between two huge dunes. On the far side, it looks as if the sand is pouring down between the trees. Soon you reach the stairway that leads to the Dune Overlook Platform.

You're only a short way from the nature center and parking area, but don't pass up the climb to the scenic overlook. Reaching the platform is no easy task, for it is 193 steps to the top. But the stairway leads you 190 feet above Lake Michigan to the top of one of the park's largest parabolic dunes. A pair of observation decks provide a sweeping view of Lake Michigan, its sandy shoreline, and, most of all, the dunes that are almost everywhere you look, whether wind-blown or well forested. The sight of these dunes is a fitting end to a day spent hiking through them.

30

Dune Ridge Trail

Place: Muskegon State Park

Total Distance: 4.2 miles

Hiking Time: 2 to 3 hours

Rating: Moderate to challenging

Highlights: Open dunes, scenic views, Muskegon Lake

Maps: Muskegon State Park Hiking Trails map from the Michigan DNR, or Dune Ridge Trail map from MichiganTrailMaps.com

Trailhead GPS Coordinates: N 43° 14' 50.05" W 086° 20' 8.42"

Located just north of Muskegon—and often overshadowed by P. J. Hoffmaster State Park just to the south—is Muskegon State Park. The 1,233-acre unit is the next in a string of state parks that preserve a slice of Lake Michigan's renowned beach and sand dunes. Muskegon features more than 2 miles of Great Lakes shoreline and another mile along Muskegon Lake.

But unlike Hoffmaster, which incorporates a stretch of the Lake Michigan beach in its trail system, the 12-mile network at Muskegon does not. Nor does the park have an impressive interpretive center like the Gillette Nature Center. The hiking at Muskegon, however, is no less impressive.

The trail system is a series of loops that wind through an amazing variety of landscapes including open dunes, stands of century-old pines, and an area called the Devil's Kitchen, where the mist rises and swirls as if Satan is stirring his caldron. The northern portion of the system surrounds the park's Winter Sports Complex and was cut as cross-country ski trails.

This hike is a 4.2-mile loop combining two of the park's most scenic footpaths: Dune Ridge Trail and Devil's Kitchen Trail. Located in the southern half of the park, the two trails wind through a series of unique intracoastal dunes, a sea of shifting sand that lies between two large bodies of water: Lakes Michigan and Muskegon. The trek is described from the trailhead in the Snug Harbor Day-Use Area but can also be hiked beginning in Channel Campground or at

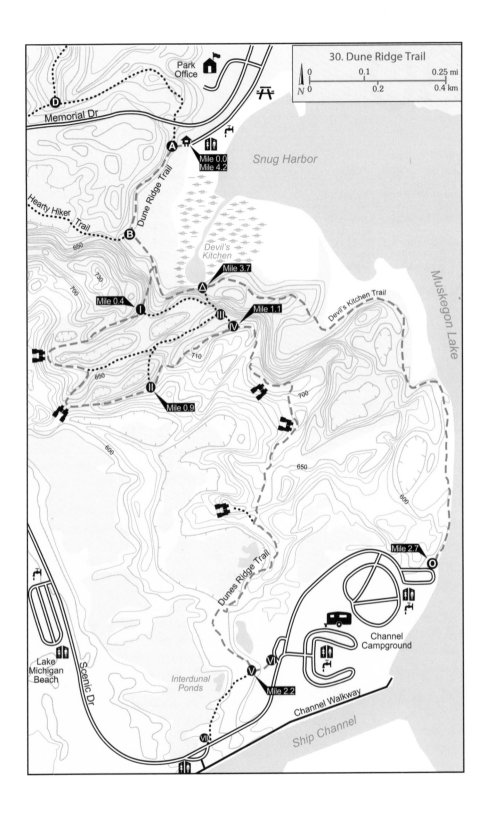

30. Dune Ridge Trail

N

0   0.1   0.25 mi
0   0.2   0.4 km

Park
Office

Memorial Dr

D

Snug Harbor

Dune Ridge Trail

Mile 0.0
Mile 4.2

A

Hearty Hiker Trail

B

650

730

700

Devil's
Kitchen

Mile 3.7

Mile 0.4

I

III

Mile 1.1

IV

Devil's Kitchen Trail

Muskegon Lake

710

650

II

Mile 0.9

700

600

650

600

Mile 2.7

O

Dunes Ridge Trail

Channel
Campground

Lake
Michigan
Beach

Scenic Dr

Interdunal
Ponds

VI

V

VI

Mile 2.2

Channel Walkway

Ship Channel

Two hikers enjoy the view from a bench along Dune Ridge Trail in Muskegon State Park.

post No. VII opposite a day-use parking area along the Ship Channel.

Muskegon's trail system is well marked with color-coded posts that correspond to a trail map available at the park office, campground contact station, or online from the Michigan DNR website (www.michigan .gov/dnr). At times the junction posts can be bit confusing—they're labeled in Roman numerals and letters in the southern half of the park, and numbers and letters in northern half. Add in the fact that the many spurs, loops, and unofficial trails in the open dunes make it easy to get turned around and you have a place that requires a map in your day pack.

As with other dune areas, the hiking at Muskegon can be challenging. Steep climbs through the soft sand of a towering dune are common on this hike. If you arrive during the height of the summer, make sure you carry along a quart of water per person.

The state park has two campgrounds for a total of 244 sites. Lake Michigan Campground (also referred to as North Campground) and Channel Campground are modern facilities with electric hookups and toilet/shower buildings. Both campgrounds are filled on weekends throughout the summer; reservations (800-44-PARKS; www .midnrreservations.com) are recommended for July and August.

ACCESS
From US 31, exit at M-120 and head southwest following park signs to Memorial Drive, which serves as the park's south entrance and passes Snug Harbor Day-Use Area.

The Blockhouse marks the highest point in Muskegon State Park.

A daily vehicle permit or annual state park pass is required to enter the park. For more information, contact Muskegon State Park (231-744-3480).

TRAIL

The Snug Harbor Day-Use Area has a shelter, restrooms, drinking water, and a boat launch. It is also conveniently located on the other side of Memorial Drive from the park office, where a map can be obtained. At the west end of the parking area is a trailhead with a path leading into the woods that immediately arrives at post A. Head south (left) to follow the Dune Ridge Trail along a wide, level path that at one time was an old road around Snug Harbor.

Within a quarter mile you reach post B, marking the junction where the Hearty Hiker Trail heads west (right) for post C. Continue south (left) and within 200 yards you'll arrive at a junction where the Devil's Kitchen Trail veers off to the left for what is posted as "South Camp" (Channel Campground). Dune Ridge Trail heads to the right, and you are immediately faced with a steep uphill climb along a soft sandy trail. Welcome to dune country.

You top off at a junction at *Mile 0.4* that may or may not be marked as post No. I. It's been missing for years. Head west (right) and the climbing continues as you skirt the top of a dune ridge with a deep ravine on the south side. You descend a bit, pass a deep depression on the right, and then climb a ridge to a scenic view of sand blowouts, often called sugar bowls, with Lake Michigan on the horizon.

The next stretch follows the ridgeline and can be confusing due to all the social trails leading into the open dunes. Stay left and follow the ridge as the path swings east and then west, opening up to views of the Ship

Channel between Muskegon Lake and Lake Michigan. The trail swings east again and begins a particularly scenic stretch. You hike along the crest of a high, ribbon-like dune where below you on one side is open sand and the other a forested hollow carpeted in last year's leaves. In the middle of the summer this contrast between shade and sun is amazing.

Post No. II is reached at *Mile 0.9*. Continue east (right) as the trail makes a descent to skirt a sandy bowl, followed by a knee-bending climb to the crest of another dune ridge. More views follow until you arrive at a junction at *Mile 1.1* where one trail makes a sharp turn to the north (left) and the other continues following the edge of the open dunes (right). On park maps this is where post No. IV is labeled, but the real post might be missing.

Head right here and keep an eye out for directional posts—they will lead you off the ridge into the open dunes with a steady descent along a soft, sandy path. Within a quarter mile you reach a bench, allowing you to sit and gaze at the open and wooded dunes stretching out to the west. You descend again and at *Mile 1.5* reach a second bench aligned in the same direction and overlooking Lake Michigan and the Muskegon South Pierhead Light. If it's the weekend and there is any wind, the lake will be a sea of colorful sails from dozens of sailboats on the water.

The trail continues in a southerly direction through an area laced with social paths due to its close proximity to Channel Campground. Keep an eye out for the directional posts—they seem to pop up just when you need one. One of the unofficial trails is passed at *Mile 1.7* and climbs northwest (right) a short distance to an open knob of a dune with 360-degree views. A directional post here keeps you heading south along the dune ridge as it skirts an interdunal pond that is dry most of the year.

At *Mile 2.2* you reach post No. V, marking a spur that heads east (left) to post No. VI in Channel Campground. Within 100 yards you pop out of the trees at the post in a small trailhead parking area and then follow the campground road for a half mile to the third and final loop where post O, the start of the Devil's Kitchen Trail, is located. Along the way you pass restrooms and drinking water.

Devil's Kitchen Trail begins by tightroping a narrow strip between the shoreline of Muskegon Lake and a bluff of dunes to the west. At *Mile 3* you leave the shoreline and swing sharply west, then north, passing the open fields that were once the site of Bay Mills Village, a Native American settlement. Within a third of a mile the level walk ends as the trail climbs a wooded dune forested with an impressive stand of hemlocks and maples, whose massive trunks indicate they escaped the saws and axes of loggers in the early 1900s.

Now a former road, the trail begins skirting above Devil's Kitchen and reaches a post marked by an enclosed triangle at *Mile 3.7*. The short spur to the left steeply climbs to the crest of the dune, topping off at the Dune Ridge Trail near post No. III. You head right for the best views of the marshy bay known as Devil's Kitchen.

The small bay forms the elongated end of Snug Harbor and is enclosed by high, forested ridges. When the conditions are right, the wind will rush in and swirl the rising mist off the water, making it look like the devil is boiling a wicked brew. This phenomenon occurs far more often in spring and fall than in summer.

From Devil's Kitchen, the trail descends the ridge and at *Mile 4* arrives at post B. Head right and Post A and the Snug harbor parking area are only a quarter mile away.

31

Silver Lake Dunes Route

Place: Silver Lake State Park

Total Distance: 6 to 7 miles

Hiking Time: 4 to 5 hours

Rating: Moderate to hard

Highlights: Sand dunes, Lake Michigan beach

Maps: Silver Lake State Park map from the Michigan DNR, or Silver Lake Dunes Route map from MichiganTrailMaps.com

Trailhead GPS Coordinates: N 43° 40' 46.69" W 086° 30' 11.25"

One of the most unusual hikes in the Lower Peninsula isn't on a trail at all. This trek is a journey through Silver Lake State Park's trailless backcountry, a mile-wide strip of dunes between Silver Lake and Lake Michigan. There's not another hike like this in Michigan—or even the Midwest—because no other stretch of dunes is so barren.

Perched on a plateau and rising more than 100 feet above Silver Lake, the heart of these dunes is totally devoid of any vegetation, even dune grass. The only thing besides sand are the stumps and trunks of ghost forests, ancient trees that the migrating dunes had buried and killed. Almost half of the hike is in this Sahara Desert–like terrain; the other half is spent strolling a stretch of Lake Michigan that is free of cottages and ice cream stands.

A rare hike indeed.

In all, Silver Lake State Park contains 2,936 acres, with 1,800 of them located in the backcountry between the two lakes. The strip of dunes is divided into three areas. Small sections at the north end are designated for off-road vehicles, and the south end is used for a dune-ride concession. But most of the acreage lies in the pedestrian area, where hikers follow the ridges of open sand out to Lake Michigan. The state park also contains almost 4 miles of Great Lake shoreline, a wide sandy beach that is rarely crowded, and a just reward for the hike out.

The rest of the park, however, attracts more than its share of users. Silver Lake draws more than 600,000 visitors a year, and the east side of the lake is a tourist

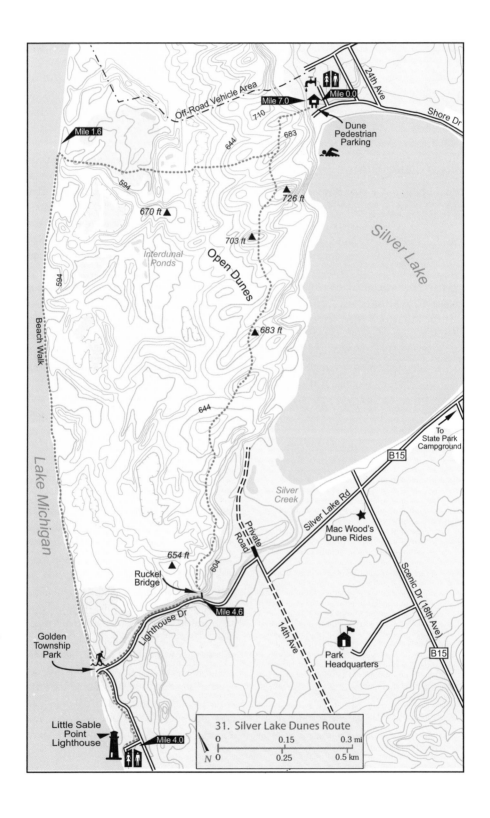

Off-Road Vehicle Area

Mile 7.0

Mile 0.0

Shore Dr

24th Ave

Dune
Pedestrian
Parking

710

683

644

Mile 1.6

594

▲ 726 ft

670 ft ▲

Silver Lake

*Interdunal
Ponds*

703 ft ▲

595

Open Dunes

▲ *683 ft*

*Beach
Walk*

644

To
State Park
Campground

B15

*Silver
Creek*

654 ft ▲

604

Private
Road

Silver Lake Rd

Mac Wood's
Dune Rides

Lake Michigan

Ruckel
Bridge

Mile 4.6

Lighthouse Dr

Scenic Dr (18th Ave)

B15

Golden
Township
Park

14th Ave

Park
Headquarters

Little Sable
Point
Lighthouse

Mile 4.0

31. Silver Lake Dunes Route

0   0.15   0.3 mi

N   0   0.25   0.5 km

mecca—a bumper-to-bumper row of motels, ice cream shops, go-cart tracks, and souvenir shops. The state park campground, featuring 200 modern sites, is also located here, and the demand for sites is heavy to say the least.

All this activity contrasts with the dunes themselves, where much of the crowding and noise of the Lake Michigan tourist season is lost among the ridges and valleys of the windblown sand. The dunes run east to west for the most part, and some tower more than 130 feet above Silver Lake. From the crest of many of them, you are rewarded with good views of this unusual area, with the inland lake on one side and Lake Michigan's endless blue on the other.

This hike begins with a trek across the dunes and then continues along Lake Michigan to historic Little Sable Point Lighthouse. From there you loop back through the open

dunes to the trailhead. The total distance ranges between 6 and 7 miles depending on the route you choose through the dunes. If this is too much of an adventure for you, then simply hike across the dunes to Lake Michigan and retrace your steps to the parking lot for a round trip of 3.6 miles.

This hike can be done in tennis shoes; in fact, that's the preferred footwear since it's easier to dump the sand out of them. Don't forget a hat, sunscreen, and a water bottle, for in midsummer trekking through the sand can be hot work.

ACCESS

The state park is south of Ludington and can be reached from US 31 by exiting at Shelby Road and heading west 6 miles to County Road B-15 (18th Avenue). Head north (right) for 5 miles. Just before reaching the lake, you pass the park headquarters (231-873-3083),

A ghost forest (trees killed by migrating dunes) in Silver Lake State Park.

Little Sable Point Lighthouse.

where additional information can be obtained. County Road B-15 swings around the east side of the lake, goes past the state park campground entrance, then heads east toward Mears. Where County Road B-15 merges with Hazel Road, turn west (left) onto Hazel Road and follow the ORV ACCESS AREA signs. These will lead you to the dune pedestrian parking area, well posted and located right next to the huge lot where off-road vehicle users park their trailers and rigs. Along with parking, the trailhead area contains vault toilets, picnic tables, grills, and a hand pump whose cold, clear water will taste like champagne after your return.

TRAIL

The route begins with a short trail through an oak and maple forest marked in the parking area by a DUNE ACCESS STAIRWAY sign. It leads to a wooden staircase that puts you face-to-face with a 50-foot-high wall of sand so steep that it's literally pouring into the forest. The climb to the top is a knee-bender and only the first of many. Once at the top you're rewarded with a view of Lake Michigan on the horizon, Silver Lake to the left, and sharp ridges of sand right in front of you. Within 10 minutes or less you have gone from the shady and cool forest at the trailhead to the world of rippled sand and brilliant sunlight. It's a striking contrast.

To reach Lake Michigan, select one of the ridges and begin scaling it. By climbing the one to the north (right) you will be able to watch the off-road-vehicle (ORV) daredevils race along dunes of their own in a variety of vehicles—trucks with oversized tires, four-wheelers, VW Bugs, and homemade dune buggies. But the dune ridge straight ahead is visibly higher than those around it, and from its sandy peak you are rewarded with the best view in the park, overlooking both Lake Michigan and Silver Lake.

Here the sand is pure, sugar-like, and there's not a plant around, not even dune grass. The sides of the dune, sculpted by the wind, form steep slopes with an incline of 45 degrees or more, while the surface at the top has a rippled wave effect to it. If there is a wind, sand will be visibly moving across the dune, making many hikers hesitant to pull out their cameras. In the troughs between the dunes are gray, stark trunks of ghost forests.

After trudging along the crest of the dune, you descend to the section where grass has taken root at *Mile 0.7*. Although the area is trailless, several routes are visible through the grass and lead into the strip of oak and jack pine. Depending on where you're cutting across, several interdunal ponds can also be seen. Although these ponds may vanish completely during a dry spell, early in the summer they are a haven for a variety of wildflowers, grasses, and animals.

It's about a half-mile walk through the sparse forest, where unofficial trails crisscross in every direction. Either put your trust in one or simply continue heading west. Eventually you depart the lightly forested strip, undertake another short climb through windblown and grass-covered dunes, and end up on the edge of a sandy bluff looking down at the Lake Michigan beach. Now, here is a true beach! The Lake Michigan shoreline, usually reached at *Mile 1.8*, is more than 30 yards wide and nothing but sand. If you have undertaken this trek in the middle of the week, you might well have a good stretch of this beach all to yourself.

Continue the route by heading south along the shoreline of the Great Lake. On one side is the endless blue horizon of Lake Michigan, while at your feet is a beach covered with tracks. A few will be footprints but most will not, making a field guide to wildlife tracks a handy thing to pack along. Within 1 mile Little Sable Point Lighthouse comes into view to the south, and at **Mile 3.7** you arrive at the mouth of Silver Creek. Kick off the shoes and cross the shallow stream.

On the other side is Golden Township Park and Lighthouse Drive. Followed the paved road for a third of a mile to reach the lighthouse, the centerpiece of a separate day-use area at Silver Lake State Park. The picnic area, reached at **Mile 4**, has restrooms and water, making it ideal for an extended break or lunch.

Built in 1873, the lighthouse was originally equipped with a third-order Fresnel lens and a three-wick lamp that burned whale's oil. Eventually an electric light replaced both the wick and the lightkeeper and in 1954 his adjoining dwelling was demolished, leaving only the conical, red-brick tower. At 108 feet in height, the light is one of the tallest on the west side of the state and a photographer's dream, thanks to its decorative black railing at the top, a handful of large trees at its base, and the low dunes surrounding it.

The second half of the hike begins by backtracking Lighthouse Drive, passing up Golden Township Park, and continuing along the road as it skirts the south side of Silver Creek. If it's early spring, keep one eye on the stream—steelhead trout are often visible spawning in it. At **Mile 4.6** you cross an old wooden bridge to the north side of the stream and then endure another gut-busting climb to return to the top of the open dunes.

Once on top, work your way northeast across the dunes toward Silver Lake. Again, there are no trails, but from the perch of any high dune you will be able to see Lake Michigan, Silver Lake, and a pair of posts topped off with bits of colored cloth. These are markers for the dune buggy concessioner and can be used to stay on course. As you hike toward the posts, grass-covered dunes will give way to huge blowouts, which will give way to those long ridges of pure sand. In the final mile of the trek, you will climb and descend four such ridges, each a little higher than the last, until you are perched on the highest grain of sand in this park. From here you will be able to view the ORV area of the state park to the north as well as a small sign pointing to the stairway that you climbed at the beginning of the hike.

32

Ridge and Island Trails

Place: Ludington State Park

Total Distance: 4.8 miles

Hiking Time: 3 to 4 hours

Rating: Moderate

Highlights: Scenic views, sand dunes

Maps: Ludington Hiking Trails map from the Michigan DNR, or Ridge and Island Trails map from MichiganTrailMaps.com

Trailhead GPS Coordinates: N 44° 2' 6.66" W 086° 29' 36.46"

Ludington State Park can be a busy place. The largest unit along Lake Michigan at 5,300 acres, it attracts more than 700,000 visitors a year, with the vast majority arriving between Memorial Day and Labor Day. At that time, the beaches are popular, the campgrounds often filled, and the paved pathways that skirt the Big Sable River between Hamlin Lake and Lake Michigan crowded with families riding bicycles to their campsites.

But don't let this discourage you from visiting this state park. With its extensive acreage, hikers can easily escape the summer heat and the crowds by following a foot trail into the wooded dunes to the north. The park's developed area, and the focus for most visitors, is concentrated along the Big Sable River, where three campgrounds contain a total of 352 sites. You'll also find a concession store, picnic area, and park headquarters.

To the north is Ludington's backcountry, featuring a terrain that ranges from open dunes and protected marshes along Hamlin Lake to towering pines and miles of undeveloped Lake Michigan shoreline, complete with a historic lighthouse. A 20-mile network of trails provides foot access into this area, ending at the edge of the park's Wilderness Natural Area, a trailless, 1,700-acre section of mostly forested dunes. This unique dune wilderness continues beyond the state park border, for to the north of Ludington is Nordhouse Dunes, the only federally designated wilderness in the Lower Peninsula (see Hike 34).

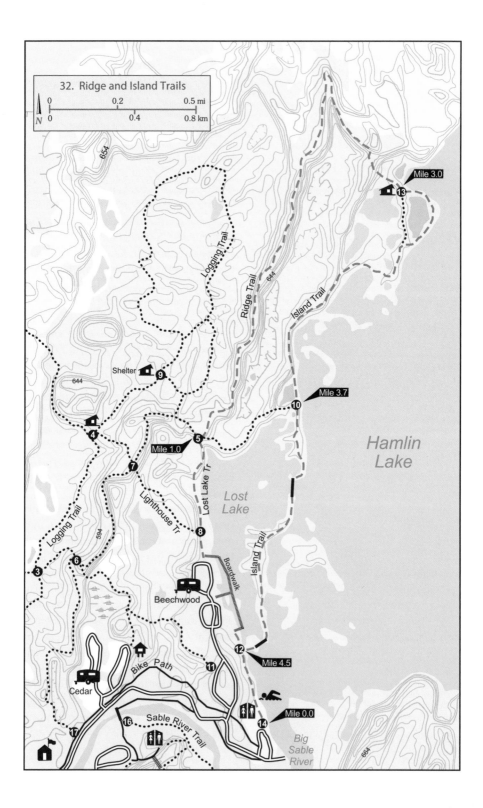

32. Ridge and Island Trails

N

0   0.2   0.5 mi
0   0.4   0.8 km

654

Logging Trail

Ridge Trail

644

Island Trail

Mile 3.0

13

Shelter 9

644

Mile 3.7

4

10

5

Mile 1.0

7

Lost Lake Tr

Lighthouse Tr

Hamlin
Lake

Lost
Lake

Logging Trail

594

8

Island Trail

Boardwalk

6

3

Beechwood

11

12

Mile 4.5

Cedar

Bike Path

17

16

Sable River Trail

14

Mile 0.0

664

Big
Sable
River

A popular hike in the park is to follow an access road out to Big Sable Point Lighthouse, then circle back along Lighthouse and Logging Trails for a 5-mile trek (Hike 33). Just as scenic, however, is the circuit formed by Ridge and Island Trails. These trails lead you to the edge of the wilderness area and past the fascinating perched dunes above Hamlin Lake. This loop makes for a pleasant day hike, and you can enjoy lunch deep in the park at a rustic CCC shelter overlooking the inland lake.

In summer, bring a quart of water per person, a hat, and sunscreen, for some stretches of the walk are through open dunes. But the vast majority of the day will be spent in the cool shade of the forest, away from beach blankets, beach balls, and the crowds that congregate along the park's designated beaches.

ACCESS

The park is located 8.5 miles north of the city of Ludington at the end of M-116. From US 31, head west on US 10 through the heart of the city to the waterfront where it merges into M-116. Just before crossing the Big Sable River, you pass a campsite reservation center where you can make arrangements to obtain a site. Keep in mind that the campgrounds are heavily booked from early July through Labor Day; reservations are strongly recommended (800-44-PARKS; www.midnr reservations.com).

A daily vehicle permit or annual state park pass is required to enter the park For more information, contact Ludington State Park (231-843-2423).

TRAIL

Begin at the Hamlin Lake Day-Use Area where you'll find parking, restrooms, drinking water, a picnic area, and a pleasant beach overlooking the inland lake, the perfect place

Hikers following the Ridge Trail in Ludington State Park.

to cool off after the hike. At the parking area the trail is marked by post No. 14 and begins as a paved walkway past the picnic area and children's play area. At **Mile 0.3** you pass post No. 12, marking the junction with the south end of the Island Trail. Continue north on Lost Lake Trail to follow a series of scenic boardwalks and docks along Lost Lake and bypass Beechwood Campground.

From the boardwalk Lost Lake Trail continues north along the shoreline, quickly passing post No. 8, marking the east end of the Lighthouse Trail. Steps lead you away from Lost Lake itself to a ridge above it at post No. 5, reached at **Mile 1**.

This is a major junction, with trails departing in almost every direction. But a display map and a rainbow of boot prints lead you

Following the Island Trail boardwalks at Ludington State Park.

from Lost Lake Trail to Ridge Trail, where purple prints continue north. Ridge Trail ascends a ridge and then follows the crest of it, passing a small pond along the way and a set of benches. The hiking here is interesting. For the next half mile, there are steep ravines on either side of the ridge, heavily forested in an old stand of maple and beech. The trees are so thick that the forest floor is almost devoid of any undergrowth.

Eventually, you come to a clearing where to the west there is a view of the open and grass-covered dunes with Lake Michigan on the horizon. The trail quickly climbs to its highest point of 712 feet—128 feet above Lake Michigan—reached at *Mile 2*. Under the shade of a large oak tree you are rewarded with an unobstructed view of the dunes and the Great Lake to the west, with a portion of Hamlin Lake to the east. More panoramic views follow for the next a third of a mile as you traverse what is basically a migrating sand dune. On its west side is open sand being pushed along by the winds off Lake Michigan. On the east side a scattering of trees try valiantly to keep this moving mountain in place.

At *Mile 2.3* the trail makes a sharp curve and descends off the ridge. To the east, you get a full view of the open and grass-covered dunes that surround Hamlin Lake, a sight just as spectacular as the views of Lake Michigan. Within another quarter mile, a purple boot directs you to descend into a shaded beech forest, but it's easy to scramble 50 yards to the top of a sand dune to the east here for the best vantage point of Hamlin Lake and the dunes perched above it on its northwest shoreline.

The trail, meanwhile, descends rapidly through the forest, swings east (left), and bottoms out at the edge of a pond. Just on the other side is the picturesque stone shelter on the shores of Hamlin Lake. The shelter, like many of the structures in state parks, was built by the CCC in the early 1930s under the direction of the National Park Service. When Ludington State Park officially opened in 1934, corps members served as trail guides to visitors from 16 states and Canada.

Just beyond the shelter is post No. 13 at *Mile 3*, marking the start of Island Trail. The trail, marked by blue boot prints, heads south, and you have a choice between taking the main route that winds between two ponds and following a somewhat obscured path that veers off to the east and hugs the shoreline of Hamlin Lake. By taking the obscure path, you can get an excellent view of the steep dunes that make up Hamlin Lake's west shore.

At *Mile 3.3* the footpaths merge and Island Trail continues south by skirting the edge of a marshy bay. Tree-studded islets separate this lagoon from the rest of the lake and make for calm water that attracts a variety of waterfowl, often seen resting among the cattails.

Eventually you round the lagoons and return to the open lake while passing a small inland pond to the west. Just south of the pond is post No. 10, reached at *Mile 3.7* and marking the junction with Lost Lake Trail. Island Trail continues south as it cuts along a scenic spit, with Lost Lake on one side and Hamlin on the other.

Just before *Mile 4* you cross an impressive bridge and hike across an island, passing well-protected coves on Hamlin Lake that often attract waterfowl and other birds. Within a half mile the trail arrives at the south end of the island. You can spot the campers on the other side of Lost Lake just before you arrive at a boardwalk and bridge to the mainland. On the other side is post No. 12. Head south (left) at the junction to return to the day-use area and beach on Hamlin Lake, reached at *Mile 4.8*.

33

Lighthouse Trail

Place: Ludington State Park

Total Distance: 4.3 miles

Hiking Time: 3 hours

Rating: Moderate

Highlights: Historic lighthouse, Lake Michigan beach

Maps: Ludington Hiking Trails map from the Michigan DNR, or Lighthouse Trail map from MichiganTrailMaps.com

Trailhead GPS Coordinates: N 44° 2' 14.69" W 086° 30' 21.10"

Within Ludington State Park, one of the most popular units in Michigan, Big Sable Point Lighthouse is without question the most popular destination for walkers and hikers. Most visitors simply follow the access road out to the historic lighthouse, snap a few pictures, then turn around and head back along the same sandy road. But the more intriguing way to reach Big Sable Point is to hike the park's Logging Trail, which winds through the woods and around interesting ponds, then head west on the Lighthouse Trail through open dune country.

You can return by hiking the Lake Michigan shoreline, where some of the best beachcombing on this side of the state can be enjoyed. This is paradise for lovers of weather-beaten, gray, faded driftwood. The loop covers 4.3 miles and is of moderate difficulty, but the only time you see the access road is when you cross it.

Although in summer the park is busy—too busy for some people—the crowds taper off dramatically once you leave the campground and hike north. The first half of the route can be buggy, but the bugs are almost nonexistent in the open dunes and along the beach. You'll see more people here than on the Ridge and Island Trail loops (see Hike 32), but the almost 2-mile stroll down Lake Michigan in August is great, especially if it's early evening and the sun is beginning to melt on the horizon.

Sturdy tennis shoes are adequate for this trip, and there are two stone shelters in the first half in case of a sudden downpour. If you're packing a lunch, the best place to

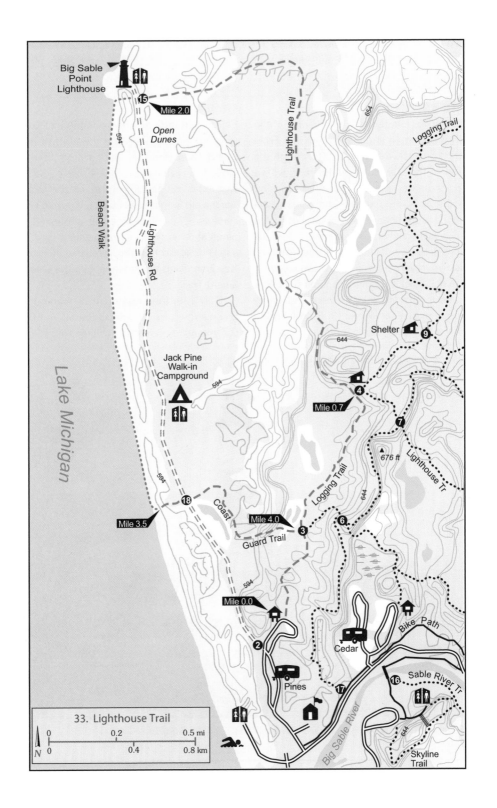

Big Sable
Point
Lighthouse

15 ◆ Mile 2.0

Open
Dunes

Lighthouse Trail

654

Logging Trail

594

Beach Walk

Lighthouse Rd

Lake Michigan

Jack Pine
Walk-in
Campground

594

Shelter 9

644

4
Mile 0.7

7

676 ft

Lighthouse Tr

Logging Trail

594

644

18

Mile 3.5

Coast

Mile 4.0

Guard Trail

3

6

Bike Path

Cedar

Mile 0.0

2

Pines

17

16 Sable River Tr

Big Sable River

644

Skyline
Trail

33. Lighthouse Trail

N

0   0.2   0.5 mi

0   0.4   0.8 km

feast is on the small dunes overlooking the lighthouse and Big Sable Point—dining with a million-dollar view.

ACCESS

The park is located 8.5 miles north of the city of Ludington at the end of M-116. From US 31, head west on US 10 through the heart of the city to the waterfront, where US 10 merges with M-116. After crossing Big Sable River, you pass the contact station. Straight ahead is a parking lot with a fish-cleaning station. The trailhead is in Pines Campground, but this is the best place to leave your vehicle if you don't have a site.

A daily vehicle permit or annual state park pass is required to enter the park, and during the summer, reservations (800-44-PARKS; www.midnrreservations.com) are strongly recommended if you want to camp. For more information, contact Ludington State Park (231-843-2423).

TRAIL

Pines Campground serves as the trailhead for the Logging Trail and the start of the Lighthouse Road, a service drive that is closed to motorized vehicles. The Logging Trail is posted next to site No. 41 and looks like the old logging trail that it once was. You immediately climb a ridge that is forested in pines and hardwoods and within a third of a mile descend to a small wetland and post No. 3, marking the junction with the Coast Guard Trail.

Stay with the Logging Trail, marked in green arrows, as it heads northwest. At *Mile 0.7* you arrive at a stone shelter built in the

Big Sable Point Lighthouse, reached on foot in Ludington State Park.

Following the Lighthouse Trail to Big Sable Point Lighthouse.

1930s by the Civilian Conservation Corps, now a scenic spot to sit out a sudden rainstorm. Just beyond it is post No. 4, marking the junction of the Lighthouse Trail. Head left to follow the brown arrows that mark it.

The Lighthouse Trail begins in the forest but with a sharp climb quickly emerges from the hardwoods and pines onto a ridge of open and grass-covered dunes. If the day is not too hot, it's a welcome change of scenery that lasts for almost a half mile before the trail descends back into scruffy pines.

After a small dune provides the first glimpse of the lighthouse, the trail swings left at **Mile 1.6** to reach a posted map. At this point the Lighthouse Trail heads almost

due west and in the next half mile winds around interdunal ponds and over dunes. It's less a trail than a series of footprints in the open sand with an occasional trail marker. It's hard to get lost, however. The distinctive black-and-white tower of the Big Sable Point House soon appears above the rolling dunes, showing the way like the guiding light it was built to be for sailors of the Great Lakes. At **Mile 2** is post No. 15 on the Lighthouse Road, with the lighthouse just to the north along with picnic tables and restrooms.

Big Sable Point Lighthouse was authorized by President James Buchanan in 1858 after the barge *Neptune* sank off the point and 37 people drowned. Actual construction didn't begin until President Andrew Johnson ordered it in 1866, and on November 1, 1867, the light was illuminated by Burr Caswell, the first resident of Mason County and the first lighthouse keeper.

The light used a third-order Fresnel lens that was almost 6 feet tall and was shipped in from Paris. The signal was fixed white, and the lamp used 179 gallons of "refined lard wick oil" during each shipping season from April to May. A lifesaving station was also established here in 1875 but was discontinued in 1921. The light was automated by the Coast Guard 47 years later.

Since 1940 government agencies have taken several steps to protect the lighthouse from the rough weather on the point and to renovate the structure. The light was placed on the National Register of Historical Sites in 1983 and, in 1990, received a grant for shore protection from Michigan's Historic Preservation Office. Today the Sable Points Lighthouse Keeper's Association (splka .org) has the task of maintaining the light and keeping it open daily May through October from 10 AM to 5 PM.

The lighthouse is one of the northernmost points of the park's trail system, making it an ideal spot for an extended break or lunch. On the first floor the association maintains an interpretive room and a gift shop that does a brisk business selling bottles of water and soda on hot summer days.

But most hikers who arrive have one thing in mind. They want to climb the tower, 130 steps and all. And for good reason. The 360-degree view from the top is spectacular. And what is most amazing about the view is that it hasn't changed since the first lightkeeper arrived in 1867 and scaled the tower. Because the lighthouse is surrounded by state land, it looks exactly as it did a century and a half ago.

That alone makes it worth the hike in.

There are two ways to return to Pines Campground. The Lighthouse Road is a 1.5-mile walk back and skirts the forest to the east and the open dunes to the west. Along the way you pass a number of ponds and wetlands; within a mile is the Jack Pine Walk-in Campground, which has 10 sites, vault toilets and drinking water.

You can also follow the beach back, a far more interesting trek. The shoreline is wide, sandy, and scattered with driftwood. You can stroll along the hard sand near the water with Lake Michigan's surf pounding one side and low, rolling dunes on the other. At *Mile 3.5* there is a depression between two dunes and a trail post with a black arrow, marking the west end of the Coast Guard Trail.

Follow the Coast Guard Trail and at *Mile 4* arrive at post No. 3, marking its junction with the Logging Trail. Head south on the Logging Trail to retrace your steps to Pines Campground, reached at *Mile 4.3*.

34

Nordhouse Dunes

Place: Nordhouse Dunes Wilderness Area

Total Distance: 6.5 miles

Hiking Time: 4 to 5 hours

Rating: Challenging

Highlights: Sand dunes, scenic overlooks

Maps: Nordhouse Dunes Wilderness Area map from the USDA Forest Service or MichiganTrailMaps.com

Trailhead GPS Coordinates: N 44° 7' 9.86" W 086° 25' 38.50"

Wilderness is such a subjective concept. To many, the only true wilderness in Michigan is on Isle Royale National Park, an island in the northwest corner of Lake Superior that is free of roads, vehicles, or, for the most part, WiFi and cell reception. To others, wilderness is anywhere without a McDonald's.

With the Michigan Wilderness Act of 1987, the federal government declared the Nordhouse Dunes area of the Manistee National Forest a wilderness, the only area designated as such in the Lower Peninsula. To some purists, this designation is debatable. Nordhouse Dunes is not a large tract—only 3,450 acres—nor is it a pristine setting. The area is crisscrossed in places by old logging tracks and Forest Service roads.

True wilderness or not, though, there is no question that this niche of windblown dunes, wetlands, and rolling hills of hardwoods and conifers is a unique spot for southern Michigan and even for the western side of the state, which is famous for having the world's most extensive set of freshwater dunes. The most striking feature of this area is its undeveloped nature, most notably along the 4 miles of Lake Michigan shoreline where you won't find a single bathhouse, ice cream stand, or paved parking lot. Paralleling the shoreline are open dunes and forested bluffs, and skirting the edge of these is a footpath that at one time was called the Michigan Trail.

In the nature of a true wilderness, Nordhouse Dunes was stripped of its signs, markings, and even names for trails. But this path is worthy of its title. Lying like a thread

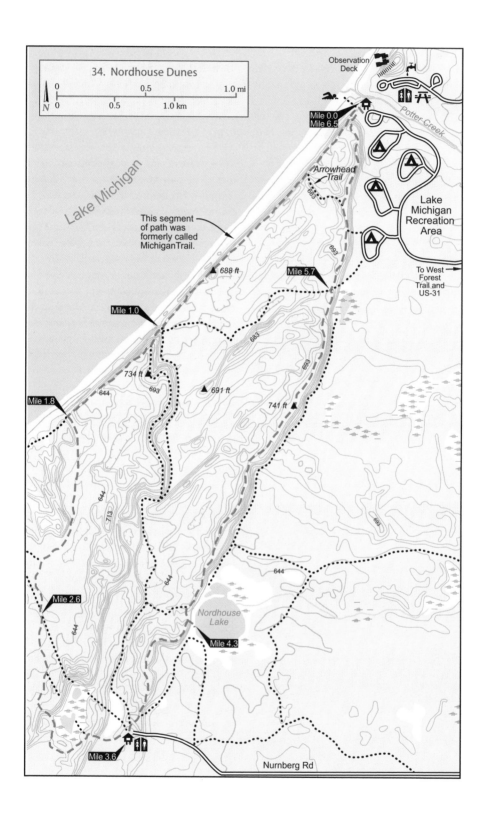

34. Nordhouse Dunes

0   0.5   1.0 mi

0   0.5   1.0 km

N

Lake Michigan

Observation Deck

Potter Creek

Mile 0.0
Mile 6.5

Arrowhead Trail

This segment of path was formerly called Michigan Trail.

Lake Michigan Recreation Area

To West Forest Trail and US-31

▲ 688 ft

Mile 5.7

Mile 1.0

734 ft ▲

▲ 691 ft

741 ft ▲

Mile 1.8

Mile 2.6

Nordhouse Lake

Mile 4.3

Mile 3.6

Nurnberg Rd

between the roar of the Lake Michigan surf and the quiet interior of the forests, this route is one of the most scenic hikes not only in Michigan but possibly in the Midwest. The actual trail stretches 1.9 miles above the shoreline between the southern observation platform in the Lake Michigan Recreation Area to a stretch of open dunes. You then complete this 6-mile loop by following a trail to the Nurnberg Road trailhead, where you pick up another path to the campground. Alternatively, spurs allow you to depart the shoreline earlier and shorten the hike to either 2.4 miles or 5.5 miles.

Any one of these return routes takes you away from the Great Lake and into the heart of this small wilderness, where solitude and encounters with wildlife will be enjoyed. The interior trails traverse numerous ridges and hills (old dunes, really) and at times are a

challenge to climb. But there are rewards for the effort. A quiet walker, especially at dusk, might sight a variety of wildlife including white-tailed deer, raccoons, porcupines, numerous squirrels harvesting nuts, maybe even a fox or coyote.

Encounters with people are also likely, especially during July and August or on trails near the Lake Michigan Recreation Area. During the firearm deer season, November 15 to November 30, hunters will often be seen along the interior trails. But Nordhouse Dunes can be something of a wilderness experience for those who venture onto the remote open dune area at the southern end of the tract. Due to the fragile nature of the open dunes, campfires and camping are discouraged, but nearby are pockets of conifers or hardwoods that are excellent places to set up camp for a night. Carry in all your water

Entering the Nordhouse Dunes Wilderness.

and a backpacker's stove to make life easy in the woods, and carry out all your trash. The backpacking effort will seem well worth it in that magic moment when the sun begins to sink into Lake Michigan, people disappear, wildlife peek out, and the "wilderness" of the Nordhouse Dunes settles in.

ACCESS
The Lake Michigan Recreation Area is at the northern edge of the federal wilderness and located almost halfway between Manistee to the north and Ludington to the south. From M-55 in Manistee, head south on US 31 for 10 miles and then turn west (right) on Lake Michigan Road for 8 miles to its end. From US 10 turn north on US 31 at Scottville, 7 miles east of Ludington. Lake Michigan Road is reached in 11.5 miles.

The recreation area features 99 rustic and wooded campsites well spaced along four loops. There are hand pumps for water, fire rings, and picnic tables, but no electricity or showers. The area is open year-round and managed from mid-May to mid-October. There is a nightly campsite fee.

The tract's 10-mile network of trails is also accessible from a trailhead at the west end of Nurnberg Road. From US 31, head west on Lake Michigan Recreation Road for 3 miles, then head south (left) on Quarterline Road for a little over 1 mile to reach Nurnberg Road. Three trails marked by USDA Forest Service signs and one with a display map depart from here. Make sure you have water before you arrive, for the trailhead contains only a parking area for your vehicle.

A Huron-Manistee National Forests vehicle permit is required to hike into Nordhouse Dunes and can be obtained at the trailhead or from the Cadillac/Manistee Ranger District. More information or maps can be obtained contacting the Cadillac/Manistee Ranger District (231-723-2211; www.fs.usda.gov /hmnf) or stopping at the ranger station located at 412 Red Apple Road just off US 31 and south of the town of Manistee.

TRAIL
To reach the trailhead at the Lake Michigan Recreation Area, drive through the campground to a parking lot at the end that features an information display and a boardwalk. One end of the boardwalk heads to the beach; the other toward the shoreline bluff to the south (left). At one time there was a long stairway up the bluff to an observation deck at the top, but these have since been removed. Now the trail sidles around the bluff, gradually ascending to the top. Within a quarter mile you pass a log stairway to the beach below and at *Mile 0.35* arrive at the posted junction with the Arrowhead Trail, which heads inland (left). Head southwest (right) to officially enter the federal wilderness.

The trail continues along a dune ridge high above the shoreline and is surprisingly level and easy walking for the first mile. On one side are dunes forested in hardwoods, pines, and an occasional paper birch; on the other, a steep drop, a strip of white, sandy beach, and the blue horizon of Lake Michigan. The contrast between the shade of the woods and the sun on the sand is remarkable.

The forest is composed mostly of northern hardwoods such as maple, beech, and white and red oaks, with hemlock and red and white pines mixed in. At *Mile 1*, however, you head through a scenic stand of paper birch and pass the second crossover trail, which is not posted and can easily be missed. This spur is a 0.7-mile walk to the return trail of this hike.

The Michigan Trail continues south (right) and immediately ascends along an embankment stairway that quickly passes

Hikers strolling the beach at Nordhouse Dunes Wilderness.

the third junction of the day. You climb several more humps along the shoreline dunes before making a long descent to the fourth junction, reached at **Mile 1.8**. This area is the most popular for backpackers to set up camp, thus the maze of social trails here that lead to the beach or farther into the woods. Though not posted, the crossover trail is a former two-track that heads south (left) and is easier to distinguish than the others.

If you continued southwest (right), the Michigan Trail would lead you out of the woods to an impressive blowout of open sand. What lies beyond is an area of wind-blown dunes, slopes of beach grass, and woody patches often populated by juniper and stunted jack pine, surrounded by open sand. All the dunes were formed within the

last 13,000 years, after the glaciers receded and the level of Lake Michigan fluctuated between a high of 640 feet and the present 580 feet. During times of low water, the prevailing winds from the west pushed the exposed lake-bottom sand into dunes onshore. The dunes stand 140 feet high in some places and are a textbook display of natural plant succession. Beginning with just sand and water at the edge of Lake Michigan, you can follow this path of succession: mosses, lichens, and grasses first appearing, only to be replaced by larger shrubs such as sand cherry, jack pine, and aspen saplings, which are finally eclipsed by a hardwood climax forest.

The southern half of the Nordhouse Dunes is trailless, but adventurous hikers can continue southwest by following the beach. In a little over 2 miles, you would leave the federal tract and enter Ludington State Park's Wilderness Natural Area, a 1,699-acre extension of this undeveloped segment of Lake Michigan shoreline, and end up at the Big Sable Point Lighthouse (see Hike 33).

This trail description, however, follows the old two-track south. The trail is wide and easy to follow, passing another former two-track that heads northwest (left) at *Mile 2.4*. Continue south and at *Mile 2.6* you'll pass yet another old road that crosses the trail and climbs steeply up a hill. This junction can be a bit confusing, but head left and then right to remain on the described route, a wide, sandy path that makes its own long ascent. You follow with an equally long descent, after which the trail curves around a large marsh with an open pond in the middle. From the trail, you can look down into the entire wetland, an excellent place to look for deer early in the morning.

The main trail then swings noticeably to the east, passes another old road, and at *Mile 3.6* descends gently to the trailhead and parking area off Nurnberg Road. The trailhead features vault toilets and an information display but no source of drinking water.

Pick up the next segment by crossing the parking area to the north to the path marked by a NO MOTORIZED VEHICLES sign. This path is the main route back to the Lake Michigan Recreation Area and is a scenic hike as you straddle the crest of a line of wooded dunes almost all the way back to the campground. You immediately pass a junction with one of the crossover spurs which heads northwest (left), and then within a few hundred yards a trail that heads northeast (right) for Nordhouse Lake. Stay on the main trail, a wide, easy-to-follow path, and at *Mile 4.3* you'll arrive at a clear view of the lake with a short spur dropping to its shoreline.

Just beyond the lake is a junction with a crossover spur to the west (left). The main trail resumes following the edge of the bluff, passing another crossover spur to the west (left) at *Mile 5.7*. Less than a quarter mile later, a spur drops sharply off the bluff to the campground below. The main trail begins climbing steadily, reaching an open high point of 713 feet, where a water tower once stood. The Arrowhead Trail departs to west (left) here. Stay right and follow the main trail as it skirts a narrow ridgeline and arrives at the spot where the observation deck was located.

You descend the bluff from here along one of two trails. Both are steep and demand caution, especially if you're hiking with young children. You bottom out at a trail and then the boardwalk that leads back to the trailhead parking area, reached at *Mile 6.5*.

Sleeping Bear Dunes

35

Old Indian Trail

Place: Sleeping Bear Dunes National Lakeshore

Total Distance: 3.2 miles

Hiking Time: 1 to 2 hours

Rating: Easy

Highlights: Open dunes, Lake Michigan beach

Maps: Old Indian Trail map from the National Park Service or MichiganTrail Maps.com

Trailhead GPS Coordinates: N 44° 42' 9.54" W 086° 11' 6.36"

Anchoring the southern end of Sleeping Bear Dunes National Lakeshore, well away from such park favorites as the Pierce Stocking Scenic Drive and the Dune Climb, is Old Indian Trail. The path picks up its name from when Native Americans used the route to access their fish camps along Lake Michigan and today draws less attention than most other trails in the park. Many hikers, especially those visiting Sleeping Bear Dunes for the first time, bypass this area for the dramatic perched dune scenery found along trails like Empire Bluff (Hike 37) or Pyramid Point (Hike 41).

But Old Indian still provides access to a beautiful beach, open dunes, and a ghost forest, and is often the only escape from the summer crowds encountered elsewhere in this popular park. The trail is a pair of loops that merge a third of a mile from the shoreline with most of it winding dips through a forest of red and white pines or a mix of hemlocks, maples, and oaks.

Old Indian was the first trail to feature one of the most unusual warnings found at any trailhead in Michigan: YOU ARE A VISITOR IN COUGAR HABITAT! It was along this trail in 2002 that several cougar sightings were reported and resulted in the National Park Service posting the unusual trail sign a year later. The trailhead sign goes on to say that seeing a cougar can be a thrilling experience—but if you do encounter one, remain calm and do not run. If approached, wave your arms and throw sticks and rocks. If attacked, fight back aggressively.

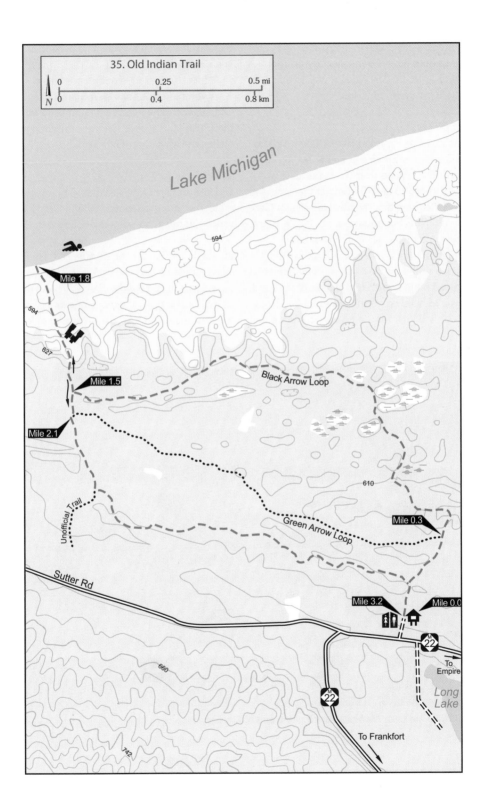

35. Old Indian Trail

Lake Michigan

Mile 1.8

594

627

Mile 1.5

Mile 2.1

Black Arrow Loop

610

Unofficial Trail

Green Arrow Loop

Mile 0.3

Sutter Rd

660

Mile 3.2

Mile 0.0

22

To Empire

22

Long Lake

To Frankfort

742

594

Keep in mind that in the past century only 13 people have been killed by cougars in North America. Still, what a way to spice up a hike.

ACCESS

The heart of Sleeping Bear Dunes National Lakeshore is Empire, a small, scenic town located 22 miles from Traverse City or 74 miles from I-75 and Grayling at the west end of MI 72. From the Philip A. Hart Visitor Center and NPS headquarters (231-326-5134; www.nps.gov/slbe) in Empire, head south on M-22 for 12 miles and look for the entrance to the trailhead parking lot, which is posted on the north (right) side of the road. If you're heading north from Frankfort, follow M-22 and look for the posted entrance just beyond Sutter Road. Within the parking area is a display sign and map box along with a vault toilet. Camping is not allowed here.

A vehicle park pass is required to hike Old Indian Trail and can be purchased from the Philip Hart Visitor Center or the ranger station at Platte River Campground.

TRAIL

The hike begins along a level trail that immediately enters the woods. In less than 100 yards you pass the posted junction with the return route west (left). Continue straight; the next junction arrives at **Mile 0.3**. Heading west (left) is the Green Arrow Trail. Continue straight to hike the Black Arrow Trail, as this loop is by far the most interesting. For the next mile, you hike over a series of low

Hiking to the Lake Michigan beach at the end of Old Indian Trail.

dunes, forested in mixed hardwoods (maple, beech, oak) and pines. Within a quarter mile the trail passes a series of open wetlands. At **Mile 1.2** is a spot where open dunes are migrating south into the forest, sand pouring down between the trees.

At **Mile 1.5** you arrive at the posted junction to Lake Michigan. Head north (right) and quickly the spur breaks out of the trees to enter an area of open dunes, where you're faced with the steepest climb of the day through loose sand. At the top you're rewarded with a view of open dunes and the shoreline, leading east to Platte River Point. Just below you is a ghost forest, trees that were buried alive during periods of active dune migrations and died. When winds push the dunes farther inland "ghost forests" appear: dead trees still standing in clusters without leaves, branches, or even bark.

At **Mile 1.8** you reach the cooling waters of Lake Michigan. This is a scenic spot, even though a handful of homes are visible to the west. To the east you view nothing but the wide expanse of low beach dunes along Platte Bay, while off in the distance are Empire Bluffs and famous Sleeping Bear Dunes. Out in Lake Michigan, you can see South and North Manitou Islands (see Hikes 42 and 43); on a clear day even the Fox Islands may be visible. The perched dunes along South Manitou's west side are clearly visible. The beach is usually 20 to 30 feet wide, depending on the lake level, and you can walk it the length of Platte Bay.

To return, backtrack the spur to Lake Michigan and at the junction continue straight. At **Mile 2.1** you reach the junction with the Green Arrow Trail heading east

Mother and son cross the open dunes along Old Indian Trail.

(left). Continuing south, the trail remains level and in the woods. At **Mile 2.3** the loop, well marked here by green arrows, curves sharply east (left) while an unofficial trail continues south. It is here that Old Indian Trail picks up its name, as it follows a path that was originally established by Native American tribes traveling the coastline between camps and fishing spots.

You stay in the woods for the remainder of the hike and at one point pass through an impressive stand of beech, with one huge tree towering above you along the trail. At **Mile 3.1** you arrive at the first junction you passed from the trailhead. Head south (right), and you'll be back at the parking lot in minutes.

36

Platte Plains Trail

Place: Sleeping Bear Dunes National Lakeshore	
Total Distance: 7.2 miles	
Hiking Time: 3 to 5 hours	
Rating: Easy	
Highlights: Lake Michigan shoreline, backcountry camping	
Maps: Platte Plains Trail map from the National Park Service or MichiganTrail Maps.com	
Trailhead GPS Coordinates: N 44° 43' 11.36" W 086° 7' 2.54"	

Until the proposed Bay-to-Bay Trail is completed across Sleeping Bear Dunes National Lakeshore, there are two walk-in campgrounds within the mainland portion of the park. Valley View is a lightly used facility north of Glen Arbor with forested sites at the end of a 1.5-mile trail; neither dunes nor Lake Michigan is nearby. The other is White Pine Campground, reached on foot from the Platte Plains Trail. This backcountry campground is a gem.

Located in a ravine between two forested dunes, White Pine is an escape from the noise and bustle of the park's busy tourist season in midsummer—yet it still lies near the three main attractions of Sleeping Bear Dunes. Within a short walk of your tent are windblown dunes, panoramas of the rugged shoreline and the Manitou Islands, and isolated stretches of Lake Michigan beach.

Platte Plains Trail is actually a 15-mile network of trails with four trailheads. The shortest route to White Pine Campground is a 1.2-mile walk that begins at the end of Peterson Road. But the most scenic route and the one described here begins at Platte River Campground and is commonly referred to as the Lasso Loop. This hike is a 7.2-mile walk, with White Pine Campground reached in 2.8 miles.

With its easy hiking and ban on mountain bike use, Platte Plains is one of the best destinations in the Lower Peninsula for anybody's first overnight adventure in which all that's needed is strapped to their back. Surprisingly, as overrun as Sleeping Bear Dunes can be in the summer, the demand for campsites at White Pine is moderately light. Often when there is a line of campers waiting for an opening at popular Platte River Campground, walk-in sites at White Pine are still available.

If you're planning to spend a night in the backcountry, pack in water along with your food, tent, sleeping bag, and other equipment. There's a community fire ring in the campground, but cooking is best done on a backpacker's stove. Don't forget the bathing suit; the swimming is excellent in Platte Bay.

To stay at White Pine, you need to obtain a backcountry camping permit at either the park headquarters or the ranger contact station at the Platte River Campground. The permits are handed out on a first-come, first-served basis and allow up to two tents and four people per site. There is a nightly fee to stay at the six walk-in sites that is above and

beyond the vehicle fee required to enter the national lakeshore.

The hiking season runs through the typical spring-to-fall period, with the heaviest demand for the walk-in sites in July and August, especially on the weekends. These summer months are popular for those who like to romp across hot dunes to cool off in the surf of Lake Michigan. October brings in the spectacular fall colors, while by late December or early January a good base of snow has formed and cross-country skiers begin arriving. Winter camping, anyone?

ACCESS
Begin the trip in Empire (see Hike 35) at the Philip A. Hart Visitor Center and NPS headquarters (231-326-5134; www.nps.gov /slbe) on the corner of MI 72 and MI 22, or 22 miles west of Traverse City. Open daily

A hiker taking in the view of Platte Bay along the Platte Plains Trail.

Platte Plains Trail

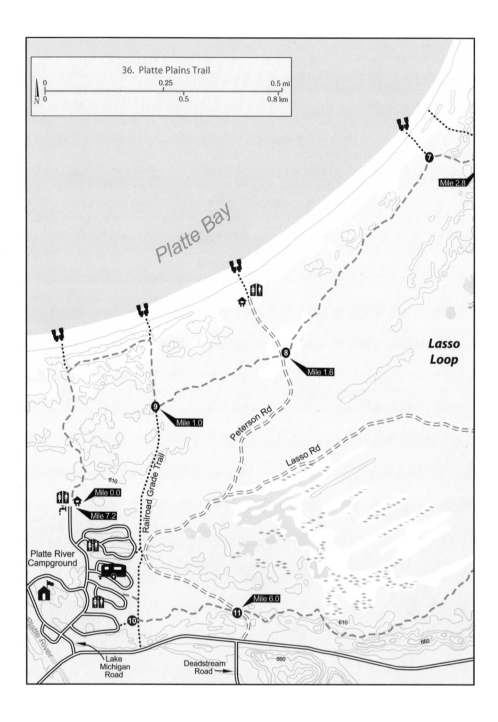

36. Platte Plains Trail

N

0   0.25   0.5 mi
0   0.5   0.8 km

Platte Bay

Mile 2.8
7

Lasso Loop

Mile 1.6
8

Peterson Rd

Lasso Rd

9
Mile 1.0

610

Mile 0.0

Mile 7.2

Railroad Grade Trail

Platte River Campground

Platte River

Mile 6.0

10

11

610

660

Lake Michigan Road

Deadstream Road

660

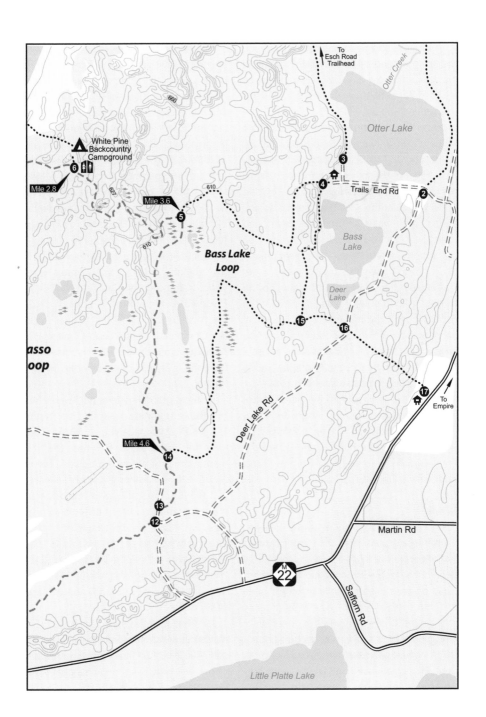

9 AM to 5 PM, and often later in the summer, the visitors center has nautical and natural displays about the Sleeping Bear Dunes as well as information on other trails and activities within the park.

From the headquarters, head south on M-22; in 9.5 miles you reach Platte River Campground. This facility features 179 sites, including those with hookups for recreational vehicles and 25 walk-in sites that are secluded in the woods at the west end. You'll also find a picnic area, water, showers, restrooms, and a ranger contact station with information. You can reserve a site through Recreation.gov (877-444-6777; www.recreation.gov).

There are actually several places in the campground to enter the trail system. At the back of loops 1 through 4 are short spurs that connect to the Railroad Grade Trail. This hike begins from the walk-in camp area, where a trail leads directly to Lake Michigan and is marked by blue (intermediate) triangles.

Alternative trailheads to the Platte Plains include the west end of Peterson Road, Otter Creek, reached 4 miles south of Empire and west on Esch Road, and Otter Lake Trailhead, 6 miles south of Empire at the west end of Trail's End Road.

TRAIL

Parking is available either in the Walk-In Camp Area loop or near the ranger contact station. From the Walk-In Camp Area a trail departs near the restrooms into the pine forest and winds past a couple of walk-in sites and into the hilly terrain. The route is easy to follow and is well marked by blue triangles. In less than a half mile, you break out of the trees and enter the low dunes along the Lake Michigan shoreline—where many discover how tiring hiking on soft sand can be. You arrive shortly at a locator map, where straight ahead are the cool breezes off the Great Lake and a scenic view of the beach.

To the east (right) is the soft, sandy path to post No. 9 and the junction with the Railroad Grade Trail. You hike over open dunes and through patches of beach grass. Here and there an odd pine or cottonwood is thriving, but for the most part you are in the heat of the sun until the trail swings sharply south at *Mile 0.8*. The views are excellent here, and a short spur heads north to the beach. In less than a quarter mile you reach post No. 9, where the trail quickly merges into an old railroad grade. You don't have to be a train buff to envision a line running along the wide and level path. The narrow-gauge line was built in the 19th century from a logging town on the west end of Platte Lake called Edgewater to docks on Lake Michigan, where ships carried the cut lumber to cities like Chicago. Railroad Grade Trail is a level path, because workers filled in every dip and flattened every rise of sand before laying the tracks.

The old grade heads south toward M-22, but those planning to spend the night at White Pine Campground should head east (left) at post No. 9, where the trail is marked by green (easy) triangles. The next half mile is yet another change in scenery, as you enter a forest that provides more solid footing than the dunes but remains a level walk. Eventually you break out into a grassy clearing and arrive at Peterson Road at *Mile 1.6*. A short walk down the road to the left you'll find a parking area, vault toilet, another stretch of beautiful beach, and sweeping views of the bay.

Northeast of Peterson Road, the trail remains in the lightly forested area for almost a half mile. You then move into a thicker stand of oak and pine, where you stay until reaching post No. 7 at *Mile 2.6*, the junction with another access spur to Lake Michigan. The views along the spur are stunning: You can see the entire bay, along with the famous

Hikers on the Platte Plains Trail.

Sleeping Bear Dunes to the north and South Manitou Island in Lake Michigan. The main trail swings east from post No. 7 and at *Mile 2.8* reaches post No. 6, marking White Pine Campground.

White Pine is located in a narrow ravine, with wooded ridges running along both sides of the secluded sites. The campground offers a vault toilet, a community fire ring, and only six sites, which explains why this area is a quiet section of the park even during the busiest weekend of the summer. There is no view of the lake from the campground, but near site 6 a path wanders west through the woods and quickly breaks out into an area of windblown dunes. From the high perch of the dunes, you are rewarded with an immense view of the Sleeping Bear Dunes and South Manitou Island. The Lake Michigan beach, with its clear waters and sandy bottom, is just a dune or two away. Return in the evening and sit on the last dune before the beach to watch the sun melt into Lake Michigan. What more could you ask for in a campsite?

For those spending the night at White Pine, the second day involves 4.4 miles of walking or a two- to three-hour trek. In other words, there is no reason not to spend the morning on the beach.

From the campground, the loop continues due east. The triangles change color, from green (easy) to black (advanced). It's rated primarily for skiers, but hikers will also notice that the walking is a little more strenuous. The approaching ridges and hills are ancient shoreline sand dunes that mark the position of Lake Michigan after each glacial ice melt. The steepest climb is within a quarter mile of post No. 6. After topping off, the trail follows the crest of the ridge around a pond filled with cattails. You descend, climb again to skirt another pond, and then drop quickly to the base of that dune. The trail levels out

somewhat to wind through an impressive stand of pines, and at *Mile 3.6* comes to post No. 5 and the junction with Bass Lake Loop.

To the north (left) is the 1.1-mile spur to post No. 4, marking the Trail's End Road trailhead. Lasso Loop continues south (right) along a level stretch that is marked by green triangles. Here's another interesting change of scenery, as on one side of the path lie towering pines, with a thick understory of ferns, while on the other side you pass one cattail marsh after another. The largest marsh is seen at *Mile 4*; often in June wild irises can be spotted from the trail. Other marshes follow for almost the entire 1.1-mile length of this stretch.

Post No. 14 is reached at *Mile 4.6*, and here Lasso Loop heads right. Within a third of a mile you break out at Lasso Road at post No. 13 and follow the two-track briefly before veering off to the west at post No. 12, a spot that is occasionally missed by hikers who continue to follow the dirt road.

The forested terrain remains level for the next mile; then the trail begins skirting more of those ancient lakeshore sand dunes. At one point there are forested ridges towering over you on both sides of the path. After swinging so close to M-22 that on a busy summer weekend you can hear the traffic, the trail climbs a ridge and skirts more marshy areas. The open wetlands and meadows remain visible until you drop back down into the forest and cross Peterson Road for the second time at *Mile 6*.

On the other side of the road, the trail swings north and eventually merges with the Railroad Grade Trail. Turn right here and follow the old line. Spurs to the campground quickly appear, with one to loop 2 posted. You emerge in that loop next to campsite 217 and can then follow the campground road to wherever you parked your vehicle.

37

Empire Bluff Trail

Place: Sleeping Bear Dunes National Lakeshore

Total Distance: 1.5 miles round-trip

Hiking Time: 40 to 60 minutes

Rating: Moderate

Highlights: Beech-maple forest, scenic vistas

Maps: Empire Bluff Trail map from the National Park Service or MichiganTrail Maps.com

Trailhead GPS Coordinates: N 44° 47' 57.54" W 086° 3' 31.13"

Few trails in Sleeping Bear Dunes National Lakeshore lead to a more spectacular view at the end than does this short path to the edge of Empire Bluff. The bluff rises more than 400 feet above the sandy shoreline of Lake Michigan and puts you in a lofty perch to view a large chunk of the national lakeshore.

Add six interpretive posts and an accompanying brochure that explains the natural and geological history of the area, and you have one of the best short hikes in the state.

The round trip is only 1.5 miles, but is rated moderate due to the amount of climbing involved. You also have to keep an eye out for poison ivy, commonly seen in the open areas along the way, and should definitely refrain from descending the sandy bluffs at the end—this will hasten erosion.

The trail is open year-round and makes for a far better trek for snowshoeing than it does for Nordic skiing, even with backcountry skis. Mountain biking is not allowed on the trail.

As a hike, Empire Bluff is an excellent choice for families and can be done by most people in under an hour. Pack along a lunch and enjoy it with a vista that would rival the tableside view at any of Michigan's finest restaurants. Better yet, bring a flashlight and arrive near dusk on a clear evening for a sunset second to none.

ACCESS

From the Philip Hart Visitor Center on the corner of M-22 and M-72 in Empire, head south on M-22 for 1.7 miles and then west

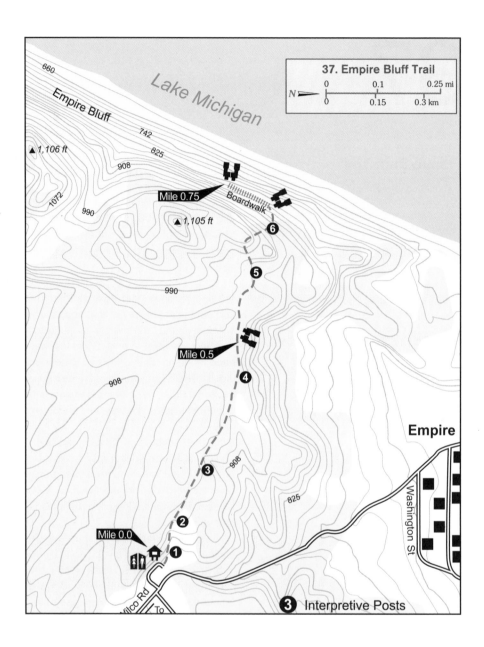

37. Empire Bluff Trail

Lake Michigan

Empire Bluff

Mile 0.75

Boardwalk

Mile 0.5

Empire

Washington St

Mile 0.0

Wilco Rd

To

❸ Interpretive Posts

(right) on Wilco Road. The trailhead is to the left, a mile down Wilco Road.

The trail is open year-round, and all visitors are required to have a weekly vehicle entrance permit, an annual park pass, or a per-person pass if they arrive on foot, bicycle, or motorcycle. Passes can be purchased from the Philip Hart Visitor Center in Empire or at the trailhead. For more information, contact the Philip Hart Visitor Center (231-326-5134) or check

Following the boardwalk along the Empire Bluff Trail.

The view from the end of the Empire Bluff Trail.

the Sleeping Bear Dunes National Lakeshore (www.nps.gov/slbe).

TRAIL

From the parking lot, the trail begins with an immediate climb past post No. 1, which marks an out-of-place boulder. Glaciers that picked up rocks and soil in Canada and the Upper Peninsula retreated from here 11,800 years ago, leaving the debris behind as bluffs, hills, and out-of-place boulders known as erratics. You move into a beech-maple forest that edges an old farm field and at post No. 2 can examine some old farm equipment left behind from the 1940s.

Another climb brings you the crest of a ridge where the trail levels out, passing two more posts. At *Mile 0.5* you arrive at the first panoramic view of the hike where a bench allows you to sit and gaze on the Lake Michigan shoreline to the north.

Eventually you descend off the ridge, bottom out at post No. 5, and then make the final climb to post No. 6, where you break out of the forest to witness a spectacular panorama. It's a breathtaking sight for anybody who never envisioned such a reward at the end of such a short walk. You are more than 400 feet above the lake and can view Platte Bay to the south and the Sleeping Bear Bluffs to the north, with the famous Sleeping Bear Dune itself appearing as a small hill on top of the high, sandy ridge. Seven miles out on the horizon is South Manitou Island, and this entire picture is framed by dune grass and weathered trees.

At this point the trail swings south and follows a boardwalk along the bluffs for 500 feet to an observation area with a series of benches reached at *Mile 0.75*. Here is a hiker's bench with a view unmatched anywhere else in Michigan. You might have walked less than a mile, but you could rest here for hours.

You simply backtrack to return to the trailhead on Wilco Road.

38

Dunes Trail

Place: Sleeping Bear Dunes National Lakeshore

Total Distance: 4 miles round-trip

Hiking Time: 3 to 4 hours

Rating: Challenging

Highlights: Sand dunes, Lake Michigan shoreline

Maps: Dunes Trail map from the National Park Service or MichiganTrailMaps.com

Trailhead GPS Coordinates: N 44° 52' 57.43" W 086° 2' 33.66"

This trail is undoubtedly the most popular and famous hike in Sleeping Bear Dunes National Lakeshore; or, at least, the beginning is. The Dune Climb, at the start of the park's Dunes Trail, attracts more than 300,000 people annually, with the vast majority making the climb during the summer. They struggle up the steep slope of open sand only to turn around and gleefully romp down it. After reaching the top of the slope, though, many continue on toward the Lake Michigan shoreline along the route marked by blue-tipped posts.

Unfortunately, a large number of these hikers start out shirtless, hatless, and, worst of all, shoeless, and never reach beautiful Lake Michigan at the trail's end. They soon discover that trudging through soft sand up steep dunes in the hot sun is not the same as walking down a beach. This hike is challenging, 4-mile round trip from the parking lot to the Great Lake and back. If you have trouble scaling the Dune Climb at the beginning, think twice before continuing; you will have to climb five more dunes of various heights.

But for those who come prepared with walking shoes, sunglasses, a wide-brim hat, sunscreen, and water, the Dunes Trail can be a most unusual trek during the summer and one of the most scenic walks at the national lakeshore. The route crosses the Sleeping Bear Plateau, a 4-square-mile field of perched dunes that extends from the Dune Climb to Lake Michigan to the west and Sleeping Bear Point to the north. The rolling dunes are beautiful and vary in cover from open sand or patches of beach grass

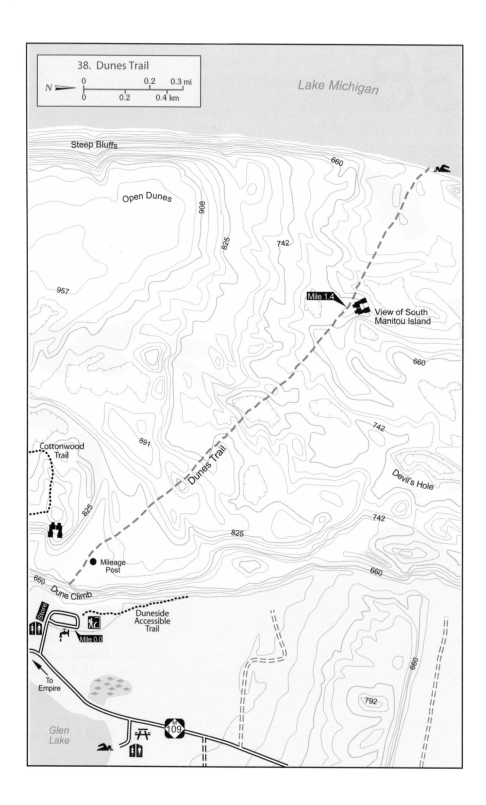

38. Dunes Trail

N

0   0.2   0.3 mi
0   0.2   0.4 km

Lake Michigan

Steep Bluffs

Open Dunes

660

908

825

742

957

Mile 1.4

View of South
Manitou Island

660

Cottonwood
Trail

891

742

Devil's Hole

Dunes Trail

825

742

825

660

Mileage
Post

660

Dune Climb

Duneside
Accessible
Trail

Store

Mile 0.0

660

To
Empire

792

Glen
Lake

M
109

and wildflowers to a lone cottonwood here and there.

By packing a bathing suit and a beach towel, you can turn this into a full-day affair. Don't forget to take along a camera. There are panoramas of Glen Lake at the beginning and the famous shoreline of the Sleeping Bear Dunes at the end.

ACCESS

At the corner of M-72 and M-22 in Empire, or 22 miles west of Traverse City, you'll find the Philip A. Hart Visitor Center and NPS headquarters (231-326-5134; www.nps.gov/slbe), a nautical-looking building. The center is open daily 9 AM to 6 PM and features historical and nature exhibits, a slide program, and trail maps for the park, including one on the Dunes Hiking Trail. You can purchase your park entry permit either here or at a contact station in the Dune Climb parking lot. From the visitors center, head north on M-22, veer left onto M-109, and in about 6 miles you'll reach the Dune Climb.

TRAIL

The steep slope of the Dune Climb is only a few yards from the parking lot, store, and restrooms. It's a knee-bending ascent of the famous Dune Climb, a sandy slope of 45 degrees that rises 130 feet above the picnic area. Take your time, and remember that you are supposed to feel winded on the way up. At the top, catch your breath and enjoy the spectacular view to the east of Glen Lake and the rolling farmland that surrounds it.

Most people then climb the slope to the southwest, which reaches to about 890 feet and features benches in a cluster of cottonwood trees. But a sign posted DUNES TRAIL clearly points the way across a sandy plain, where the first blue-tipped marker appears. Soon you're faced with a second dune, though it's not nearly as steep as the Dune

Climb. At the top you get your first view of the Great Lake. From this high point, you descend quickly, only to climb another dune that provides a much better view of what lies ahead, a rolling terrain of dunes covered with sparse beach grass. For the next mile you follow the posts, climbing up and down hills of sand. The trail is little more than a path of soft sand, and here is where most barefoot and shirtless hikers give up and turn around.

At *Mile 1.4* you scale a dune and are greeted with the best view of South Manitou Island, on Lake Michigan's horizon. You can even see the island's historic, 100-foot-high lighthouse, built in 1871 to mark the entrance of Manitou Passage. At this point the

Beginning the Dunes Trail toward Lake Michigan.

Hikers returning from the trek out to Lake Michigan along the Dunes Trail.

trail descends, makes one more short climb, and then crosses a somewhat level area for a half mile. Throughout much of June, this area is colored with wildflowers ranging from the bright yellows of hoary puccoon to the distinct oranges of wood lilies.

You don't see the beach until you're almost in the surf, but near the end of the trail the breeze becomes cooler and the sound of the waves is more distinguishable. Suddenly you're on a low bluff, looking straight down at the water and the wide band of sand making up the beach. Most people flop down on the beach right at the end of the trail, reached at *Mile 2*, but if you walk in either direction, you should soon have a stretch all your own. To return, backtrack to the last blue-tipped post and retrace your steps.

39

Dunes Trail–Sleeping Bear Point

Place: Sleeping Bear Dunes National Lakeshore

Total Distance: 2.8 miles

Hiking Time: 2 hours

Rating: Moderate

Highlights: Open dunes, Lake Michigan shoreline

Maps: The Dunes Trail map from the National Park Service, or Dunes Trail–Sleeping Bear Point map from MichiganTrailMaps.com

Trailhead GPS Coordinates: N 44° 54' 33.33" W 086° 2' 20.12"

Without question, the most scenic trails in the Lower Peninsula are at Sleeping Bear Dunes National Lakeshore. And the most scenic corner of this park, a spot with ghost forests, windswept dunes, and the clearest views of Lake Michigan, is Sleeping Bear Point. So why does it always take people so long to discover the other half of the Dunes Trail, a 2.8-mile loop that skirts the bluffs above the point?

Who knows?

The Dunes Trail is actually two separate routes through the dunes in this corner of the national lakeshore, and most visitors head to just one of them—the park's popular Dune Climb and its 2-mile route west to Lake Michigan (see Hike 38). Not nearly as many people make their way to the other trailhead at the end of M-209 located on Sleeping Bear Point itself. Yet step for step, few trails anywhere in the state are as interesting as this route, where the open dunes create excellent vantage points and the Manitou Passage provides a good reason to stop and gaze.

Don't underestimate this short hike. Walking in sand can be strenuous, and in the middle of the summer sunglasses, a wide-brim hat, suntan lotion, and a quart of water are needed to survive the desert-like heat that radiates off the dunes.

But this trek is not nearly as long or strenuous for young children as the trail from the Dune Climb. And when combined with a visit to the park's Sleeping Bear Point Coast Guard Station Maritime Museum and a dip in the cooling waters of Lake Michigan after

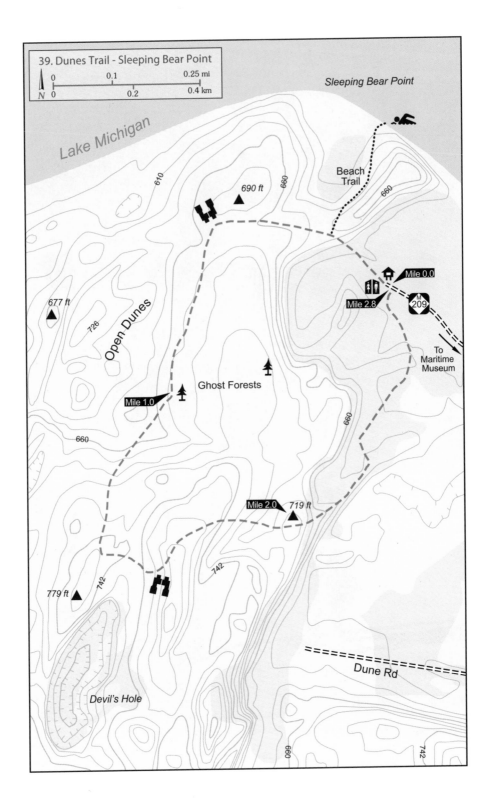

39. Dunes Trail - Sleeping Bear Point

N

0   0.1   0.25 mi
0   0.2   0.4 km

Sleeping Bear Point

Lake Michigan

Beach Trail

690 ft

610

660

660

Mile 0.0

Mile 2.8

M 209

To Maritime Museum

677 ft

726

Open Dunes

Ghost Forests

Mile 1.0

660

660

Mile 2.0   719 ft

779 ft

742

742

Devil's Hole

Dune Rd

660

742

Admiring a ghost forest along the Dunes Trail–Sleeping Bear Point.

the hike, I can't think of a better way for a family to spend an afternoon in the park.

ACCESS

An annual or weekly vehicle permit is required to enter the national lakeshore and can be purchased from the Philip Hart Visitor Center (231-326-5134; www.nps.gov /slbe) at the corner of M-22 and M-72 in Empire or at the trailhead. From the headquarters, head north on M-22 and veer off onto M-109. When M-109 turns east toward Glen Arbor, continue on M-209 and follow it to the end. The trailhead parking area is just beyond the park's maritime museum.

TRAIL

Despite the shifting sand, following the route is easy due to a series of tall, blue-tipped posts. You begin in the woods but quickly are climbing out of the trees near a posted junction. The spur to the right leads a quarter mile through a blowout carved by the wind to a stunning beach along Lake Michigan. The loop heads left.

Just beyond *Mile 0.5* you top off at the first panorama of the day; there are views in every direction you look. To the west are the Manitou Islands, to the northeast the towering bluffs of Pyramid Point, to the south rolling dunes. At your feet are the many shades of Lake Michigan.

The trail skirts the dune above the point, and the panoramic views get even better. Eventually you swing south, descend to a plain of windswept sand, and follow blue-tipped poles in crossing it. At the end of *Mile 1* you pass a ghost forest where trees were killed by the migrating dunes and then bleached white by the sun. Another ghost forest is passed and then the trail takes you on a long uphill march, topping off on a series of grass-covered dunes and views of this barren corner of the park. To the south you can peer into Devil's Hole, a rugged ravine forested at the bottom by stunted trees.

At almost *Mile 2* the trail begins to loop back and you begin heading in a northerly direction along the crest of another high dune, where the views of Glen Lake are good and any wind off Lake Michigan refreshing. In less than a half mile you drop into the quiet, protected spruce and birch of the forest. There is a sense of relief if you're hiking in the middle of the summer, as the cooling shade of the trees is a welcome change from the hot sand. At *Mile 2.8* the trail emerges from the forest at the trailhead and parking area.

A hiker begins the trek around Sleeping Bear Point.

40

Alligator Hill Trail

Place: Sleeping Bear Dunes National Lakeshore

Total Distance: 4.3 miles

Hiking Time: 2 to 3 hours

Rating: Moderate

Highlights: Beech-maple forest, scenic vistas

Maps: Alligator Hill Trail map from the National Park Service or MichiganTrail Maps.com

Trailhead GPS Coordinates: N 44° 53' 25.58" W 086° 1' 15.72"

The best cross-country ski area in Sleeping Bear Dunes National Lakeshore is Alligator Hill, whose 8.3-mile trail system offers skiers three loops that range from easy to advanced and feature plenty of long downhill runs and equally long climbs. But during the rest of the year Alligator Hill can be a destination for anybody looking for a walk in the woods—albeit a hilly one—that includes the kind of sweeping Lake Michigan panorama this national park is famous for.

The hill picks up its name from a long ridge and bluff at its southeast corner that resembles the silhouette of an alligator's snout, best seen from the top of the Dune Climb (Hike 38). Alligator Hill is the result of glacial activity when two lobes of ice that gouged out Big Glen Lake and Little Glen Lake dumped their load of sand and rock between them. An ancient Lake Michigan, which was much higher than today's Great Lake, went on to erode bluffs and cut terraces and notches on the flank of the hill, including the alligator's snout.

The most unusual aspect of Alligator Hill is the remains of an 18-hole golf course on its north side. The course dates back to the 1920s when David Henry Day, a prominent lumber baron who was responsible for the company town of Glen Haven, developed an elaborate resort that included golfing. The venture failed during the Great Depression, but you can still see the outlines of fairways today from aerial and satellite photos such as those found on Google Earth.

The trails that wind up and down Alligator Hill are wide, well-marked paths that

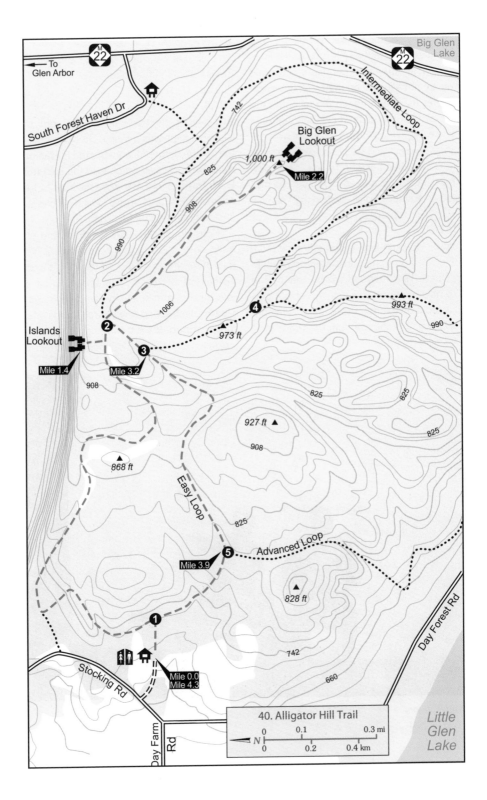

To
Glen Arbor

Big Glen
Lake

South Forest Haven Dr

742

Intermediate Loop

Big Glen
Lookout

1,000 ft

Mile 2.2

825

908

990

1006

993 ft

990

2

Islands
Lookout

Mile 1.4

3

Mile 3.2

4

973 ft

825

825

825

908

927 ft ▲

825

908

868 ft ▲

Easy Loop

825

Advanced Loop

5

Mile 3.9

828 ft ▲

Day Forest Rd

1

742

Stocking Rd

Mile 0.0
Mile 4.3

660

Day Farm Rd

Little
Glen
Lake

40. Alligator Hill Trail

0		0.1		0.3 mi

N

0	0.2	0.4 km

are used by Nordic skiers, day hikers, and equestrians—this is the only area of the lakeshore where horses are permitted. Mountain bikes are not allowed on the trails, however.

Other than to increase the mileage, the Advanced Loop and Intermediate Loop hold little interest to most hikers. Thus the walk described here is the Easy Loop along with the spur to Big Glen Lookout for a 4.3-mile day. Although the trek is rated moderate, be prepared for a steady uphill climb in the first half.

ACCESS

From M-109, just east of the entrance to D. H. Day Campground, head south on Stocking Road. The trailhead will be reached in 0.75 mile. An annual or weekly vehicle permit is required to enter the national lakeshore and can be purchased from the Philip Hart Visitor Center (231-326-5134; www.nps .gov/slbe) at the corner of M-22 and M-72 in Empire or at the trailhead.

TRAIL

Just beyond the trailhead are the concrete kilns that lumberman Pierce Stocking built in the 1950s before he constructed his famous road. Stocking had purchased the area from D. H. Day in 1948 and used the kilns to turn scrap wood into charcoal, which he bagged and sold throughout Michigan.

Post No. 1 is quickly reached, and you head north (left) to reach post No. 2. You pass through one of the old fairways, though it's hard to distinguish from the ground, then in a third of a mile swing east and begin a steady climb along a wide trail that is a former roadbed. It's a gentle ascent through

Two hikers enjoy the Islands Overlook along Alligator Hill Trail.

Sleeping Bear Dunes

A junction along the Alligator Hill Trail.

the beech-maple forest, but it lasts for a half mile before the trail swings away from the edge of the ridge at **Mile 1**. At **Mile 1.4** you arrive at the posted Islands Overlook, a short walk from the main trail.

A bench is located at the edge of the bluff so you can plop down to gather in the spectacular view. Below you a forest stretches north to the sandy Lake Michigan shoreline, while floating on a watery horizon are North and South Manitou Islands and Beaver Island. On a clear day you might even see South Fox Island, and at any time a freighter might be passing through the Manitou Passage. In the fall this magnificent view will be framed in by shades of autumn.

Post No. 2 is just up the main trail and clearly points out the spur to Big Glen Lookout. A wide and level path along the crest of a ridge, this segment comes as something of a relief for hikers. At the end the spur becomes narrow and is marked by blue blazes just before you arrive at the overlook and another bench. Needless to say this view is not nearly as spectacular as Islands Overlook—you can see only a small portion of Big Glen Lake and the ridges that enclose it to the east.

You backtrack to post No. 2, reached at **Mile 3** of the hike, and then head west (left), gently descending to post No. 3 within a quarter mile. Head for post No. 5 as the descent becomes even more mellow and within a third of a mile levels out. Post No. 5 is reached at **Mile 3.9**; the remaining 0.4 mile resumes its gentle descent through the beech-maple forest almost all the way back to the parking lot.

41

Pyramid Point Trail

Place: Sleeping Bear Dunes National Lakeshore

Total Distance: 2.6 miles

Hiking Time: 1.5 to 2 hours

Rating: Moderate

Highlights: Lake Michigan overlook, sand dunes

Maps: Pyramid Point Trail map from the National Park Service or MichiganTrail Maps.com

Trailhead GPS Coordinates: N 44° 57' 43.09" W 085° 55' 47.81"

It used to be that, if you were very lucky, you'd see a hang glider while hiking Pyramid Point Trail. The pilot would be strapped onto his colorful glider on the edge of a steep dune, 260 feet above Lake Michigan, and with one short leap begin a silent journey, soaring over the light-blue water of the Manitou Passage—beautiful.

The hang gliders are long gone now but that blue panoramic that they leaped into is still there. In an area of the state known for its stunning views of sand dunes, islands, and the pastel blues of Lake Michigan, Pyramid Point is one of the best. Part of the Sleeping Bear Dunes National Lakeshore, the point is a 2.6-mile trail that also traverses old farm fields and century-old beech-maple forests.

But to many the trail's most distinctive aspect isn't habitat or hang gliders. It's the off-the-beaten-path location of Pyramid Point. When the famous Dune Climb is crawling with people, it's still possible to lace up a pair of hiking boots and escape the summer crowds in this corner of the park.

The vast majority of people who do find their way to the Pyramid Point Trailhead merely hike to the Lookout for the view and then return, a round trip of only 1.2 miles with a bit of climbing at the end. Beyond that you'll usually have the trail to yourself and in early October will be dazzled by the fall forest. Along the way a crossover spur allows you to shorten the walk to 2 miles.

ACCESS

From Glen Arbor, head on M-22 for 5 miles to the park's Port Oneida Historic Farm

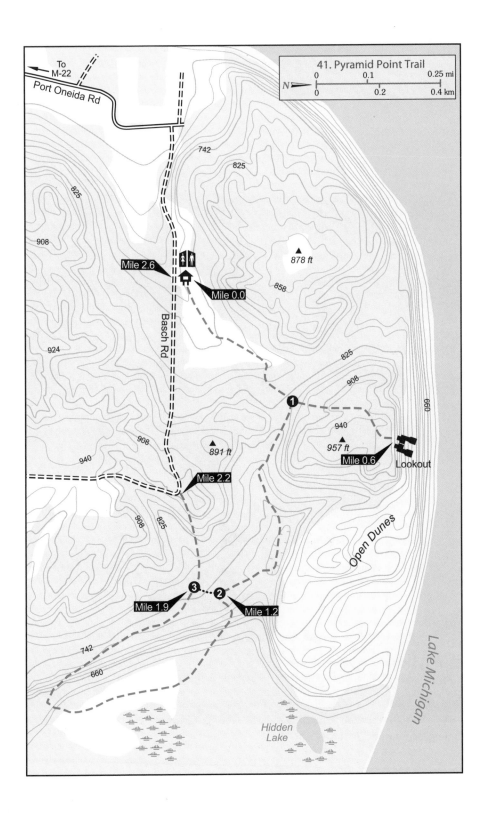

To
M-22
Port Oneida Rd

41. Pyramid Point Trail

N

0   0.1   0.25 mi
0   0.2   0.4 km

742
825

908

825

878 ft

858

Mile 2.6
Mile 0.0

Basch Rd

924

825
908

660

940

940
908

Mile 2.2

891 ft

957 ft
940
Mile 0.6

Lookout

908
825

Open Dunes

Mile 1.9
3 2
Mile 1.2

742

660

Hidden
Lake

Lake Michigan

Admiring the view from Pyramid Point.

District. Within this 3,000-acre tract are more than a dozen farmhouses and barns that date back to the 1850s and are currently being restored by the National Park Service. When M-22 swings sharply to the east, you continue north along Port Oneida Road for 2 miles, then go east (right) on Basch Road. The dirt road climbs steadily for a third of a mile until it levels out at the trailhead parking area, where you can find a vault toilet, display board, and map box.

An annual or weekly vehicle permit is required to enter the national lakeshore and can be purchased from the Philip Hart Visitor Center (231-326-5134; www.nps.gov/slbe) at the corner of M-22 and M-72 in Empire or at the trailhead.

TRAIL

The trail begins in a grassy field, the remnants of one of those 19th-century farms, but quickly enters the woods and begins climbing. At **Mile 0.4** you reach post No. 1, where you head left for the viewing point known as the Lookout. The final stretch is a bit steeper. At **Mile 0.6** from the parking lot you break out of the trees on the edge of a perched dune.

The dune puts you 260 feet almost straight above the lapping waters of Lake Michigan, which is why it attracted the hang gliders when their sport was peaking in popularity in the late 1970s. The daredevil pilots would haul their equipment to the Lookout and then use the wind currents that came up the side of the steep dune to soar for an hour or two over the lake.

If they were good they could land back at their car in the parking lot. If not, they would end up on the beach and be faced with an even steeper climb than the trail to the Lookout.

A hiker snaps a photo from Pyramid Point.

You never see hang gliders anymore because they fly inland, where they are towed up by an airplane. The view, however, is still the same. One reason the overlook is so dramatic is because the point is the closest spot on the mainland to the Manitou Islands. You get an eyeful of not only North and South Manitou Islands but also any freighter in the area—Pyramid Point forms the south side of Manitou Passage, a popular shipping lane.

From the Lookout you backtrack to post No. 1, follow the left-hand fork, and continue the descent through a beech-maple forest. After dropping 130 feet you bottom out where a migrating dune is slowly spilling its sand among the hardwoods and quickly arrive at post No. 2 at *Mile 1.2*. To the west (right) is the crossover spur that shortens the hike to 2 miles. Head southeast (left); another rapid drop ends in an open area created when farmers arrived here after the Civil War. The last farm was gone by the 1930s. Today the meadow is a beautiful spot, a grassy area hemmed in by forested dunes on one side and framed by birch and beech on the other. Blue standards lead you through the length of the meadow and redirect you back into the woods at its south end.

The trail now regains all the elevation lost on the previous leg. But the 0.4-mile ascent is a scenic one if the leaves have already dropped, for you can view the entire meadow along with the Lake Michigan shoreline. At post No. 3, reached at *Mile 1.9*, you head west (left) for the final leg to Basch Road. This stretch holds the steepest climb of the day, with a deep ravine running along the south side of the trail. At *Mile 2.2* you emerge at the dirt road, where a post directs you to head west (right). It's a downhill walk along Basch Road for 0.4 mile to the trailhead parking area.

Normally I detest any hike that ends at a road, but Basch Road makes for a scenic finish. It's a narrow dirt road that winds and curves through a forest so thick, its foliage forms a canopy overhead. Even on the hottest days this is cool end to a hilly hike.

42

South Manitou Island

Place: Sleeping Bear Dunes National Lakeshore

Total Distance: 9.7 miles

Hiking Time: 4 to 5 hours (2-day stay)

Rating: Challenging

Highlights: Scenic vistas, beach hiking, shipwrecks

Maps: South Manitou Island map from the National Park Service or MichiganTrailMaps.com

Trailhead GPS Coordinates: N 45° 0' 40.88" W 086° 5' 40.64"

No other hike in southern Michigan matches this trek on South Manitou Island. Within a 9.7-mile loop, you pass a shipwreck, travel through a virgin stand of white cedar, trudge up sand dunes to spectacular views, rest on isolated beaches, and end it all by climbing up the tower of a historic lighthouse. What more could you possibly want in a hike? How about backpacking opportunities at some of the most scenic campsites in the state? An inland lake that never experiences much fishing pressure? Spectacular sunsets?

South Manitou Island is a day hiker's paradise much as its sister island, North Manitou, is a haven for backpackers. The 5,260-acre island is administered by the National Park Service as part of the Sleeping Bear Dunes National Lakeshore but is only about a third of the size of North Manitou. Located 7 miles off Sleeping Bear Point on the mainland, South Manitou is the southernmost island of a Lake Michigan archipelago that stretches to the Straits of Mackinac. The island's west side features perched dunes that rise more than 400 feet above Lake Michigan. Florence Lake lies on the south side, old farms and other remains of the island's past are scattered throughout, and some of the most beautiful beaches in Michigan form the shoreline.

As at North Manitou, the vast majority of campers and hikers reach the island on a ferry that departs from Leland's Fishtown. It's a 90-minute trip, and along the way you will view Sleeping Bear Dunes, North Manitou's scenic west shore, and North Manitou Shoal Light in the middle of the Manitou Passage.

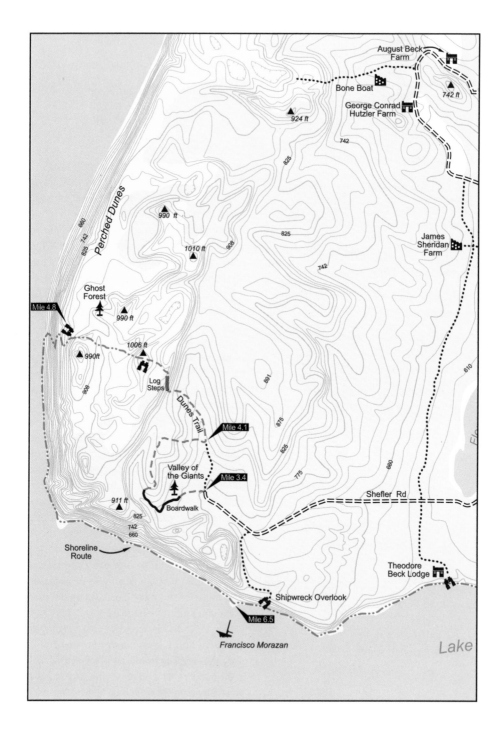

August Beck Farm

Bone Boat

George Conrad Hutzler Farm

742 ft

924 ft

742

825

James Sheridan Farm

Perched Dunes

660

742

825

990 ft

1010 ft

908

825

742

610

Ghost Forest

Mile 4.8

990 ft

990ft

1006 ft

868

Log Steps

Dunes Trail

891

Mile 4.1

825

875

825

775

660

Valley of the Giants

Mile 3.4

Shefler Rd

911 ft

Boardwalk

825

742

660

Shoreline Route

Shipwreck Overlook

Theodore Beck Lodge

Mile 6.5

Francisco Morazan

Lake

El

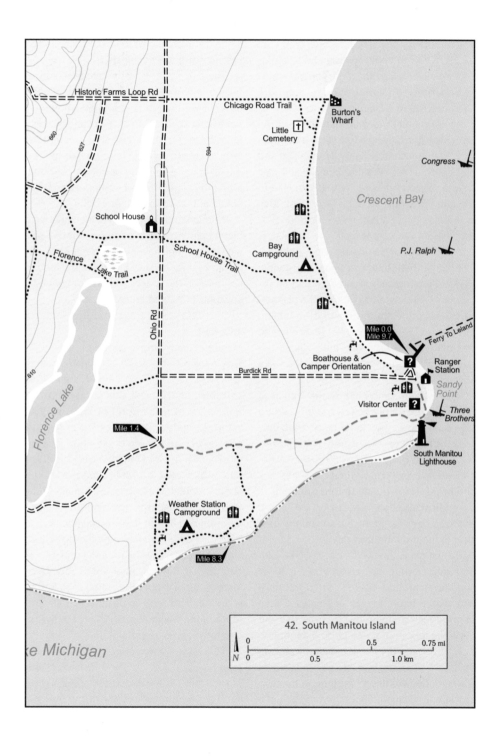

Historic Farms Loop Rd

Chicago Road Trail

Burton's Wharf

Little Cemetery

Congress

Crescent Bay

School House

Florence Lake Trail

School House Trail

Bay Campground

P.J. Ralph

Ohio Rd

Mile 0.0
Mile 9.7

Ferry To Leland

Boathouse & Camper Orientation

Ranger Station

Sandy Point

Burdick Rd

Visitor Center

Three Brothers

Mile 1.4

South Manitou Lighthouse

Florence Lake

Weather Station Campground

Mile 8.3

Lake Michigan

42. South Manitou Island

N   0   0.5   0.75 mi
     0   0.5   1.0 km

627
660
594
610

The trip is very scenic on a nice day and an excellent way to begin any island adventure.

Unlike North Manitou, here you can camp in only three designated campgrounds: Weather Station, Bay, and Popple. But all three are extremely scenic, each overlooking Lake Michigan or lying a few steps away from its golden beaches. All provide fire rings and numbered sites; Weather Station and Bay have sources of drinking water. You hike to the campgrounds from the ferry dock. Bay is the closest at a half mile, Weather Station is 1.3 miles, and Popple, the farthest, is 3.8 miles away and the least used. Although camping is restricted to the campgrounds, they are strategically located so that an excellent 11-mile, two-day trek can be planned by following the shoreline and overnighting at Popple. The only potential problem with this beach hike would be the logjams between the steep shoreline bluffs and Lake Michigan.

Most visitors simply hike to the *Francisco Morazan,* the shipwrecked freighter along the south shore, then head back. Thus they miss the most impressive area of the island—the perched dunes. The 9.7-mile hike described here extends beyond the shipwreck and crosses the dunes before returning to Lake Michigan. You return along the shoreline for an excellent beach hike and the best view of the grounded freighter.

Technically, this walk is a day hike. But note that the ferry arrives around 11:30 AM and leaves around 4:30 PM. Thus you have less than 5 hours to walk 9.7 miles. Those in good hiking shape will be able to complete the loop, but some people might find themselves standing on the shore, watching the boat head back toward Leland. The best way to undertake this route, then, is to camp at Weather Station. That afternoon you can hike the rest of the loop, timing your return

along the shoreline so that you catch the sun setting over Lake Michigan.

There is a per-night, per-site fee to camp on the island as well as the national lakeshore's vehicle entry fee (either a weekly pass or an annual permit). You can pay these fees at the ranger desk where you board the ferry in Leland's Fishtown. You can pick up a backcountry camping permit at the South Manitou ranger station in the former boathouse at the foot of the ferry dock.

Also located here is a visitors center with historical displays, a modern restroom, picnic tables, drinking water, and the historical South Manitou Island Lighthouse. There is no store on the island, so bring all your own supplies, food, and equipment.

ACCESS

Manitou Island Transit provides passenger ferry transportation to South Manitou Island. The ferry departs from Leland, a small resort town on the west side of the Leelanau Peninsula 24 miles north of Traverse City via M-22 and M-204. Tickets can be purchased at The Pot Hole gift shop, located in Leland's quaint Fishtown area. The ferries depart from the wharf right behind the shop. Contact Manitou Island Transit (231-256-9061; manitoutransit.com) to get exact sailing times and to make reservations. The boat runs daily from mid-June through Labor Day, and daily, except Tuesday and Thursday, June 1 through June 15. In May, September, and October the schedule is further reduced. The ferry departs at 10 AM and reaches the island around 11:30 AM; the return ferry leaves at 4:30 PM.

There are approximately 7 miles of dirt road on South Manitou, and Manitou Island Transit runs a motorized tour past sights such as the old school, the farms, and the cemetery of a farming community that once

The Francisco Morazan, *a freighter that sank in 1960 just offshore of South Manitou Island.*

A hiker heads to the South Manitou Island Lighthouse.

place for Great Lake shippers, who used Manitou Passage to shave off 50 to 60 miles of travel. The bay where you landed was the only deep-water harbor from here to Chicago, and from 1860 to the early 1900s, so many ships sought its protection that it was often referred to as the Forest of Masts.

The surf boat used to rescue sailors still sits inside the boathouse, but of more interest to many hikers is the three-dimensional map that shows the rugged contour of the island. Rangers conduct a brief orientation for both hikers and campers, hand out backcountry permits and maps, and send the newly arrived visitors on their way. Head toward the lighthouse, going past the visitors center with the old farm equipment on display outside, and within 200 yards you'll reach the posted junction to Weather Station Campground.

The trail quickly leaves the open shoreline of the island and becomes a cool forest walk. At *Mile 1.2* you come to a posted junction with a spur that heads south (left) to the campground. It's still another half mile to the facility, which features more than 30 group and individual sites along with a water pump and vault toilets. Some of the sites are in a lightly shaded area where you can stand on the bluff and view the Sleeping Bear Dunes across the passage or a beautiful bay and beach below you. These are spectacular campsites, some of the best in the state, and are always the first to be occupied.

The main trail continues west and within a quarter mile reaches a second spur that heads south (left) to Weather State Campground. The campground's hand pump for water is a third of a mile south on this trail. Continue west (right) and in a few steps you reach a second junction at *Mile 1.4*, where a sign says that the perched dunes are still a 2.1-mile walk away. Even though there is no cars on the island, the main trail is Shefler

existed here. Check with transit officials on the way over for details.

For more information on South Manitou before your trip, contact the Philip Hart Visitor Center (231-326-5134; www.nps.gov /slbe) at the corner of M-22 and M-72 in Empire or at the trailhead.

TRAIL

After stepping off the ferry, you head up the dock to a boathouse that was built in 1901 as part of the lifesaving station established here. South Manitou was once a crucial

Sleeping Bear Dunes

Road. As an official county road it's rutted and narrow; as a path for hikers, wide, level, and easy to follow.

You skirt the south end of Florence Lake, a long, narrow, but scenic lake with an undeveloped shoreline, and at *Mile 2.4* arrive at a posted trail. To the north (right) this trail leads to the island's farms and to south (left) to Theodore Beck's Lodge, whose front porch still overlooks Lake Michigan. The main route continues west, passing an open field that was the site of the first farm on the island and further testimony to the rich farming history South Manitou enjoyed from the turn of the century until the late 1940s. The early settlers quickly discovered that the island was an excellent place to raise experimental seeds and crops, because the plants were isolated from alien pollens on the mainland. South Manitou farmers soon became known throughout the Midwest as producers of prize Russian rye and hybrid beans and peas. At the 1920 Chicago International Livestock Exposition, a crop of South Manitou Russian rye won top honors. By 1948, however, due to the dwindling shipping traffic, only two farms were still active.

At *Mile 3.1* you reach the spur to the shipwreck. The side trail is a third-of-a-mile walk and ends at an overlook and interpretive display, with the boat visible out in Lake Michigan. If you're taking photos, keep in mind that the best views of the wreck are from the beach on the return portion of the trip.

In another quarter mile Shefler Road ends at the loop through the Valley of the Giants. Head west (left) at the posted junction. Bugs can be murderous here, but these trees should not be missed. The stand of virgin white cedar, estimated to be more than 500 years old, is impressive, especially the North American champion white cedar that is only 90 feet tall but has a trunk measuring more than 17 feet in circumference.

Just the fact that these trees are still standing is amazing. From 1840 to 1917 South Manitou was an important refueling stop for the wood-burning steamships that sailed the Great Lakes. Almost all the island's original timber was cut for those boilers, except for this stand. Why the sailors passed over these cedars has been debated. Some believe they were too remote from the docks at Sand Point, while others say that the dune sand embedded in the bark discouraged loggers.

The trail through the Valley of the Giants passes benches and a boardwalk and at *Mile 4.1* pops out at the Dunes Trail. Head north (left); within a quarter mile, a steep climb begins with a series of log steps before turning into a soft, sandy path. You ascend almost 150 feet, then break out of the trees and into the perched dunes. It's an amazing scene. When you top off on a dune at 1,006 feet, you can view all of South Manitou as well as North Manitou to the north, the bluffs of Sleeping Bear Dune to the south, Pyramid Point and Leland to the east, and much of the mainland shoreline. It's a million-dollar view that cost you only the price of a ferry ticket.

Most of the dunes are covered by grass, but here and there are the stark white trunks of the ghost forests, stands of trees that were killed by the migrating sand. Continuing west toward Lake Michigan, you see one dune crowned by trees. Referred to by some as the Island of Trees, this is South Manitou's high point at 1,014 feet. Even more impressive is the bow of sand you climb through that ends at the edge of the steep bluff at *Mile 4.8*. More than 300 feet almost straight down is the Lake Michigan shoreline. The bluff is as impressive as those seen at Pyramid Point, Sleeping Bear Dune, or the Log Slide at Pictured Rocks in the Upper Peninsula. This high ridge was formed by a tilted layer of limestone that the glaciers buried under a blanket of glacial debris. Winds off Lake Michigan have built these rare perched dunes, and their existence is fragile.

When descending to the beach, avoid running straight down, which promotes erosion, and instead hike diagonally toward the water to avoid disturbing the sand as much as possible. At the bottom you'll discover one of the most remote beaches in Michigan, and if you're not in a hurry to catch the ferry, plan to spend a few hours here.

By following the beach to the north, you will reach Popple Campground after a 5.3-mile hike. To the south (left) is the shipwreck and a quick return to the ferry dock. Hike south along the beach, with that impressive bluff towering over you on one side and Lake Michigan lapping at your boots—or maybe by now your feet—on the other. In a half mile the sandy beach becomes more rocky as you begin to hike around the southwest corner of the island, and eventually you clear the point to see the wreck.

At **Mile 6.5** you are directly across from the grounded ship, the middle third of which still stands above the water less than 100 yards offshore. The *Francisco Morazan* departed Chicago on November 27, 1960, and was bound for Holland with 940 tons of cargo, a crew of 13, its captain, and his pregnant wife. The next day it ran into 40-mile-per-hour winds, snow, and fog that created a virtual whiteout. The captain thought he was rounding Beaver Island, more than 100 miles away, when he ran aground. A Coast Guard cutter and helicopter rescued the 15 persons, but the wreck was left behind to be forever battered by Lake Michigan. Now it's probably the most popular destination for hikers on the island.

The wreck moves out of view when you round the next point south. Continue the beach walk, passing Theodore Beck's Lodge (though hard to see from the beach) then rounding a point and reaching the access trails down the bluff from Weather Station Campground at **Mile 8.3**, roughly a 3-mile walk from where you descended from the dunes. You'll know when you're near the campground because you'll spot more than one camper lying out on the beach.

Unless you have a tent pitched on the top of the bluff, continue along the shore. The beach is actually the shorter route to Sand Point, and maybe a more scenic one. For most of the way, you can see the top of the lighthouse sticking out above the trees. Reached at **Mile 9.5**, the original tower of the lighthouse was built here in 1839—the first light on Lake Michigan and one of the earliest ones on the Great Lakes. This one replaced it in 1871, and its 100-foot tower and Fresnel lens from Paris made it a superior structure. It could well withstand the violent winds of Lake Michigan. The walls of the tower are 18 feet thick at the base and taper to 28 inches at the top, and they are hollow inside, allowing them to sway in the wind. The spiral staircase inside is not attached to the walls, which allows it to move as well.

It's 125 steps to the top platform, but the view is worth every one of them. The lighthouse is usually locked, but several times a day rangers give a presentation about it that ends with a climb to the top. Check the bulletin board near the boathouse for the exact times each day.

43

North Manitou Island

Place: Sleeping Bear Dunes National Lakeshore

Total Distance: 8.8 miles

Hiking Time: 5 to 6 hours (2-day stay)

Rating: Moderate

Highlights: Lake Manitou, historic relics, backcountry camping

Maps: North Manitou Island map from the National Park Service or MichiganTrailMaps.com

Trailhead GPS Coordinates: N 45° 7' 20.58" W 085° 58' 30.17"

North Manitou Island offers backpackers and hikers the best wilderness experience in the Lower Peninsula. The island is not only isolated from the mainland and undeveloped but managed as a wilderness by the National Park Service (NPS) as part of the Sleeping Bear Dunes National Lakeshore. Among the strict rules the NPS enforces is a ban on motors, off-road vehicles, mountain bikes, and even the wheeled carts used for portaging boats to Lake Manitou.

Although some visitors reach the island in private boats, the island offers no protected anchorage, and the vast majority of hikers arrive at this Lake Michigan wilderness through a ferry service out of Leland. The ferry operates daily from July through Labor Day and with a reduced schedule in May, June, September, and October. Most hikers stay at least two nights—anything less would be a mistake.

The 14,753-acre island is 7.7 miles long, 4.2 miles wide, and laced with 30 miles of designated trails and secondary trails, most of them either old roads or railroad grades. The trails wind through impressive stands of maple and beech, through clearings that used to be farm fields, past serene Lake Manitou, and over the open dunes at the southern end of the island. The highest point on North Manitou is 1,001 feet above sea level, a rather remote spot in the northwest corner that few hikers ever reach. Overall, the hiking is surprisingly level, and the trails are not difficult to follow; maintained trails are posted with directional and mileage signs.

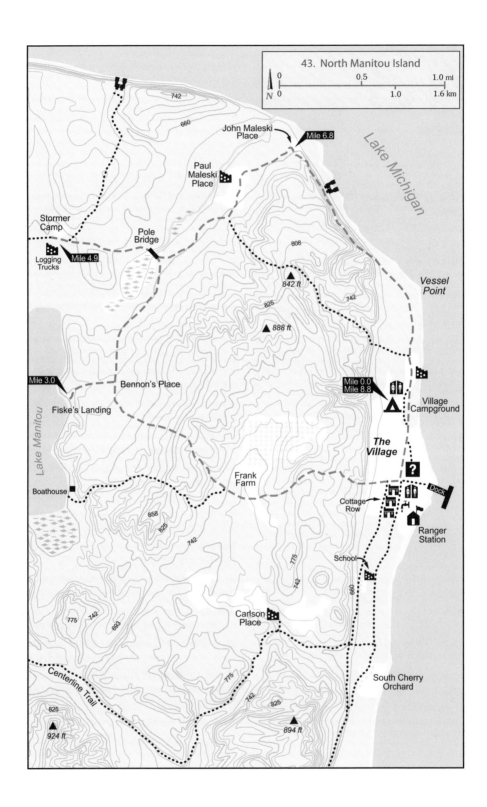

0.5   1.0 mi

0   1.0   1.6 km

N

Lake Michigan

742

660

John Maleski
Place   Mile 6.8

Paul
Maleski
Place

Stormer
Camp   Pole
                              Bridge

Logging   Mile 4.9
Trucks   808

                                      ▲ 842 ft   742   Vessel
                                                                 Point

                              ▲ 888 ft

825

Mile 3.0   Mile 0.0
                                                   Mile 8.8
                 Bennon's Place   Village
Lake Manitou   Fiske's Landing   ▲   Campground

                                                   The
                                                   Village

Boathouse   ?

858   Frank   Cottage
825   Farm   Row

742   Dock

                                                   Ranger
                                                   Station

                                                   School
775

742   775

693   742   660

                                    775
         Carlson
         Place

Centerline Trail   South Cherry
                                    775   Orchard

825   742

825

▲   ▲
924 ft   894 ft

North Manitou also had a history of residents farming, logging, and saving sailors. But the leftover buildings and remnants are not as numerous or as well preserved as you'll find on South Manitou. The lack of a natural harbor delayed the first woodcutter arriving at North Manitou until 1850, or 10 years after they began cutting on South Manitou. Farming soon followed, and in 1860 North Manitou recorded its largest population: 269 residents, with almost a dozen families maintaining farms. In 1877 a U.S. lifesaving station, including a lighthouse on Dimmick's Point, was built on the island. For 23 years the North Manitou Light was the only source of guidance for ships in the treacherous Manitou Passage until stations were established later at South Manitou (Hike 42) and Sleeping Bear Point (Hike 39).

Even summer cottages began appearing on the island at the turn of the century; many are still standing today in the Village, where the NPS maintains a ranger station and backpackers step ashore from the ferry. But by the 1920s most of North Manitou was under single ownership, and used primarily as a private hunting preserve until the park acquired control in 1984. To improve the hunting, 9 white-tailed deer were released in 1927, and the small herd, without any natural predators, exploded to more than 2,000 by 1981. The state of Michigan began staging special deer hunts on the island in 1985, and today the herd numbers less than 100.

Other wildlife that might be seen includes garter snakes and especially chipmunks, which are encountered too frequently to be natural. Chipmunks have become so troublesome to backpackers—they invade packs and food supplies—that rangers urge visitors to hang their food in the trees, almost as if you were in bear country.

The classic North Manitou trek is a three-day, 17-mile walk around the island. But with the arrival of daily ferry service to the island in 2013 a growing number of visitors elect to stay at Village Campground and explore the island with day hikes. This hike is an 8.8-mile loop through North Manitou's northeast corner that can easily be done in a day or turned into a overnight adventure with a night spent at Lake Manitou.

Keep in mind that fires are not allowed on the island outside of a community fire ring in the Village Campground. Bring a backpacker's stove or feast on cold meals. The only safe water supply is at the ranger station; all other water should be treated. You can camp anywhere on the island except within sight or sound of a building, a major trail, or another camper; within 300 feet of an inland water source (lake or stream); or on the beach along Lake Michigan. Pack all trash out and don't bring your pet.

Within the Village, a cluster of buildings on the east side of the island, is the ranger station. There are no stores in the Village and, other than the eight-site campground, no accommodations. The ferries from Leland land at the Village; NPS rangers greet all visitors to give a quick orientation and issue backcountry permits.

ACCESS

Manitou Island Transit provides ferry transportation to both Manitou Islands and departs from Leland, a small resort town on the west side of the Leelanau Peninsula, 24 miles north of Traverse City via M-22 and M-204. Tickets can be purchased at The Pot Hole Gift Shop, located in Leland's quaint Fishtown area, and ferries depart from the wharf right behind it. Contact Manitou Island Transit (231-256-9061; manitoutransit.com) for reservations, which are strongly recommended in July and August. Service to North Manitou is offered from May 1 to early October including daily runs from July 1 to Labor Day. During

A backpacker pauses along the beach on North Manitou Island.

the summer the boat departs North Manitou at 12:40 PM and 2:55 PM as part of a loop that includes a stop at South Manitou Island.

There is a per-night fee to camp on the island as well as the national lakeshore's vehicle entry fee (either a weekly pass or an annual permit). You can pay these fees at the ranger desk where you board the ferry in Leland's Fishtown. For more information on North Manitou before your trip, contact the Philip Hart Visitor Center (231-326-5134; www.nps.gov/slbe) at the corner of M-22 and M-72 in Empire or at the trailhead.

TRAIL

From the ferry dock you enter the Village, which is surrounded by a 27-acre clearing, much of it an old airstrip. The ranger station is a former lightkeeper's residence built in 1887 and today a National Historic Landmark. On the side of it is a water faucet and next to it is the original boathouse for the U.S. lifesaving station, the oldest building on the island—it dates back to the 1870s. At the head of the dock you'll find another water faucet, trash containers, and vault toilets while just to the north is a small visitors center where rangers hold their camper orientation. The beach near the Village, as is true through most of the island, is a beautiful stretch of sand littered with small pebbles and bleached driftwood. Across the lake is the light-blue water of the Manitou Passage with the mainland on the horizon.

On the west side of the Village, near Cottage Row, is a posted four-way junction. A 0.4-mile walk to the north (right), past the maintenance buildings, is Village Campground, where you'll find eight numbered sites, two community fire rings, and vault toilets. The description and mileage for this hike begins here and starts by backtracking to the four-way junction; here you to head west (right) to Lake Manitou.

The trail to the serene lake begins with a gentle climb across the old airstrip and then returns to the woods. You break out into an opening that was the Frank Farm apple orchard, dating back to the 1890s, with some trees still around. At one point North Manitou supported more than 3,000 apple trees as well as pear and cherry trees scattered in small orchards across the island. Just beyond the farm, at **Mile 1.5**, is a posted side trail that heads west (left) to a spot on Lake Manitou known as the Boathouse. Though the original structure is long gone, the park staff still maintain canoes here and the area is a nice spot to camp.

From the Boathouse junction, the trail makes a steady climb in the woods and then descends to Bennon's Place, a posted junction reached at **Mile 2.6**. To the west (left) is a 0.4-mile spur to Fiske's Landing overlooking beautiful Lake Manitou and a popular area to set up camp. Rough trails skirt the lakeshore in both directions from the landing, the best indication that the fishing here for smallmouth bass is outstanding. Only artificial lures can be used and there is a daily limit of one bass, which must be at least 18 inches long. Boats are allowed on the lake—canoes and rubber rafts being the most popular choices—but not motors or wheeled carts to carry them the 2.2 miles from the Village to the lake.

Backtrack to the Bennon's Place junction and head northwest (left) on the main trail. You pass through another clearing and at **Mile 4.3** (including the side trip to Fiske's Landing) you reach the posted junction at Pole Bridge, which really isn't a bridge at all but rather a culvert over a stream flowing out of a large swamp. This loop eventually heads north (right) here to Paul Maleski's farm and then back to Village Campground, but an excellent side trip is to continue another 0.6 mile west (left) to the clearing posted as Stormer Camp.

Old logging trucks left behind on North Manitou Island.

From 1913 to 1923 Peter Stormer maintained a family farm at the south end of North Manitou and operated a widespread timber operation across the island. He used this camp in the 1920s; in the 1950s the Lake Michigan Hardwood Company arrived and built a sawmill here. What remains is just south of the trail in the woods: a handful of old logging trucks from that era, some of North Manitou's most interesting and photogenic relics.

Backtrack to Pole Bridge, reached at **Mile 5.5**, and head north (left) at the junction. At **Mile 6.1** you arrive at another junction. The main trail heads southeast (right) as the most direct route for Village Campground, reached in 1.8 miles. A much more scenic route to the campground is to take the side trail north (left) posted for MALESKI.

You soon break out in a large clearing that was the Maleski homestead. Adam Maleski arrived on North Manitou in 1875 and purchased this property in the 1880s. Eventually he passed the family farm on to

his oldest son, Paul Maleski, who continued to live here until the 1950s. The farm has the distinction of being the longest uninterrupted homestead on the island, as the Maleski family lived here more than 70 years. There are some remains of the home, but you have to look hard to find them.

The trail continues northwest to reenter the woods and at **Mile 6.8** breaks out in a small clearing that was the site of John Maleski's homestead, brother to Paul. In the clearing the trail takes a sharp swing to south, putting you within sight of Lake Michigan; you can hear its surf on a windy day. This trail continues in a southeast direction to skirt a bluff, providing more views of the Great Lake and opportunities to access its lakeshore.

At **Mile 8.4** you reach the junction with the main trail heading west (right) to Pole Bridge. Continue south (left) on it and you'll quickly pass more island ruins and an old home, arriving at Village Campground at **Mile 8.8**.

44

Lake Michigan and Mud Lake Loop

Place: *Leelanau State Park*

Total Distance: *5 miles*

Hiking Time: *2 to 3 hours*

Rating: *Moderate*

Highlights: *Lake Michigan shoreline, scenic overlook*

Maps: *Leelanau State Park map from the Michigan DNR, or Lake Michigan & Mud Lake Loop map from Michigan TrailMaps.com*

Trailhead GPS Coordinates:
N 45° 10' 22.64" W 085° 34' 25.17"

Most people heading to Leelanau State Park drive to the northern tip of Michigan's Little Finger to view the historic Grand Traverse Lighthouse, look for Petoskey stones along the pebbled beach, or pitch a tent in the rustic campground. Hikers, however, stop 4 miles short of Lighthouse Point and head west toward Cathead Bay. Surrounding the scenic bay is the bulk of the 1,300-acre park, including its 6-mile network of trails.

Other than a parking lot, this nonmotorized area is undeveloped, consisting of low dunes forested predominantly in hardwoods of maple, beech, white ash, and paper birch. Toward the water, the forest gives way to open dunes covered by only patches of beach grass, shrubs, and a few cottonwoods. Then, at the shoreline itself, you find a beautiful beach with fine sand and often a gentle surf. The other spectacular aspect of this area is the sunsets, where on a clear evening the fiery orb melts in Lake Michigan, silhouetting the nearby Fox Islands.

Although there are five named trails within the network, the system basically forms a 5-mile loop using the Lake Michigan Trail and Mud Lake Trail, with three crossover spurs in the middle. The Lake Michigan Trail out to the beach is a 1.7-mile loop while the trek described here makes for a pleasant three-hour walk or even a full-day outing if combined with an extended break on Lake Michigan.

The trail is easy to follow as it is well marked with locator maps and numbered junctions that feature benches. The hardwoods, whose colors generally peak in early

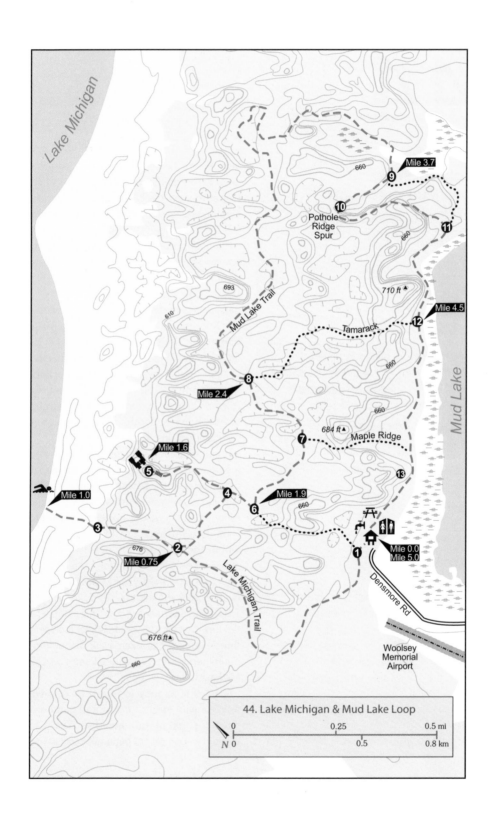

Lake Michigan

Mud Lake Trail

693

610

Pothole
Ridge
Spur

660

Mile 3.7

⑨

⑩

⑪

710 ft ▲

Tamarack

Mile 4.5

⑫

660

660

⑧

Mile 2.4

684 ft ▲

Maple Ridge

⑦

⑬

Mile 1.6

⑤

Mile 1.0

④

Mile 1.9

⑥

660

③

676

②

Mile 0.75

Lake Michigan Trail

Mud Lake

⑬

①

Mile 0.0
Mile 5.0

Densmore Rd

676 ft ▲

660

Woolsey
Memorial
Airport

44. Lake Michigan & Mud Lake Loop

0   0.25   0.5 mi

N 0   0.5   0.8 km

October, make this trail an excellent choice in the fall while a popular use of this undeveloped tract is for cross-country skiing in the winter. But come summer, it's hard to imagine a better destination for a hike than the somewhat isolated beaches of Cathead Bay.

ACCESS

The park is located at the northern tip of the Leelanau Peninsula, a 30-mile drive from Traverse City along M-22. In Northport, continue north along M-201 and then County Road 629 for another 4 miles. A sign for the trailhead is posted on County Road 629, jut past Woolsey Airport, and is reached by turning left on Densmore Road and following it to a parking area at the end.

The rest of the park and the park office (231-386-5422, summer only) is another 4 miles north on County Road 629. A daily vehicle permit or annual state park pass are required to enter either section, and there is an additional fee for those who want to spend a night in the campground at Lighthouse Point. No camping or mountain bikes are allowed in the Cathead Bay area.

TRAIL

In the parking area is a large display map of the trail system along with a vault toilet, drinking water, and picnic tables. Three trails depart from near the trailhead sign: Mud Lake Trail; a direct route to the overlook; and Lake Michigan Trail, which is marked by blue boot-print symbols and departs the area due west (left).

Lake Michigan Trail provides the shortest avenue to the beach and begins as a level walk through a pine and hardwood stand that keeps you well shaded from the sun. In less than a half mile, you pass the first of several benches and then gently climb into a series of forested dunes. At **Mile 0.75** from

the trailhead, you arrive at post No. 2, the junction with the beach access trail.

It's a quarter mile out to the bay, along a path that begins in the forest but suddenly breaks out of the trees into open dunes. If it's summer, you'll make the transition from cool forest to the brilliant sunlight and hot sand of the dunes in three steps or less. A sandy path leads you across the low, rolling dunes first to post No. 3, where you'll find a series of benches, and then to Cathead Bay, a spectacular spot to unroll a beach towel. Only a few cottages are visible to the east; to the west is Cathead Point, and out on the horizon of Lake Michigan lie the Fox Islands.

A hiker enjoys the view of Lake Michigan from the overlook along Mud Lake Trail in Leelanau State Park.

Backtrack on the spur trail and turn left at post No. 2 to continue on Lake Michigan Trail. The trail climbs over a low dune via a long boardwalk and at *Mile 1.4* reaches post No. 4. The spur to the left is an uphill walk, including a long staircase at the end, to a wooden observation platform and bench from where you can view the edge of the forest, open dunes, and the shoreline. The most prominent landmarks you see in Lake Michigan are the Fox Islands, and in the still of a quiet morning, they often appear to be floating on a layer of mist and fog. If the day is exceptionally clear you might even see Beaver Island to the northwest.

Backtrack to post No. 4 and continue straight to reach post No. 6 at *Mile 1.9*; this is the junction with Mud Lake Trail. Marked by orange boot prints, Mud Lake Trail heads left and within a quarter mile reaches post No. 7 and the Maple Ridge Cutoff, a crossover spur that allows you to reach the parking area in a half mile south. The Mud Lake Trail continues in a northerly direction as a wide and level path, reaching post No. 8 and the junction to Tamarack Cutoff at *Mile 2.4*.

Mud Lake Trail remains surprisingly level beyond the junction even though it is now winding through a series of forested dunes. There's no views of the water, but the terrain is interesting and at *Mile 3.3* you begin a steady climb, topping off at a well-placed bench where you can rest and gaze down into a pothole, a natural amphitheater forested in hardwoods. You descend to a marsh, skirt it, and at *Mile 3.7* arrive at post No. 9.

This post marks the junction to Pothole Ridge Spur. Mud Lake Trail heads south (left) and is a shorter and more level route. Pothole Ridge begins with the steepest climb of the day. Despite what common sense tells you, start climbing. This segment of trail is a scenic walk along the crest of a dune that includes a pair of boardwalks built to prevent excessive erosion to the delicate sides. The second features a pair of built-in benches. You pass post No. 10 and then descend to post No. 11 and the marshy north end of Mud Lake, reached at *Mile 4.2*.

Returning to Mud Lake Trail, you head southeast along what was an old two-track that parallels a towering dune on one side while providing glimpses of the marshy shoreline of the lake on the other. Keep an eye on Mud Lake; a variety of birds and wildflowers, including wild irises, can often be spotted. Within a third of a mile you arrive at post No. 12, marking the junction with Tamarack Cutoff and one end of a handicapped-accessible segment of trail. There are also picnic tables among the trees. From here, it's a half mile until Mud Lake Trail emerges into the open field and then enters the east end of the parking lot.

Pere Marquette

45

Manistee River Trail

Place: Manistee National Forest	
Total Distance: 11 miles	
Hiking Time: 6 to 8 hours	
Rating: Moderate	
Highlights: Scenic vistas of the Manistee River, waterfall, backpacking opportunities	
Maps: Manistee River Trail map from the USDA Forest Service or MichiganTrail Maps.com	
Trailhead GPS Coordinates: N 44° 21' 29.38" W 085° 48' 38.37"	

In 1990, while flagging the new Manistee River Trail, forest rangers stumbled on a previously unknown waterfall and only the second cascade to be located in the Lower Peninsula. But be forewarned: What was described in one newspaper as a "spectacular discovery" is often little more than a stream leaping toward the Manistee River below.

In the middle of the summer the cascade may be ho-hum, but that's it. With or without the thunder of whitewater, the rest of the 11-mile trail is nothing short of spectacular. Extending from Seaton Creek Campground near Mesick to Coates Highway's Red Bridge, this trail offers backpackers an easy route through a semi-primitive, nonmotorized area where there are stunning vistas of the Manistee River valley almost every step of the way.

The trail itself was completed in late 1992 and is laid out with mileposts beginning at the national forest campground and ending at the Red Bridge Access Area on Coates Highway. Here a 1.3-mile spur extends north to merge with the Manistee Segment of the North Country Trail (NCT; see Hike 46). The official dedication of the Manistee River Trail didn't take place for another four years, however.

That's when the Forest Service unveiled a footbridge that connected the north end of the new trail with the NCT on the west side of the river. Built just below Hodenpyl Dam Pond, the $125,000 cable bridge extends 245 feet across the Manistee River, including a 165-foot main span. The impressive structure was the last link in a 23-mile loop with the Manistee River Trail featuring spectacular views and the NCT offering a challenging trek through the hills and ridges on the west side. The end result is one of the best backpacking trips in the Lower Peninsula, a two- to three-day trek as scenic and wild as the Jordan River Pathway or North Manitou Island.

If you're not up for an overnight backpack, the most common day hike along the trail is the trek from Seaton Creek Campground to the waterfall, a round trip of 6.4 miles.

The NCT is open to mountain bikes but the Manistee River Trail is for foot travel only, with bicycles and pack animals banned from it. Backcountry camping is permitted but you cannot pitch your tent closer than 200 feet to the trail or any source of water. That includes the Manistee River. The Forest Service has designated seven camping sites along the trail for backpackers and canoeists. Each site is marked by a post with a tent symbol on it. If you do spend the night, pack along a water filter—the only sources of safe drinking water are at Seaton Creek Campground and Red Bridge Access Site.

ACCESS

To reach Seaton Creek Campground, head north on M-37 for 9 miles after it intersects with M-55 and then turn left on 26-Mile Road for 1.7 miles. Turn right on O'Rourke Drive for 1.3 miles then right on Forest Road 5993 where Seaton Creek Campground is posted. It is a half mile to the campground on FR 5993.

The south end at the Red Bridge river access site is reached from M-37 via 30-Mile Road. Turn west on 30-Mile Road and follow it to the end, where you bear left at

Taking in the view of the Manistee River along the Manistee River Trail.

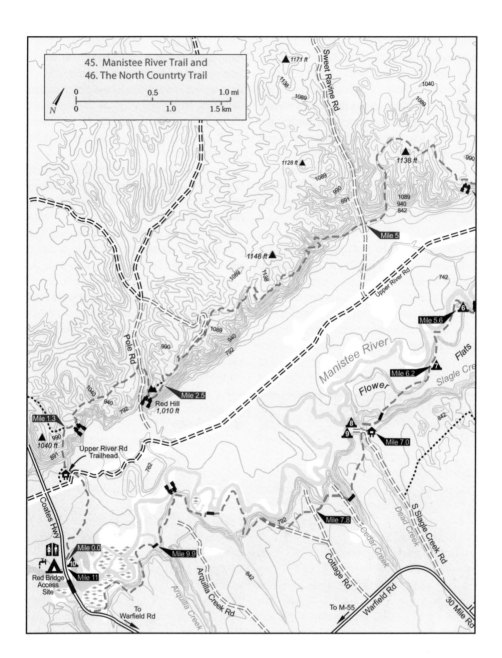

45. Manistee River Trail and
46. The North Countrty Trail

N

| 0 | 0.5 | 1.0 mi |
| 0 | 1.0 | 1.5 km |

Sweet Ravine Rd

▲1171 ft

1138
1089
1040
1089

1128 ft ▲

▲1138 ft

1089
990
891

1089
940
842

Mile 5

742

Upper River Rd

▲1148 ft

1089
1138

Mile 5.6 ▲6

Manistee River

Flats

Slagle Cre

Mile 6.2 ▲

Flower

1089
940
792

Pole Rd

990

Mile 2.5
Red Hill
1,010 ft

842

1040
940
792

▲8
▲9

Mile 7.0

Mile 1.3

▲1040 ft
990
891

Upper River Rd
Trailhead

762

S Slagle Creek Rd

Dead Creek

Coates Hwy

Mile 7.8
792

Cedar Creek

Mile 0.0

Mile 9.9

Cottage Rd

10

To M-55

Warfield Rd

30 Mile Rd

Red Bridge
Access
Site

Mile 11

Arquilla Creek Rd

842

Arquilla Creek

To
Warfield Rd

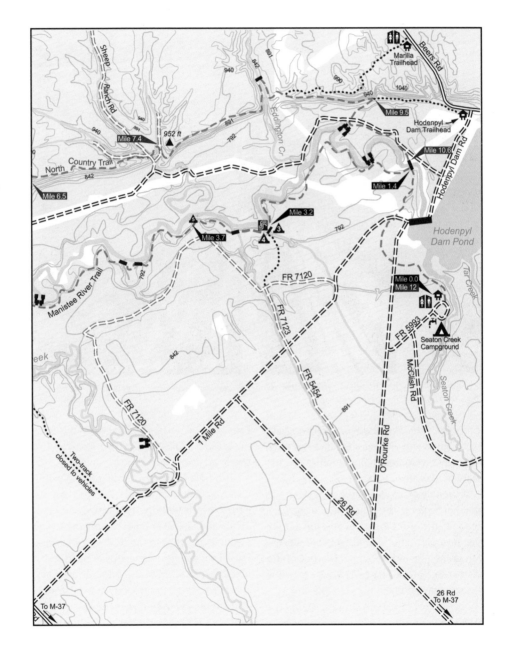

Marilla
Trailhead

Beers Rd

891

940

942

990

1040

940

Mile 9.5

Hodenpyl
Dam Trailhead

Sheep
Ranch Rd

940

891

891

940

952 ft

Mile 7.4

792

Mile 10.6

Hodenpyl Dam Rd

North   Country Trail

842

Mile 6.5

Mile 1.4

Mile 3.2

3

Mile 3.7

792

Hodenpyl
Dam Pond

Tar Creek

FR 7120

Manistee River Trail

792

842

FR 7123

FR 7120

Two-track
closed to vehicles

To M-37

1 Mile Rd

842

FR 5454

891

26 Rd

Mile 0.0
Mile 12

FR 5993

Seaton Creek
Campground

O'Rourke Rd

McClish Rd

Seaton Creek

26 Rd
To M-37

A backpacker crosses the swing bridge that connects the Manistee River Trail and the North Country Trail.

the curve onto Warfield Road. Drive south for 1.5 miles and watch for Coates Highway. Turn right on Coates Highway to Red Bridge over the Manistee River.

A weekly or annual vehicle pass to the national forest is required and can be purchased at the trailhead in Seaton Creek Campground. The best source of information is the Manistee Ranger District of the Manistee Forest (231-723-2211; www.fs.usda.gov/hmnf).

TRAIL

At Seaton Creek Campground the trail is posted in the picnic-area parking lot; from there gray diamonds lead you along bluffs above the sluggish creek. There is a great view of Hodenpyl Dam Pond from its south end just before the trail swings away and

crosses O'Rourke Road at **Mile 0.6** from the trailhead, followed by No. 1 Road and an overhead power line.

The trail, an old two-track at this point, swings north and at **Mile 1.4** reaches the impressive footbridge that spans 245 feet across the Manistee River. On the other side a spur heads west to the NCT. The Manistee River Trail swings south (left) here and within a half mile returns to the edge of the Manistee River and begins a very scenic stretch. You stay in view of the water as you skirt the flat river bluffs along a trail that is a surprisingly easy hike considering how rugged the NCT is on the other side.

At **Mile 3.2** the trail arrives at those "previously unknown" waterfalls. It's a spot where a spring-fed brook is leaping its way down the bluff to the river. If it's raining, the stream might even live up to its billing as an 8-foot-tall cascade. If not, then you're assured of pleasant weather and an afternoon of great views. Campsites No. 3 and No. 4 are located on both sides of the stream and make for a pleasant place to spend the night for those who arrive at Seaton Creek Campground late in the day.

The easy trekking along the bluff and the good view of the river continue as you pass the next two mileposts. Campsite No. 5 is passed in another half mile. At *Mile 5.5* comes perhaps the best vista of the day. Standing on the edge of a 50-foot bluff that drops steeply to the water, you can gaze down on where the Manistee sweeps through a long oxbow bend. Bordering the river on the west bank is a series of rolling hills.

A little farther down the trail is campsite No. 6, followed by the longest descent of the day. Here the trail finally reaches the edge of the Manistee, only to begin climbing the bluff again. You pass campsite No. 7 at *Mile 6.2* and then swing away from the Manistee River to arrive at Slagle Creek. The creek flows through a beautiful cedar-filled ravine and can be crossed by a unique arch-timber bridge. The trail climbs out of the ravine and at *Mile 7* crosses South Slagle Creek Road, a primitive two-track. Nearby is a trailhead post and parking for a handful of cars. From the parking area two trails head into the woods and quickly break out at campsites No. 8 and No. 9, each perched on the edge of the river bluff. Side trails from each lead

down to the river below, making this an incredibly pleasant spot to camp.

The main trail never passes through the campsites; rather it climbs a bluff and then resumes its southerly direction to climb in and out of the scenic Cedar Creek ravine within a half mile and cross Cottage Road, a primitive two-track, at *Mile 7.8*. You will also cross two other tracks in this area and at *Mile 8.4* follow a two-track briefly to a viewing point of the river.

Another fine viewpoint is passed before the trail descends to cross a footbridge over Arquilla Creek at *Mile 9.9*. More climbing continues as the trail uses the river bluff to avoid the marshy islands that the Manistee flows around. A view of Coates Highway pops into view for those with sharp eyes; then the trail make a long climb to reach paved road at *Mile 10.6*. Head west (right) and Red Bridge Access Site is less than a half mile away.

Reached at *Mile 11*, Red Bridge features a large parking area, boat ramp, vault toilets, and drinking water. There are also three camping spots in the access site, but keep in mind that at times it can be a busy place with anglers launching their driftboats. A better place to set up camp is campsite No. 10, located by itself on the north side of Coates Highway, overlooking a quiet stretch of the river.

To reach the NCT, briefly follow Coates Highway until a sign directs you into the woods. This side trail reaches the junction with the NCT (see Hike 46) in 1.3 miles.

46

North Country Trail– Manistee Segment

Place: Manistee National Forest

Total Distance: 12 miles

Hiking Time: 6 to 8 hours

Rating: Moderate

Highlights: Scenic vistas, backcountry camping

Maps: Manistee River Trail map from the USDA Forest Service or MichiganTrail Maps.com

Trailhead GPS Coordinates: N 44° 17' 4.72" W 085° 51' 47.64"

For years one of the least hiked trails in this book was the Manistee Segment of the North Country Trail (NCT). Not because it wasn't worth the walk. This trail is one of the most scenic routes in the Lower Peninsula. Few trails match the natural beauty, scenic vistas, or rugged or remote character that this section of the national trail has. The fact that it was a point-to-point path is what stopped many hikers from enjoying it. Unless you arrive with two cars, getting back to your vehicle is a hassle.

The problem was solved in 1996 when the Forest Service completed the Manistee River Trail (see Hike 45) on the east side of the river. When combined with this segment of the NCT, the new trail created a 23-mile backpacking loop that begins and ends at Seaton Creek Campground. Now this stretch of trail is part of one of the most popular backpacking routes in the Lower Peninsula.

The loop is usually walked in two to three days. For an overnight adventure, most backpackers begin at Seaton Creek National Forest Campground, cover 11 miles the first day, and often spend the night at the dispersed campsites at the Red Bridge Access Site, where there is drinking water and vault toilets. The second day would be a 12-mile return to Seaton Creek that includes backtracking the 1.4-mile spur from the campground to the footbridge across the Manistee River.

You can also camp anywhere on the NCT portion as long as you pitch your tent 200 feet off the trail. There are many scenic camping spots; the problem with the NCT

Looking over the Manistee River valley from the North Country Trail.

is having access to a source of water. For that reason many set up camp at Eddington Creek or by the streams that converge at Sheep Ranch Road. Red Hill is also a popular place to camp, but you must carry in water as there is no nearby source. All water from streams or the Manistee River needs to be treated before you drink it.

If hauling a backpack around doesn't appeal to you, the most rugged terrain with the most impressive vistas, including the Red Hill outlook, is the first leg from Coates Highway, and can be turned into a round-trip hike of 5 miles from Red Bridge Access Site. Or you can shorten a walk to the high point to 3 miles by starting at the Upper River Road Trailhead.

ACCESS

If you're starting from Seaton Creek Campground, see Manistee River Trail (Hike 45)

for directions to the USDA Forest Service facility. Red Bridge Access Site also provides overnight parking and is reached by turning west on 30-Mile Road from M-37. Follow 30-Mile Road for 3 miles, where it curves south (left) and becomes Warfield Road. Follow Warfield for 1.5 miles and then turn west (right) on Coates Highway to reach Red Bridge at the Manistee River. To reach Upper River Road Trailhead, continue north on Coates Highway from Red Bridge for a half mile and turn right on Upper River Road. Follow the dirt road for a quarter mile; the trailhead will be posted on the left.

A weekly or annual vehicle pass to the national forest is required and can be purchased at the trailheads at Seaton Creek, Red Bridge, or Upper River Road. The best source of information is the Manistee Ranger District of the Manistee Forest (231-723-2211; www.fs.usda.gov/hmnf). For more information about the NCT, contact the North Country Trail Association (866-445-3628; www.northcountrytrail.org).

TRAIL

To reach the NCT from Red Bridge Access Site, briefly follow Coates Highway until a sign directs you into the woods. This side trail crosses Upper River Road and then makes a steady climb up the ridge, reaching the junction with the NCT at *Mile 1.3*. Just beyond it is your first scenic viewing point of the day.

From the junction the NCT skirts the ridge for a spell then descends to cross Pole Road, an overgrown two-track that is posted. On the other side you climb steadily to the posted spur to Red Hill Overlook at *Mile 2.5*. The hill is 200 yards to the south

and though it's only 1,010 feet in elevation, it still provides a sweeping view of the Manistee River valley to the south even during the summer. Camping is possible at the top of Red Hill or the small saddle where the junction is located. Keep in mind there is no nearby water source.

The next 4 miles are the most interesting stretch of the NCT, especially if you're hiking it in early spring. Most of it skirts a steep-sided ridge where through the trees you'll find views of the Manistee River valley and beyond. Three times the trail climbs in and out of a ravine before crossing Sweet Ravine Road at *Mile 5*. From the two-track the trail makes a half-mile climb into Sweet Ravine and reaches a high point of 1,128 feet before swinging east back toward the river.

A backpacker skirts a ridge along the North Country Trail.

The trail passes a scenic viewing point, one of the best of the day, at *Mile 6.5* and then descends to cross Sheep Ranch Road. There are actually three two-tracks in this area, but trail signs keep hikers on course. At *Mile 7.4* you cross one of the three streams in the area. The trail then climbs out of ravine and tops off in an area often used by campers due to its close proximity to the stream below.

Beyond Sheep Ranch Road, the NCT resumes skirting a ridge and climbs into the Eddington Creek ravine before crossing the large stream on a footbridge at *Mile 8.6*. Less than a half mile beyond the bridge is the junction with the spur to the Marilla Trailhead.

The NCT follows a former railroad bed to reach a well-posted junction with the spur to the suspension bridge and the Manistee River Trail at *Mile 9.5*. The spur descends from the ridge, crosses Upper River Road, and parallels the east side of the road. This section can be confusing; look for the trail signs! Eventually the trail merges into Upper River Road briefly at Woodpecker Canoe Access and then descends to the suspension bridge, reaching it at *Mile 10.6*. On the east side, you pick up the 1.4-mile spur to return to Seaton Creek Campground. See Hike 45 for a description of this stretch of the Manistee River Trail.

47

Marl Lake Trail

Place: South Higgins Lake State Park

Total Distance: 5.5 miles

Hiking Time: 2 to 3 hours

Rating: Easy

Highlights: Inland lake

Maps: South Higgins Lake State Park map from the Michigan DNR, or Marl Lake Trail map from MichiganTrail Maps.com

Trailhead GPS Coordinates: N 44° 25' 24.32" W 084° 40' 31.32"

South Higgins Lake State Park is an amazing place. A slice of it lies north of County Road 100, and within those 300 acres you find the park's campground, beach, boat launch, picnic area, and the vast majority of the 450,000 annual visitors who come here. On the south side of the road is Marl Lake, the park's other half. The shallow lake is in the middle of a 700-acre forest, and wrapped around most of its shoreline is a 5.5-mile trail of three loops that makes an easy and level day hike.

Talk about apples and oranges. In mid-summer, when the campground is filled and Higgins Lake is buzzing with motorboats and Jet Skis, when there's a line of cars waiting to get into the beach area, you can cross the road and enjoy a quiet, wooded path and encounter only a handful of other people. In the winter the loops are groomed once a week for skiers, and in October the hardwoods mixed in with white and red pine provide brilliant fall colors.

Not only does Marl Lake lie totally in the park, freeing its shoreline from cottages and resorts, but its deepest section is only 3 feet, limiting anglers to canoes or small motorboats. The lake does hold populations of perch, bass, and northern pike and has an unimproved boat launch, but angling activity is light and shore fishing is usually unproductive due to the shallow depth.

All this works to the advantage of the hiker looking for a quiet retreat. The trail is divided by two crosscuts, with the shortest route marked in green dots. That route is only a 2-mile walk, making it ideal for children

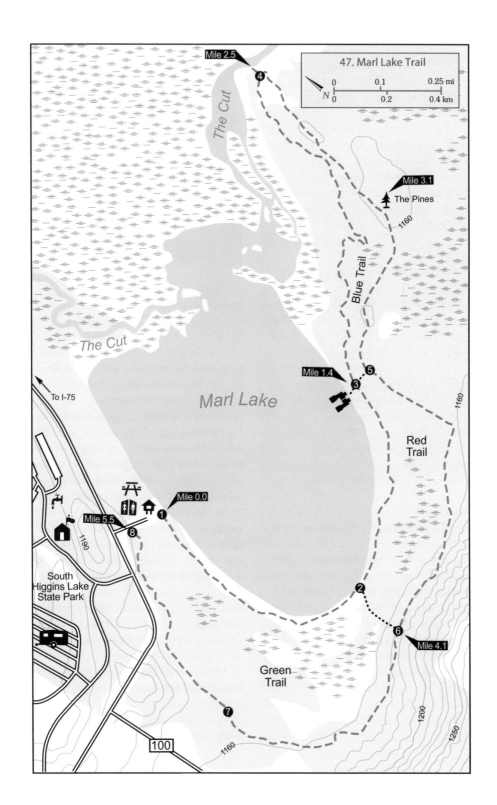

Mile 2.5

The Cut

47. Marl Lake Trail

N   0   0.1   0.25 mi
    0   0.2   0.4 km

Mile 3.1
The Pines

1160

Blue Trail

Mile 1.4

5

3

1160

Red
Trail

To I-75

Marl Lake

1190

Mile 0.0

1

Mile 5.5

8

South
Higgins Lake
State Park

2

6
Mile 4.1

Green
Trail

7

1200

1160

1250

100

as young as three or four years old. The red loop is 3.5 miles and reaches a bench on the lakeshore, a scenic spot for lunch. The entire trail, which is described here, is a 5.5-mile round trip out to the Cut River. Sections near the lake can be muddy in spring or after a recent rainstorm, but otherwise the blue loop is a pleasant walk and a great escape from the campers, crowds, and congestion north of the road. Mountain biking is permitted on the trail, but the number of cyclists is generally low.

ACCESS

To reach the trail from I-75, exit at Roscommon (exit 239). Head south, away from the town, and immediately turn west (right) onto County Road 103, where there is a state park sign. Follow County Road 103 for 3 miles, then turn south (left) onto County Road 100 for 3 more miles. The Marl Lake parking lot is located right before the main entrance to the state park on the east (left) side of County Road 100. To enter the park, you need a vehicle permit, which can be purchased at the main entrance contact station or from the park headquarters (989-821-6374), across from the boat launch parking area.

TRAIL

From the parking area you can see the lake, picnic tables, and a large display sign next to a footbridge that marks the beginning of the trail. From here, the trail heads south. The first leg of the walk is delightful as you hug the lake for a good view of the water through the fringe of pine trees. Right before the first cutoff, reached at **Mile 0.8**, you cross two long bridges that provide dry access between the lake to the east and an interesting swamp to the west. The cutoff is posted with green dots that swing south (right) to reach the return trail; the red and blue dots continue along the lakeshore.

A variety of waterbirds, including blue herons, can be seen on Marl Lake and the wetlands that surround its north end.

The red-and-blue loop stays close to the lake for a short way, then swings away from it slightly. You can still catch slivers of blue between the green pines and the white trunks of the paper birch trees, as well as any wind off the lake. The next cutoff is reached at **Mile 1.4**, where a short path leads left down to the shoreline. At the bench here, you can sit and look across the weedy lake to watch others just starting out at the parking area.

At this point the vast majority of hikers begin their return, which is too bad. The longer blue loop takes you past the oldest and most impressive trees of the forest, and it is from this section of the trail that hikers have their best chance of sighting white-tailed deer, especially in the early morning or at dusk. Even if you don't see the animals themselves, their tracks often cover the path.

The blue loop immediately moves out of view of the water into a mixed forest of pine, maple, oak, and beech. It can get wet and muddy in places, but it's not too bad as long as you're not worried about the color of your hiking boots. The blue diamonds embedded in the trees are mostly 6 to 7 feet off the ground. In the winter skiers might have trouble following the route after a fresh snowfall, but hikers encounter few problems.

At *Mile 2.5* you arrive at a spot where the trail merges with an old two-track road and begins its return journey. But to the north (left) is a short trail that leads down to the Cut, the channel that flows between Higgins Lake and Houghton Lake, passing through the north end of Marl Lake along the way. The waterway is a popular canoe route, and you might hear or see a few rental canoes banging their way down the channel. The river also holds populations of bass and pike, and from the few rubber tails and jigs that can be seen on the riverbank, it's evident that an occasional angler stops here to fish.

The return trip on the loop follows an old vehicle track and is considerably wider, and drier, than the first half. It winds through mostly hardwoods, but at *Mile 3.1* passes through a stand of pine with one particularly impressive white pine towering right above the trail. At *Mile 3.4* is the junction with the second cutover spur (you can actually see the bench on the lake). The main trail continues southwest along the old two-track road. A post with blue and red dots clearly marks the trail where another old road merges with it, and at *Mile 4.1* you arrive at the first cutover spur.

At this point you are 1.4 miles from the parking lot. The return loop swings near a gravel pit, winds through some clearings, and ends up paralleling County Road 100, where on a summer weekend the traffic roars by. The alternative is to follow the cutover spur to the right past an interesting marsh and then to rehike the most scenic stretch of the trail. For most hikers, that's no choice at all.

48

Lake Ann Pathway

Place: Pere Marquette State Forest	
Total Distance: 3.4 miles	
Hiking Time: 2 hours	
Rating: Moderate	
Highlights: Views of lakes and Platte River	
Maps: Lake Ann Pathway map from the DNR's Forest Management Division or MichiganTrailMaps.com	
Trailhead GPS Coordinates: N 44° 42' 44.86" W 085° 51' 47.66"	

Lake Ann Pathway lies in the Pere Marquette State Forest and is known primarily as an excellent Nordic ski trail, featuring many loops and a rolling terrain. When it was built in the late 1970s, however, it was called Chain O' Lakes Pathway, was part of the Betsie River State Forest, and was designed as an interpretive trail, not a ski run.

Much has changed over the years. The old interpretive posts are nowhere to be found. Trail users now include a growing number of mountain bikers, and the path has even been widened and rerouted in places to make the hills more manageable for novice skiers. What hasn't changed, and what is most important to hikers, are the scenic overlooks from the trail and the quiet nature of the area. In less than 4 miles, you view four lakes, skirt three bogs, and follow a stretch of the Platte River. From swamps and lakes to a trout stream, few trails in southern Michigan display so much water in such a short distance.

The hiking season runs from early May to late November, but keep in mind that the low-lying swamps and bogs found here are bug factories during the summer, especially from mid-June through July, and that a potent insect repellent is a requirement then. Fall colors are excellent, and the bogs are a profusion of wildflowers in the spring. Anglers will find the fishing difficult in the Platte, but Shavenaugh and especially the deeper Mary's Lake can be productive at times for panfish and perch.

The network is actually four loops. The first loop encircles the state forest campground for 1.6 miles on the east side of

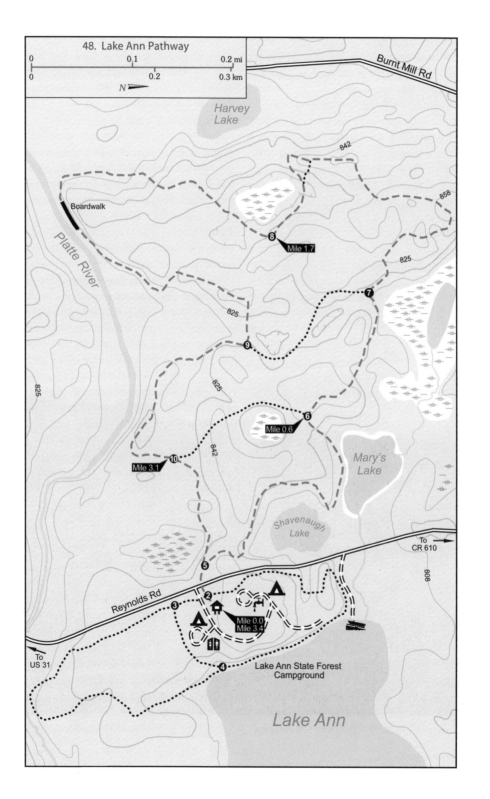

48. Lake Ann Pathway

0   0.1   0.2 mi

0   0.2   0.3 km

N▸

Burnt Mill Rd

Harvey
Lake

842

858

Boardwalk

8 Mile 1.7

825

Platte River

825

7

825

9

6 Mile 0.6

Mary's
Lake

825

842

Mile 3.1 10

Shavenaugh
Lake

To
CR 610

5

808

Reynolds Rd

2

3

Mile 0.0
Mile 3.4

To
US 31

4

Lake Ann State Forest
Campground

Lake Ann

Reynolds Road and, while scenic in places, is not nearly as interesting as what lies on the other side of the road. West of Reynolds Road, the first loop is a trek of 1.2 miles from the posted trailhead; the second is a 1.8-mile walk. The entire circuit on the west side of the road is a 3.4-mile hike and, without a doubt, makes for the most interesting afternoon in the woods. The entire perimeter of the trail system on both sides of Reynolds Road is a 5-mile trek.

ACCESS

The trailhead is located in a Lake Ann State Forest campground, a rustic facility of 30 sites, many of which are on a high, wooded bluff overlooking the water. The campground has a boat launch but no developed swimming area, and there is a per-night fee for campers.

From US 31, 18 miles southwest of Traverse City, turn north onto Lake Ann Road (County Road 665). This road ends in the small town of Lake Ann, where you turn west (left) onto Almira Road for 1.5 miles to skirt the north end of Lake Ann. Then turn south (right) onto Reynolds Road and travel a half mile to the campground. The campground is posted from both Almira and Reynolds Roads, and the trailhead is in a small parking area where post No. 1 with a map is located.

TRAIL

From the trailhead parking area, the trail heads west, immediately crosses the first loop, then Reynolds Road, and arrives at post No. 5. By heading north (right) at this junction, you'll skirt a bluff forested in maples and oak, spot Shavenaugh Lake, and descend to the water. You climb away from

Shavenaugh Lake from the Lake Ann Pathway.

Pere Marquette

Shavenaugh then descend to the shoreline of Mary's Lake, skirting it briefly before climbing a ridge to post No. 6, reached at **Mile 0.6**. Mary's Lake, connected to Lake Ann by a stream, is a beautiful and completely undeveloped body of water with crystal-clear water that is framed by paper birches leaning over the shoreline.

A skier's bench is located at post No. 6, which marks the first cutoff spur. If you do head back, note the small bog the spur passes from above. A pond many years ago, this and other bogs in the area have no outlets. Marsh grass gradually filled in the open water and, in turn, is being replaced by shrubs and trees such as red osier dogwood, black spruce, tamarack, cedar, and aspen.

Turn right at post 6 if you're continuing with this hike. The trail travels along a bluff above Mary's Lake, but only quick glimpses of the water are possible most of the summer due to the foliage. Along the way, the trail passes by a few remnants of the white pine that once covered most of northern Michigan. These pines are thought to be more than a century old, and they possess the size and straightness that made the species so desirable to loggers in the late 1800s. The trail crosses more hilly terrain and at one point breaks out to views of the low-lying wetlands that stand between Mary's and Tarnwood Lakes before descending to post No. 7 just before **Mile 1**.

This is good area to look for deer tracks or even the animals themselves, for they are frequently seen moving between the swamps and small lakes to the uplands to feed on acorns. The second cutoff spur departs here for Post 9, which lies a quarter mile to the south. Head west (right) as the main loop resumes climbing, crossing a couple of hills before reaching the high point of 860 feet. There it's possible to see both bodies of water that make up Tarnwood Lake and the swamp that lies between them. In spring or after a heavy downpour, the swamp will be flooded and Tarnwood will look like one lake.

At this point the trail swings 180 degrees to the south and follows the crest of a ridge, with steep slopes on each side. Within another a third of a mile you approach another swamp, thick with marsh grass and standing dead trees, and arrive at an unmarked junction. The trail to the west (right) is primarily a bypass to assist skiers down the ridge. The trail to the south (straight ahead) is a rapid descent to the bog below. Here is another great spot to search for wildlife (if the bugs allow you to), especially for deer.

The trail skirts the wetlands, quickly arrives at post No. 8 at **Mile 1.7**, then heads due south. You continue through the hilly terrain before descending to the Platte River for the first time. The headwaters for this trout stream lie only 1.5 miles to the east where Lake Ann and several smaller streams feed it. Because this stretch is so close to the lake, the stream tends to be too warm for most trout. Downstream, closer to the hatchery, springs and feeder creeks have lowered the temperature of the river enough to support a good fishery for brown trout. But the Platte is best known around the state as the first Michigan river to receive a planting of coho salmon. This occurred in 1966 and marked a new era in Great Lakes fisheries.

The trail swings east here and follows the river for the next a third of a mile, which includes a long stretch of boardwalk and a bench. On one side of you is a steep hillside covered with beech and maple, and on the other is the Platte River forested in cedar and tamarack. Eventually the trail swings away from the clear, gently flowing river, ascends the ridge it has been skirting, and arrives at post No. 9 at **Mile 2.7**. Turn south (right), and the trail drops into the river valley again.

The Platte River along the Lake Ann Pathway.

Along the way, observant hikers might spot a large stump or two. These are the remains of the white pines that were logged in the late 1800s and pulled out by horses to the north across frozen Tarnwood Lake. Within a quarter mile of post No. 9, you climb to a bench along the trail overlooking the river valley. It's a scenic spot even though trees prevent a clear view of the river itself. But if it's a windless day, you can hear the Platte flowing through the valley below.

The trail follows the ridge above the river and shortly arrives at post No. 10, reached at *Mile 3.1*. The last leg back to post No. 5 (straight ahead) reenters the woods and passes a second bog, though this one is hard to identify due to the bigger shrubs and trees that have already taken hold. The trail skirts the bog from above and then ascends to the junction, where you head east (right) to return to the parking lot or your campsite.

49

Old Mission Point

Place: *Old Mission Point Park*
Total Distance: *5 miles*
Hiking Time: *2 to 3 hours*
Rating: *Easy*
Highlights: *Mission Point Lighthouse, Grand Traverse Bay*
Maps: *Old Mission Point Park map from Peninsula Township or MichiganTrail Maps.com*
Trailhead GPS Coordinates: *N 44° 59' 26.11" W 085° 28' 48.40"*

From Traverse City, scenic M-37 stretches along Old Mission Peninsula, passing vineyards, orchards, and views of Grand Traverse Bay. Along the way you pass a dozen or more roadside stands selling quarts of sweet cherries, bottles of cherry juice, even homemade pies with tart cherries and a dark red syrup seeping out of a flaky lattice crust.

Go ahead devour those sweet cherries like popcorn, and enjoy a swig or two of the cherry juice—but hold off on that pie.

The 20-mile-long finger that splits Grand Traverse Bay in half may be best known for its cherry orchards and vineyards, but at its tip are a pair of parks that combine for 650 acres on the 45th parallel, include a historic lighthouse, and are laced by almost 10 miles of trails.

The 120-acre Lighthouse Park preserves the very tip of the peninsula and is home to Mission Point Lighthouse. Built in 1870, the lighthouse lies halfway between the North Pole and the equator and for 63 years warned mariners of the rocky and dangerous waters at the north end of the West Arm of Grand Traverse Bay. In 1933 it was replaced with an automatic buoy light just offshore and in 2008 reopened as a museum.

Adjoining Lighthouse Park to the south is the 520-acre Old Mission Point Park. Much of this land was cherry orchards before the state purchased the acreage in the 1980s and at one point designated it Old Mission Point State Park. But locals protested, fearing that a state park would lead to a busy campground and heavy traffic in their quiet corner of Grand Traverse County, and

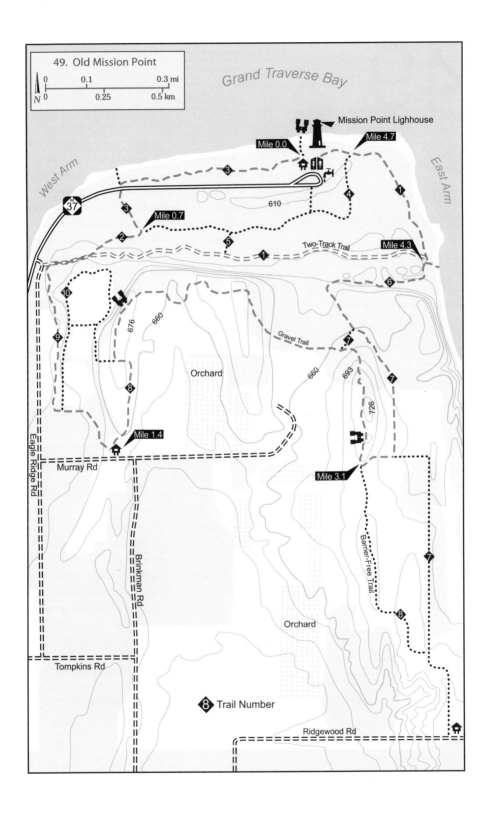

49. Old Mission Point

Grand Traverse Bay

0   0.1   0.3 mi
0   0.25   0.5 km
N

Mission Point Lighhouse

West Arm

Mile 0.0

Mile 4.7

③

M 37

③

Mile 0.7

②

④

①

⑤

610

Two-Track Trail

Mile 4.3

East Arm

⑥

⑩

676   660

Gravel Trail

⑦

⑨

660

693

⑧

Orchard

726

⑦

Mile 1.4

Mile 3.1

Murray Rd

Eagle Ridge Rd

Brinkman Rd

Barrier-Free Trail

⑦

Orchard

⑧

Tompkins Rd

◆8 Trail Number

Ridgewood Rd

eventually the land was leased to Peninsula Township.

With help from the Michigan DNR, Peninsula Township developed the current trail system, merging the existing trails in Lighthouse Park with new segments in Old Mission Point Park. Three trailheads serve the interconnecting trails. The most popular by far is Lighthouse Park, within a stone's throw of the historic lighthouse.

This hike, a 5-mile loop through both parks, is a mix of footpaths and old two-tracks that passes through a variety of terrain and scenery, including both the West Arm and the East Arm of Grand Traverse Bay, before returning to Mission Point Lighthouse. Afterward you can tour the first floor of the lighthouse or for a small fee climb its tower for views of both bays. Mission Point Lighthouse is open 10 AM to 5 PM daily from April through October and 10 AM to 5 PM on Saturday and Sunday in November and December.

ACCESS

From Traverse City head north on M-37, following the state highway for 18 miles until it ends at Lighthouse Park. Another trailhead and parking area is located in the middle of Old Mission Point Park along Murray Road at the end of Brinkman Road; you can reach this from M-37 by heading east on Tomkins Road.

A third trailhead is near the hamlet of Old Mission and reached from M-37 by heading east on Swaney Road. Within 1.5 miles the pavement ends; turn right on Ridgewood Road, where in a half mile you'll find a small parking area and a display map.

For more information on the parks, contact Peninsula Township (231-223-7322; www.peninsulatownship.com/parks) or visit the website of Mission Point Lighthouse (www.missionpointlighthouse.com).

TRAIL

Within Lighthouse Park are restrooms, drinking water, and access to the West Arm of Grand Traverse Bay. Within both parks trails are identified by a number and posted that way at the junctions. This hike begins with Trail 3, picked up next to the Hessler Log Cabin, a classic log cabin built in 1854 and eventually restored as a small museum.

Trail 3 heads west through the narrow wooded strip of Lighthouse Park bordered by the West Arm to the north and M-37 to the south. You pass numerous unofficial spurs

A hiker pauses to check a trail map at Old Mission Point.

Mission Point Lighthouse, built in 1870.

that extend in both directions to the bay and the highway before Trail 3 swings south and crosses M-37. Just on the other side, at *Mile 0.7*, you arrive at the posted junction with Trail 2. Head west (right); shortly the trail merges into a well-defined two-track that is Trail 1. Just before *Mile 1* you arrive at an unofficial parking area just off Eagle Ridge Road. This corner can be confusing, but Trail 9 departs south from the parking area.

You begin in the woods but eventually break out in an open field where the trail swings east and passes the junction with Trail 10 before returning to its southern direction and reaching the Murray Road Trailhead at *Mile 1.4*. A display board and parking are located here while Trail 8, a two-track designated as a barrier-free trail, heads north. Trail 8 climbs a low ridge, passes a spur to Trail 10 in a third of a mile, and then comes to views of the West Arm of Grand Traverse Bay.

The trail swings east off the ridge and becomes more of the gravel surface it was designed to be. It borders the woods here where to the south you can see rows of grapes outside the park, no doubt destined to become bottles of the renowned Mission Peninsula wine. At *Mile 2.7* you reenter the forest and arrive at a junction with Trail 7. Head right to stay on Trail 8, which quickly swings south to climb a ridgeline.

Glimpses of orchards below and the West Arm on the horizon begin appearing, and then at *Mile 3* you're rewarded with views of both bays and a bench to rest and enjoy them. From the viewing point Trail 8 descends and within 200 yards arrives at a junction with a crossover spur that heads east (left) to Trail 7. Use the spur to begin looping back north. The terrain from here south to the Ridgewood Road trailhead is mostly open fields and uninspiring.

Continuing north on Trail 7, you'll reach a posted junction at *Mile 3.7* where Trail 6 heads north (right) to reenter Lighthouse Park. The terrain and the older forest that covers it is much more interesting as Trail 6 swings east to wind through a series of moraines before merging into Trail 1 at *Mile 4.3*. Here a side trail provides easy to access the shoreline of the East Arm.

Continue north on Trail 1, no longer a former two-track, as it skirts the East Arm. Even if you can't see the water through the trees, you can often hear the surf on a windy day. At *Mile 4.7* the trail swings west to arrive at a junction with Trail 4, which heads south (left). Continue west (right) on Trail 1 and within a quarter mile you'll pop out of the trees at Mission Point Lighthouse with the parking lot a short walk away.

Time for a slice of that sour cherry pie.

50

Wakeley Lake

Place: Wakeley Lake Semi-Primitive
Nonmotorized Area

Total Distance: 3.9 miles

Hiking Time: 2 hours

Rating: Easy

Highlights: Inland lake, backcountry
camping

Maps: Wakeley Lake map from the
USDA Forest Service or MichiganTrail
Maps.com

Trailhead GPS Coordinates:
N 44° 37' 38.92" W 084° 30' 45.57"

Most of the people who know and visit Wakeley Lake are anglers looking for a quality fishing experience. Because of special regulations such as walk-in access, the lake has developed a loyal following of fishermen who stalk its waters for trophy bluegill, bass, and northern pike.

The same regulations that allow the lake to produce 12-inch bluegill also make the area surrounding it a hiker's delight. Walk-in access means that there are no motor homes or off-road vehicles in this 2,000-acre tract of the Huron National Forest. A ban on outboard motors means that the mornings are quiet and the water is still, even when a handful of anglers are working the shoreline. And the fact that you can't use live bait and have to carry your boat in keeps most fishermen out of the area.

For hikers, Wakeley Lake Semi-Primitive Nonmotorized Area makes for a quiet walk around a scenic body of water, with a good chance of encountering a variety of wildlife. I once watched three white-tailed deer bound through the woods from the trail here while I was listening to a loon's eerie laugh across the water. Birding is so good within the preserve that the Michigan Audubon Society maintains a daily field checklist at the trailhead. As many as 150 different species have been spotted in the area, including blue herons, bald eagles, and loons that nest on the lake.

As the name implies, there are no cottages or other developments along the shoreline, for the entire lake was owned by a single family until the USDA Forest Service

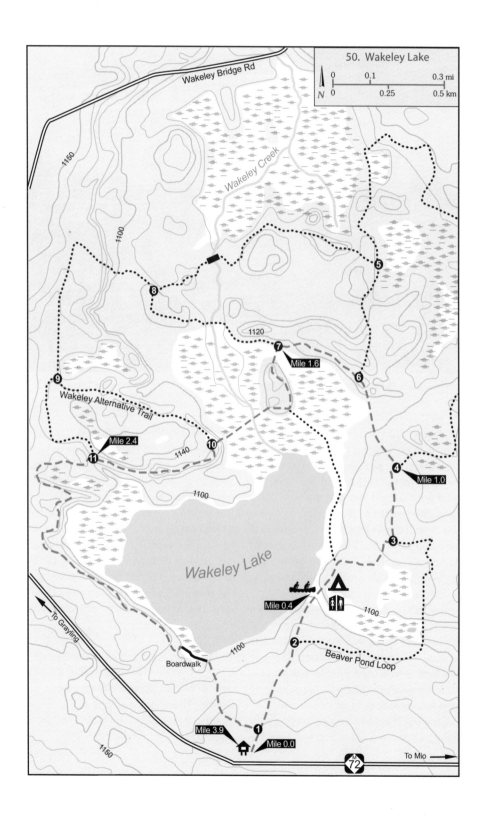

50. Wakeley Lake

Wakeley Bridge Rd

0   0.1   0.3 mi
0   0.25   0.5 km

N

1150

1100

Wakeley Creek

5

8

1120

7
Mile 1.6

6

9

Wakeley Alternative Trail

1140

10

4
Mile 1.0

11
Mile 2.4

1100

3

Wakeley Lake

Mile 0.4

To Grayling

2   Beaver Pond Loop

1100

1100

Boardwalk

Mile 3.9

1

Mile 0.0

1150

M 72   To Mio

Wakeley Lake, the centerpiece of the Wakeley Lake Semi-Primitive Nonmotorized Area.

purchased the tract in 1986. The area is laced with old logging roads and two-track forest roads, but an 8.5-mile network of trails has been marked. The most scenic walks by far are the trails that skirt the lake, occasionally referred to as the lakeshore or inner loop. This 3.9-mile trek begins and ends at the trailhead off M-72 and follows almost the entire shoreline of the lake, where you can enjoy good views of the water as well as measure anglers' successes.

The fishing season on Wakeley is from June 15 to August 31. The fishery is good not only because of the walk-in access, but also because of other strict regulations. Only artificial lures can be used, and there is a no-kill, catch-and-release regulation for all fish caught in the lake regardless of species or size.

Camping is allowed anywhere in the tract as long as you're at least 200 feet from the shore. A handful of campsites have been set up on a hill on the lake's east side, the best spot to pitch a tent. Mountain biking is allowed in the area, and the trails attract a moderate number of off-road cyclists.

Part of hike described here also crosses a loon nesting area and is closed to the public from February 1 to July 15. The area is well posted, and, if you are walking the trail at that time, signs point out the Wakeley Alternative Trail, a route that bypasses the closure. The detour adds 1.2 miles to the hike.

ACCESS

The trailhead is posted on the north side of M-72, 10 miles east of Grayling, 22 miles west of Mio, or about a 3.5-hour drive from Detroit. There is a map box at the display board in the parking area, but it's not always filled.

A weekly vehicle permit or an annual pass from the USDA Forest Service is required to hike, fish, or camp at Wakeley Lake. You can pay at the trailhead or, if you're passing through Mio, at the Mio Ranger District office (989-826-3252) on M-72.

TRAIL

On the north side of the parking area, a trail with a locked gate across it—which still looks like the road it once was—heads north to the lake. You quickly pass post No. 1, the junction with the return trail heading west (left), and then in a quarter mile arrive at post No. 2, marking one end of Beaver Pond Loop. The 0.7-mile spur heads east (right) as a true footpath and loops past a wetland and beaver pond before returning to the main trail.

This trek continues north (left) and at **Mile 0.4** will reach the lake itself. It's amazing that such a short distance is enough to keep the fishing pressure light on Wakeley Lake. You enter a grassy area that includes a canoe launch, vault toilet, and—on a small hill overlooking the lake—a camping area with five sites, fire rings, and picnic tables in a stand of red pines.

From this shore, you can view the entire lake. The best way to fish this 160-acre lake is from a boat, for it is only 12 feet at its deepest point, and much of it is choked with lily pads and aquatic weeds. The trail leaves the clearing as an overgrown two-track and swings sharply to the east (right) to the skirt the campground. You quickly pass a junction with a shoreline trail that veers off to the right, then wind through a predominantly pine forest to arrive at post No. 3 at **Mile 0.8**, marking the other end of the Beaver Pond Loop.

The main trail remains an old two-track marked by blue diamonds and within a

A shoreline boardwalk at Wakeley Lake.

quarter mile reaches post No. 4, where it swings northwest (left) to climb a low rise for a view of the wetlands that make up the lake's north shore. You pass post No. 6 and remain in view of the marshland, birds, and Wakeley Lake for a quarter mile until the trail descends to post No. 7 at *Mile 1.6*, featuring a wooden barrier. Beyond the barrier is the sensitive wildlife area that is closed from February 1 to July 15 when the loons are nesting. If you arrive during that period continue west (right) to post No. 8 and then post No. 9, where you can pick up the Wakeley Alternative Trail. This will return you to the lakeshore loop at post No. 10, a trek of 1.6 miles.

If you are hiking outside that period then the lakeshore loop continues south (left) beyond the barrier, where it crosses an earthen dike between two swamps. You then climb and cross a forested island in the middle of this marsh. The high point keeps your feet dry while providing good views of the lake to the east and the huge cattail marsh to the west. You pass one trail that heads east (left) on along a dike back to the campground area and then come to a second dike heading west. The trail follows this long dike through another stretch of wetlands; on the other side it climbs a sandy slope to reach post No. 10 at *Mile 2*. The Wakeley Alternative Trail splits off to the west (right).

The lakeshore loop continues in the southwest direction (left) where it follows a ridge for the next third of a mile, allowing you to enjoy views of the lake through the trees along this scenic stretch. If you're out early on a still morning, you can often see mist rising off the surface of the water with an angler casting from a motionless canoe in the middle of it.

Post No. 11 is reached at *Mile 2.4* with the lakeshore loop continuing west (left), where it makes a steady climb to leave Wakeley Lake behind. At *Mile 2.8* you return to views of the lake that continue for more than a half mile as the trail skirts another ridge along its south shore before descending to a long boardwalk. From the boardwalk the trail ascends to post No. 1, where you are just 100 yards from the trailhead parking area to the south (right).

51

Mason Tract Pathway

Place: Au Sable River State Forest

Total Distance: 9.5 miles one-way

Hiking Time: 4 to 6 hours one-way

Rating: Moderate

Highlights: Blue-ribbon trout stream

Maps; Mason Tract Pathway map from the Michigan DNR or MichiganTrail Maps.com

Trailhead GPS Coordinates: N 44° 37' 2.64" W 084° 28' 16.97"

The most famous trout waters in Michigan are the Holy Waters, a stretch of the Au Sable River east of Grayling that is revered by fly anglers throughout the Midwest. But auto magnate George Mason loved the river's South Branch.

Mason made his fortune in the automobile industry and, in the 1930s, purchased a large tract of land that borders the South Branch from another auto magnate, Clifford Durant of the Durant Motor Car Company. It became his personal wilderness, an area of undeveloped woods and clear water where he would go with a fly rod in hand to escape the daily routines of Detroit. Mason loved to fish his river. The grayling were no longer there, having been obliterated by the loggers in the mid-1800s, but the stream had been stocked with brook and brown trout, which thrived in the cold, clear water of the South Branch.

Mason loved his river so much that upon his death in 1954 he bequeathed it to the state of Michigan—on three conditions. The land had to be a permanent game preserve, never to be sold; camping was to be banned for 25 years; and the state had to accept the gift within two years of Mason's death. The conservationist's plan was to preserve his wooded retreat by opening it up to everyone who loved the North Woods, and Michigan accepted the responsibility to maintain it that way.

The original gift of 1,500 acres has since been enlarged to 2,860 acres, and officially it's called the South Branch Au Sable River Area. Anglers and canoeists, however, know it simply as the Mason Tract, a beautiful spot

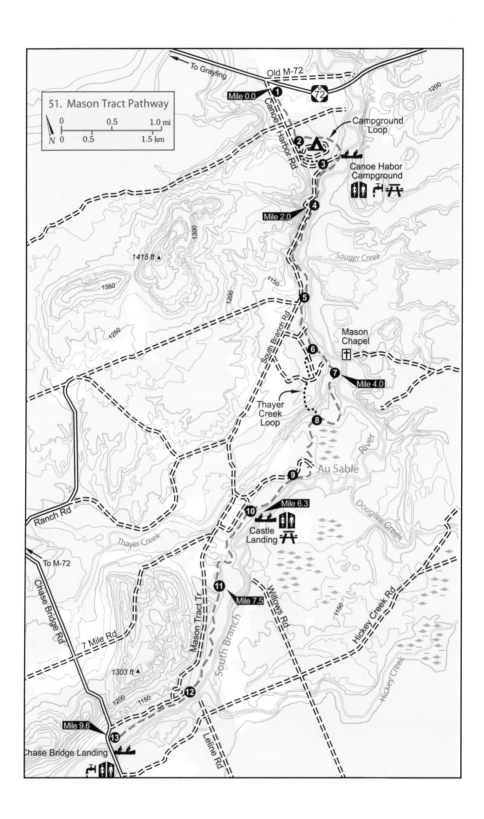

51. Mason Tract Pathway

To Grayling
Old M-72
Mile 0.0 — 1
72

Campground Loop
2
3
Canoe Habor Road
Canoe Habor Campground

4
Mile 2.0

Sauger Creek

1415 ft ▲
1350
1300
1250
1200
1150

South Branch Rd

5

Mason Chapel
6
7
Mile 4.0

Thayer Creek Loop
8

River
Au Sable

9

Ranch Rd

Thayer Creek

10
Mile 6.3
Castle Landing

Douglas Creek

To M-72

Chase Bridge Rd

Mason Tract Tr

11
Mile 7.5

Willows Rd

South Branch

Hickey Creek Rd

7 Mile Rd

1303 ft ▲

1200
1150

12

Leline Rd

Hickey Creek

1150

Mile 9.6
13
Chase Bridge Landing

in northern Michigan that is undeveloped, forested in pines and hardwoods, and split in the middle by 11 miles of some of the finest trout waters in the state. These qualities and the fact that mountain biking has been banned on the pathway have made the area a good destination for hikers.

Paralleling the west bank of the river is the Mason Tract Pathway, an 11.5-mile network of trails, most of which is a 9.5-mile, one-way hike from M-72 to Chase Bridge on Chase Bridge Road (also known as County Road 519). The river moves in and out of view along this trek as the trail works its way across the bluffs the South Branch flows between. For many, beginning at one road and ending at another presents a transportation problem. Beyond backtracking the entire way or using two vehicles, the only other solution is to walk only a portion of the pathway. The best section of trail for this choice is the northern half, where two small loops have been set up. This stretch is also the most scenic. A hike from the M-72 trailhead, along the small loop around Canoe Harbor and back, is 2.8 miles. Adding the next loop, around Thayer Creek, would make an 8.7-mile day from M-72.

Few hikers attempt this trail carrying waders, a fly rod, and a fishing vest. But even if you don't know a dry fly from a housefly, the trout and the fly fishing that goes on here add an intriguing aspect to this walk. Tackle the trail in the morning or early evening after canoeists have departed for the day, and you can sit quietly on the banks and watch trout rise to feed on insects. Or spend some time studying a fly angler work a floating line and delicate fly with such precision that he or she is able to drop it in the smallest pockets of water between deadheads and sweepers.

Watch that angler hook and land a trout, and you'll be stopping at the first fly shop on the way home.

A hiker on the Mason Tract Pathway.

ACCESS

The pathway is within a 30-minute drive of Grayling and Roscommon and is less than a three-hour journey from such major metro areas as Detroit, Flint, Lansing, and Grand Rapids (undoubtedly the reason for its heavy use by canoeists during the summer). From I-75, depart at Roscommon (exit 239) and head east on M-18 through town. To leave a car at the southern trailhead, turn north (left) on Chase Bridge Road (County Road 519) 2.5 miles out of Roscommon. The South Branch is 2 miles up the road, and the posted trailhead is on the north side of the river. On the south side of the bridge you'll find a canoe landing, vault toilet, and a well.

To reach the northern trailhead (where this description starts), continue on M-18, and the road will swing north and reach

A fly angler on the South Branch of the Au Sable River in the Mason Tract.

M-72. Head 2 miles west (left) on M-72 to reach the posted entrance to the Mason Tract. Turn south (left) on the dirt road into the area, and you will soon pass a parking lot and large trail sign to the east (left). If you continue on the dirt road past the trailhead, within a half mile you will pass the posted entrance to Canoe Harbor Campground, the only place where camping is allowed in the river retreat. Canoe Harbor was exempt from Mason's camping ban because the area was federally owned at the time and not part of the original gift. The state forest campground has 54 sites, well water, vault toilets, and a canoe landing on the river.

A state park vehicle pass is required for hiking in the Mason Tract, and there is a nightly fee for staying at Canoe Harbor State Forest Campground. For more information or a map, contact the DNR Roscommon field office (989-275-5151).

TRAIL

The Mason Tract Pathway is well marked with blue dots and triangle pathway markers, and along the way there are 13 numbered posts with locator maps, though some might be missing. The trail begins by winding through a sparse stand of pines and then crossing a two-track dirt road with a half mile, moving into a thicker forest on the other side. In another quarter mile, you reach post No. 2 with the loop around Canoe Harbor Campground. Heading east (left), you begin by following a two-track road, then veering off it where a pathway map has been posted. The trail is now skirting the campground and soon dips down to provide the first sight of South Branch.

Here is a classic Michigan trout stream. The river is 20 to 30 yards wide, less than 4 feet deep in most places, bordered along the banks by sweepers and deadheads, and crystal clear. The trail follows the river briefly

then, at **Mile 1.2**, comes to the campground's canoe landing, picnic area, and vault toilets. The trail heads southwest, skirts a high bank forested in red pine and hardwoods, and arrives at post No. 3, the return loop to the campground, at **Mile 1.6**. Located here is a bench, where on a quiet morning you can sit and listen to the river below.

Continuing south (left), the pathway winds over several small hills and swings away from the river to within sight of the dirt access road. It then descends back into view of the South Branch and arrives at post No. 4 in a parking area at **Mile 2**, from which several trails lead to the water's edge. This is the Dogtown access point and marks the spot where market hunters in the 19th century used to gather. Dogtown picked up its name from all the dogs the market hunters used to kill grouse, pheasant, and other wildlife for sale to restaurants in the cities.

For the next half mile, the trail stays within sight of the river as it passes through a pine-beech forest with a thick understory of ferns and then arrives at the Downey's Access Site, another parking area for anglers. Charles Downey was one of the first sportsmen to own the tract after buying the land from an exclusive fishing club of which he was a member. The trail heads southeast from the parking area and in 200 yards arrives in an open, grassy area marked in the middle by post No. 5 at **Mile 3**. Nearby a pair of stone stairways, left over from Downey's Place, lead down to the river, while just downstream in the water are the rocky remains of an old bridge.

The trail is marked along the grassy bluff with 6-foot posts. In another quarter mile you arrive at another parking area and QUALITY FISHING AREA. The sign marks a cedar stairway that leads down to the river. Post No. 6 marks the junction to the Thayer Creek Loop and is reached at **Mile 3.5**. Stay left here, and the pathway reenters a forest of primarily paper birch, beech, and assorted pine. Most of the time you are close to the river, but you can't see it until the trail swings past the riverbank and you get a splendid view upstream. On the other side of the South Branch, but nearly impossible to see, is the Mason Chapel, built in 1960 as a place of reverence for anglers.

The trail swings away from the South Branch, enters a low-lying wet area, and at *Mile 4* passes post No. 7 and then crosses a bridge over Thayer Creek. After ascending from the creek slightly, the trail merges into an old logging road. At *Mile 4.7* you arrive at post No. 8, the return spur of the Thayer Creek Loop.

The main trail swings to the southwest (left) from the junction as it follows a logging road briefly, then veers to the left at a well-posted spot. You climb into a small, grassy clearing, reenter the woods, and eventually emerge at a parking area and access. On the other side of the lot, the trail reenters the forest and quickly begins skirting the bluffs known to fly fishermen as the High Banks—and for good reason. The South Branch is far below you, seen every now and then between the towering pines.

At *Mile 5.7* the pathway arrives at post No. 9, a prominent hill overlooking the river where there is a bench and a long stairway to the water. The South Branch forms a sharp bend here, and the view from the bench is of flowing water and towering red pines that shade the bluffs. This is the High Banks access site, and from here the trail gradually descends until it cuts across a low-lying wet area and comes to the banks of the South Branch.

Follow the river briefly until the trail arrives at the remains of Durant's Castle at *Mile 6.3*.

Only parts of a stone foundation and a fireplace are left, but in 1931 this site held a $500,000 home built by the automaker. The 42-room castle was a retreat for Durant, and included a drawing room, music room, library, barbershop, gymnasium, and seven fireplaces. What amused locals the most, though, was a ticker tape that kept the millionaire in contact with the New York stock market even in this getaway in the woods. The house only lasted a year, for it was destroyed by fire in February 1932.

From the ruins, you ascend to a parking area with vault toilets and an interpretive display. A well-built spur leads down to a wooden landing deck on the river for canoeists. The pathway resumes in the woods directly across from the covered display sign, where it resembles a two-track road. You follow it through the forest, passing a bench at the edge of a steep bluff. Just beyond, the trail veers off the logging road and ascends into an old clear-cut that takes a half mile to cross and then arrives at post No. 11 at *Mile 7.5*. Stay left at the post and reenter the woods.

The trail descends to an access to the South Branch and then crosses several low-lying wet areas, some with boardwalks, with the river in view to the south. At *Mile 8.6* you arrive at post No. 12 where a spur leads down to the river. The trail levels out in the final mile, staying in the woods and close to Mason Tract Trail, the two-track that anglers use to access many of the access sites on the river. You do pass two more road access points before the final half mile. Finally the traffic on Chase Bridge Road becomes louder with every step and you emerge at the paved road, just north of the bridge and the canoe landing.

52

Au Sable River Foot Trail

Place: Hartwick Pines State Park

Total Distance: 3.1 miles

Hiking Time: 1 to 2 hours

Rating: Easy

Highlights: Trout stream, virgin pines

Maps: Au Sable River Foot Trail Map brochure from the Michigan DNR, or Au Sable River Trail map from MichiganTrailMaps.com

Trailhead GPS Coordinates: N 44° 44' 31" W 084° 39' 2.11"

At 9,672 acres, Hartwick Pines is the largest state park in the Lower Peninsula, but its best-known trail, Old Growth Forest Trail, is its shortest. Only 1 mile long, the path winds through the park's interpretive area, which includes virgin white pines, a reconstructed logger's camp, and a museum dedicated to Michigan's lumbering era. The trail allows a fascinating look at lumberjacks, but for a quieter, less crowded, and true escape into the woods, many hikers choose the Au Sable River Foot Trail on the west side of M-93.

This 3.1-mile trail crosses the East Branch of the Au Sable River twice, passes through its own stands of virgin timber, and sports 23 interpretive posts with an accompanying brochure available at the Michigan Forest Visitor Center or contact station. A bit of climbing is involved, and a few wet spots must be crossed; but overall the trail is not difficult and can easily be hiked in running shoes. It also serves as an access for anglers who enjoy the challenges of fishing small trout streams.

A daily vehicle permit or an annual state park pass is required to enter the park, and there is an additional fee to stay overnight in the modern, 100-site campground, located on the east side of M-93. Hartwick is a popular stop for travelers; campsite reservations through the Michigan State Park Central Reservations (800-447-2757; www.midnrreservations.com) are strongly recommended for most weekends from late June through late August.

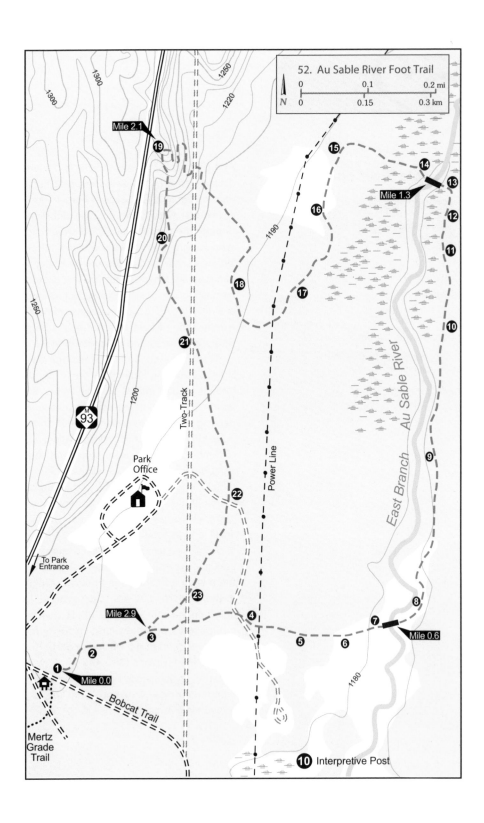

52. Au Sable River Foot Trail

0   0.1   0.2 mi

N   0   0.15   0.3 km

1300
1300
1250
1220
1250
1300
1250
1200

Mile 2.1
⑲
⑳
㉑

1190

⑮
⑭   ⑬
Mile 1.3
⑯   ⑫
⑪
⑰
⑱   ⑩

Au Sable River
East Branch

Two-Track
Power Line

Park
Office
㉒
⑨

To Park
Entrance
㉓   ⑧
Mile 2.9   ⑦   Mile 0.6
③   ④
⑤   ⑥
②
①   Mile 0.0
1180
Bobcat Trail

Mertz
Grade
Trail

⑩ Interpretive Post

M 93

ACCESS

Hartwick Pines is 9 miles north of Grayling and is reached from I-75 by departing at exit 259. Head north on M-93 for 2 miles. The park's main entrance is on the west side of M-93 and leads to the campground, park headquarters, and the Michigan Forest Visitor Center. You can actually begin this hike at the interpretive center by hiking the Old Growth Forest Trail and a portion of the Mertz Grade Trail.

For simplicity it is easier to start the Au Sable River Trail at the clearing where the old campground was located, a mile north of the main entrance at the corner of M-93 and a dirt road called Bobcat Trail.

The Michigan Forest Visitor Center (989-348-2537) makes for an interesting stop before hiking this trail. From Memorial Day to Labor Day the center is open daily 10 AM to 6 PM. From September through May the center is open 9 AM to 4 PM. For more information about trails or camping, contact Hartwick Pines State Park headquarters (989-348-7068).

TRAIL

Au Sable River Trail is marked on the north side of Bobcat Trail and begins as a level path that enters the pines and quickly moves into a red pine plantation. Within a quarter mile—at post No. 3—you reach the junction with the return loop. Continue straight to follow the loop in a counterclockwise direction and follow the posts in the correct numeric order. The trail crosses a two-track, then a power line before arriving at a footbridge across the East Branch of the Au Sable River at *Mile 0.6*. Interpretive Posts 7 and 8

A hiker admires the East Branch of the Au Sable River.

An old-growth pine along the Au Sable River Foot Trail in Hartwick Pines State Park.

are located here. There is also a bench, and if you sit quietly for long enough, you might see the rings of rising trout dissipate down the stream. Post 8 marks an old CCC swimming pool, and trout fingerlings can often be seen darting around in its still water.

The East Branch flows 16 miles from its source to the southwest and into the main stream of the Au Sable River, the most famous trout stream east of the Mississippi. It was on the shores of the Au Sable River's Holy Waters that Trout Unlimited was founded. In Hartwick Pines, the East Branch is especially scenic, a crystal-clear stream that gurgles between gravel banks and through cedar swamps, undercutting the banks around deadheads. Too narrow to be a good canoeing waterway, the stream ranges between 15 and 20 feet wide in most places and holds a good brook trout fishery that many anglers overlook. Fly anglers turn to short rods and roll casts exclusively, but still much of their time is spent picking flies out of overhanging branches. Most anglers are spin or bait fishermen using worms or small spinners to entice the brookies and, sometimes, brown trout.

From the bridge, the trail swings north and moves away from the stream into a mixed forest of white, red, and jack pines. A few of the trees are notably large. The trail arrives at the second bridge across the East Branch at *Mile 1.3* and then enters a white cedar swamp where the ground cover is a soft cushion of sphagnum moss. The best stand of trees, however, is reached at *Mile 1.6*, when the trail arrives at post No. 17, located in a cathedral of tall hemlocks where there is little underbrush due to the lack of sunlight. This stand of huge eastern hemlocks towers above the trail, enjoyed today only because in the 19th century the market price of tanbark fell before they did. The low return on hemlock bark, which was used for tanning leather, no longer paid the loggers even to cut them.

The relatively level walk passes underneath the power line a second time and arrives at a two-tracks posted ALTERNATIVE ROUTE, which you can be followed south (left) if you want to bypass climbing the ridge. The trail, posted as OVERLOOK, continues straight and switchbacks steadily up to post No. 19, reached at *Mile 2.1*. The post marks the crest of a glacial moraine that is almost 1,300 feet in elevation and near enough to M-93 that occasionally you can hear traffic rumble by. There was once a scenic overlook here, but saplings have long since filled in the view with foliage.

A sharp descent from the ridge follows. The final leg of the trail is a level walk past a railroad grade of the Lewiston Railroad and a rectangular-shaped mound that many believe was once a barn. The trail continues crosses a pair of two-tracks and at *Mile 2.9* returns to the only junction along the route. Head right to reach the trailhead at *Mile 3.1*.

53

Platte River Springs Pathway

Place: Pere Marquette State Forest

Total Distance: 1.6 miles

Hiking Time: 1 hour

Rating: Easy

Highlights: Platte River, old-growth maple and beech trees

Maps: Platte River Springs Pathway map from the Michigan DNR or MichiganTrail Maps.com

Trailhead GPS Coordinates:
N 44° 38' 36.97" W 085° 58' 49.29"

Located in Benzie County, near Honor, the Platte River Springs Pathway is short loop packed with adventure, starting with a ford you'll reach minutes after leaving your car. On the south side of the river the trail winds through 35 acres of rugged bluffs, from which a handful of springs emerge to keep the Platte cold and clear. Lining the trail is a handful of towering beech and maples, making this pathway an especially delightful place to hike in the fall.

Although rated easy, the route does involve a bit of climbing and path finding. The trail is not easy to distinguish at times, meaning you have to keep a sharp eye out for blue blazes and an occasional trail marker. The entire hike may be only 1.6 miles, but the Platte River Springs Pathway is harder than most trails twice its length. Nor is it conducive to mountain biking or cross-country skiing, even if skiers were willing to endure an icy ford in midwinter.

The pathway begins in the Platte River State Forest Campground. In the fall you can enjoy a wonderful weekend camping on one side of the river and hiking on the other. In the spring the pathway would be an excellent place to search for morels. At either time of the year, after dashing across the Platte you can warm up your toes with a campfire back at your site.

ACCESS

From Honor head east on US 31 and for a mile and then south on Goose Road for 1.5 miles to reach the Platte River State Forest Campground. The trail is marked along the

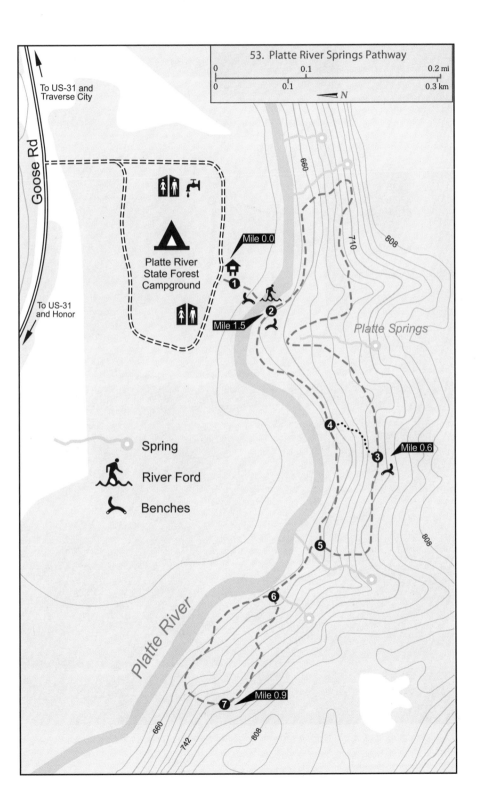

53. Platte River Springs Pathway

0   0.1   0.2 mi
0   0.1   0.3 km
N

To US-31 and
Traverse City

Goose Rd

Mile 0.0

Platte River
State Forest
Campground

To US-31
and Honor

Mile 1.5

Platte Springs

660
710
808

Spring

River Ford

Benches

Mile 0.6

808

Platte River

660
742
808

Mile 0.9

A hiker descends a spur of the Platte River Springs Pathway.

campground loop. There is a nightly fee to camp at the state forest campground. For more information, contact the Traverse City DNR field office (231-922-5280).

TRAIL

Platte River State Forest Campground is a rustic facility with 26 sites that can accommodate tents and small trailers; it also has vault toilets and hand pumps for water. The Pere Marquette State Forest campground borders the Platte River but none of the sites is directly on the water.

The pathway is marked on the south side of the campground loop. Within 100 yards of the trailhead you arrive at the Platte River. There's a bench here to kick off your boots for the watery crossing. The trail is easy to spot on the other side, where post No. 2 and another bench are located. You can do the ford in bare feet but there are patches in of stones and mud to contend with. Slipping on a pair of sport sandals is better.

You head upstream briefly and then swing sharply south (right) to climb the river bluff along the first of many springs encountered in the area. After topping off the trail descends the ridge and climbs again along a stretch where it's easy to wander off course. Follow the blue blazes! Post No. 3 is reached at *Mile 0.6*, where there is a bench and just beyond it a huge maple that is stunning in October. The post also marks a cutoff spur down the bluff to post No. 4, though it's hard to distinguish.

The main trail continues to cling to the steep bluff, providing glimpses of the Platte River below between the trees. You pass more giant beeches and maples before descending sharply to post No. 5. Head west (left) to cross a pair of springs and follow the

Fording the Platte River at the beginning of the Platte River Springs Pathway.

separate loop where post No. 7 is located, reached at *Mile 0.9* after a another climb up the bluff.

You backtrack to post No. 5 and then follow the trail as it winds through a stand of cedar along the river back to post No. 2, reached at *Mile 1.5*. The Platte is so clear that in the summer you can watch trout feeding during a hatch; in the fall, you can see coho salmon spawning upstream. One more dash across the river and you're back at the campground.

54

Thompson's Harbor

Place: Thompson's Harbor State Park

Total Distance: 5.2 miles

Hiking Time: 2 to 3 hours

Rating: Easy

Highlights: Lake Huron beach, orchids, wildflowers

Maps: Thompson's Harbor State Park map from the Michigan DNR or MichiganTrailMaps.com

Trailhead GPS Coordinates: N 45° 20' 33.47" W 083° 35' 18.83"

Much like Negwegon State Park to the south, Thompson's Harbor is an undeveloped and lightly used state park that contains miles of spectacular Lake Huron shoreline. The difference between the two is the drive getting there. Negwegon is reached via a sandy two-track where more than one car has lost a muffler. The entrance to Thompson's Harbor is right on US 23, the main route up the sunrise side of Michigan. That alone makes it worth exploring.

Located 20 miles northwest of Alpena, the 5,247-acre park includes 7.5 miles of Great Lake shoreline and is the largest unit on the east side of the state. Thompson's Harbor was created in 1988 thanks in part to the generosity of Genevieve Gillette, the renowned conservationist who was instrumental in establishing the Porcupines Mountains Wilderness. Gillette had died two years earlier but in her will instructed that her estate should be used to purchase "a scenic site to give to the people of Michigan." The $260,000 gift was the key to securing this undeveloped Lake Huron shoreline, best known for having the world's largest population of dwarf lake iris.

Despite two master plans that recommended everything from a lodge to a swimming pool, development of Thompson's Harbor has been almost nonexistent since its dedication. For the most part the facilities at the park are limited to a trailhead parking area, two vault toilets, and a pair of rustic cabins that were added in 2009 and are available for rent. The park's 6-mile trail system, partly composed of old two-tracks,

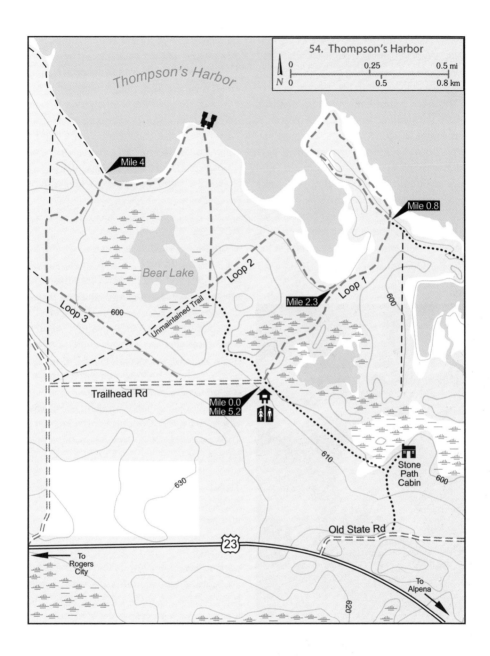

54. Thompson's Harbor

| 0 | 0.25 | 0.5 mi |
| 0 | 0.5 | 0.8 km |

N

Thompson's Harbor

Mile 4

Mile 0.8

Bear Lake

Loop 2

Loop 1

Mile 2.3

Loop 3

600

Unmaintained Trail

600

Trailhead Rd

Mile 0.0
Mile 5.2

610

Stone
Path
Cabin

600

630

Old State Rd

23

To
Rogers
City

620

To
Alpena

is centered on three interconnecting loops ranging in length from 1.4 miles (Loop 2) to 2.6 miles (Loop 3); they can easily be combined for a 5.2-mile hike.

This is a scenic hike because of the limestone character of the land, the reason it was once owned by U.S. Steel Corp. The terrain includes whitish marl marshes, shallow lakes, and old shorelines of cobblestone. Wildlife ranges from more than 100 species of birds, including nesting eagles, to deer, coyotes, and even black bears.

The park's best-known natural feature, one that attracts a number of naturalists, is its colonies of dwarf lake iris. The smallish purple flower is a federally threatened species found only in Michigan, Wisconsin, and parts of Ontario along the shores of Lake Michigan and Lake Huron. The flower is easy to spot in Thompson's Harbor because its preferred habitat is old beach ridges of limestone, something that is abundant in the park. But arrive in June and you'll more likely

Yellow lady's slipper, an orchid commonly seen at Thompson's Harbor State Park.

be overwhelmed by the large number of lady's slipper orchids encountered here.

If you do arrive in spring or fall, pack along a jacket. The park is often windy and 10 to 15 degrees cooler than trails that are only 10 miles inland. In the summer bring insect repellent; any time of year fill up the water bottles before you arrive, as there are no pumps at the trailhead. Mountain biking is allowed on the trails, but the park attracts few cyclists.

ACCESS

Thompson's Harbor is reached by US 23, 24 miles north of Alpena or 5 miles south of the junction with M-65. The entrance is marked with a highway sign that says THOMPSON'S HARBOR DAY-USE AREA. Turn onto the dirt road here and then head right (east) at the intersection on what is labeled on park maps as Trailhead Road. This dirt road ends at the trailhead parking area, where there is a large display map of the trails.

For more information, contact P. H. Hoeft State Park (989-734-2543) or the Friends of Thompson's Harbor (www.friendsofthompson harbor.org).

TRAIL

All three loops are posted in the parking area and head in different directions. Begin with Loop 1, which departs into the woods as a two-track from the northeast corner of the parking lot. The hiking is level and easy as you enter a typical northern forest of white birch, balsam fir, white spruce, and aspen. If it's early summer, yellow lady's slippers and other wildflowers will line the trail.

At **Mile 0.6** you arrive at a junction with Loop 2. Head east (right) to stay on Loop 1 and enjoy the most scenic portion of the hike. In a quarter mile you reach a second junction near the shoreline of Lake Huron. Here the shore is typical of what is found

Thompson's Harbor State Park is best known for having the world's largest population of dwarf lake iris.
COURTESY OF MICHIGAN DEPT. OF NATURAL RESOURCES

throughout the park: a cobblestone beach overlooking a bay enclosed by a pair of rocky points. Stay right at the junction as the trail becomes a small loop along the point to the west, the largest peninsula jutting out into Thompson's Harbor. Lake Huron remains in view for the next half mile as the trail follows ancient shorelines that make for a gravelly walk.

Eventually you backtrack a short section of Loop 1 to arrive at the junction with Loop 2 for the second time at *Mile 2.3*. Stay right to continue on Loop 2. The trail swings away from the views of Lake Huron and remains in a forest predominantly of red pine. At *Mile 3* a beautiful stand of towering red pine marks

the junction with Loop 3. Stay right to continue with the hike; head left to return to the trailhead in a half mile.

Heading north on Loop 3, the trail immediately passes Bear Lake, one of several inland lakes in the park. You can spot the shallow body of water through the trees but will need to depart the trail and cut through the stands of cedar to examine it closely. The marshy lake features a limestone bottom, the reason for its grayish color, and an extensive bog around it that bounces with every step you take. Pitcher plants by the hundreds grow along the shore.

Once you're past Bear Lake the trail continues heading due north until it returns to the shoreline, where there is a bench overlooking the harbor. For the next half mile you skirt Lake Huron again, along first a cobblestone beach and then a rare stretch of sand. At either stretch of shore, you can often find pieces of a wooden ship that went down inside Thompson's Harbor and is now slowly breaking up.

At *Mile 4* the trail departs the shoreline for the last time and uses planking to cross a rich conifer swamp. You then head southwest to merge with a two-track. The rocky two-track heads due south and then, at a rusty barrier, southeast for almost a mile through an area of scrub. Be careful—poison ivy thrives along this stretch. At *Mile 5* the trail arrives at another barrier that blocks it at Trailhead Road. Head east (left) and follow the entrance road to arrive back at your car in a quarter mile.

55

Sinkholes Pathway

Place: Mackinaw State Forest	
Total Distance: 2 miles	
Hiking Time: 1 hour	
Rating: Easy	
Highlights: Sinkholes, Shoepac Lake	
Maps: Sinkhole Pathway map from the Michigan DNR or MichiganTrail Maps.com	
Trailhead GPS Coordinates: N 45° 14' 31.83" W 084° 10' 12.67"	

This summer, take the kids kamping in karst-land. *Karst* is a geological term for a limestone region where underground streams dissolved the rock into a series of large circular caves. These caverns eventually collapsed under the overwhelming weight of sand, rock, and clay left by the last glacier 10,000 year ago, resulting in deep conical depressions, called sinkholes, throughout the forest.

Located between Onaway and Atlanta, less than a three-hour drive from Saginaw, is Michigan's Sinkhole Area, a 2,600-acre slice of the Mackinaw State Forest. This is the state's best karst region, and clustered near the collection of sinkholes there are three lakes, four rustic state forest campgrounds, and numerous opportunities to hike, swim, or cast a lure for northern pike and smallmouth bass.

The closest campground to the sinkholes is Shoepac Lake, itself a sinkhole that eventually filled with water. Anglers prefer to pitch a tent in the East Unit and West Unit campgrounds on Tomahawk Creek Flooding. Both campgrounds have improved boat launches on the flooding, which is fished for bluegill, smallmouth bass, and northern pike.

Then there is Tomahawk Lake Campground, which features 25 sites, more than half of them directly on the lake, as well as the best beach and swimming area. From the campground you can follow the High Country Pathway for a mile to reach the trailhead of Sinkhole Pathway, a 2-mile loop around the five deepest sinkholes in the area and the hike described here.

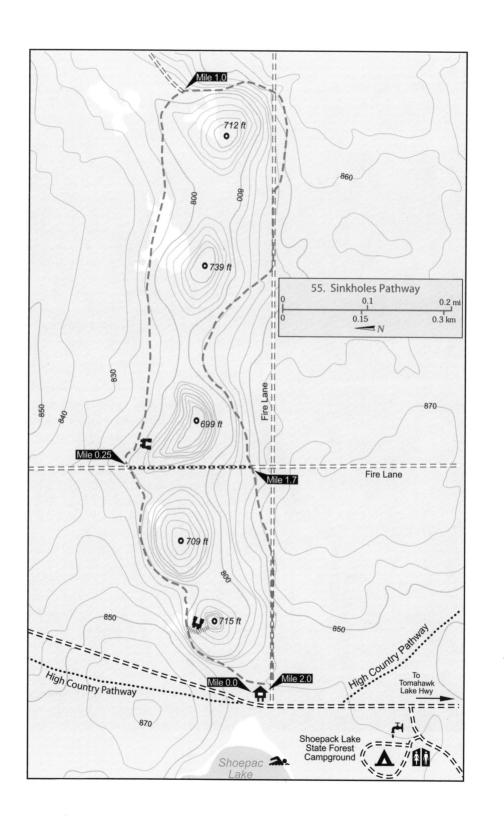

55. Sinkholes Pathway

Mile 1.0

712 ft

860

800

800

739 ft

0   0.1   0.2 mi

0   0.15   0.3 km

N

Fire Lane

830

870

699 ft

850

840

Mile 0.25

Fire Lane

Mile 1.7

709 ft

800

715 ft

850

850

850

High Country Pathway

Mile 0.0

High Country Pathway

Mile 2.0

High Country Pathway

To
Tomahawk
Lake Hwy

870

Shoepac
Lake

Shoepack Lake
State Forest
Campground

On an observation deck looking into a sinkhole.

ACCESS

From M-32 in Atlanta, head north 16 miles on M-33 and then east on Tomahawk Lake Highway. When you're 2.2 miles from M-33, turn north on a dirt road posted SHOEPAC LAKE CAMPGROUND. In a mile this road leads past the entrance of the rustic campground and then reaches a parking area within view of Shoepac Lake, which is really a sinkhole. The trailhead for Sinkholes Pathway is located across the dirt road.

For more information, contact the DNR Gaylord Operations Service Center (989-732-3541).

TRAIL

You can see the first sinkhole from the trailhead, and from here the pathway begins by skirting its northern rim. In a couple hundred yards the trail comes to an observation deck and junction with a spur into the 100-foot-deep sinkhole. For the most part the spur is a stairway—of 180 steps and three benches—to the bottom of this forested pit. The view from the floor of this geological oddity is unusual, but it's a knee-bending climb back up to the pathway.

From the stairway, you skirt the rim of the second sinkhole and then a quarter mile from the trailhead arrive at the junction with a crossover spur that shortens the hike to less than a mile. The pathway continues east and immediately arrives at the third sinkhole, this one featuring an observation platform but not steps to the bottom. Before you race

down into it, keep in mind that it's a tough climb out without a stairway.

You swing away to cross an area of scattered pines, the result of a 1939 forest fire, then arrive at a log fence that marks the fourth sinkhole, with the fifth and final one quickly following. At **Mile 1** you arrive at a junction. Head right and follow the blue blazes as the pathway climbs a wooded hill and remains in the thick forest after topping out. You stay above and out of view of the fifth sinkhole for a short spell until the trail swings sharply west and begins its return to the parking lot.

At **Mile 1.3** the pathway passes the south edge of the fourth hole and then swings inland. It's easy at this point to unwittingly continue on the fire lane, which looks like a wide, arrow-straight trail. At **Mile 1.7** you reach the junction with the crossover spur, and then finish the hike by rounding the south side of the first two holes and viewing the sandy edge on the other side where you were just an hour earlier.

In the last quarter mile, the pathway follows the fire lane and you can look down what is now a straight trail and see the shimmering waters of Shoepac Lake. Eventually you arrive at the forest road where to the north is the trailhead for the Sinkhole Pathway, to the south is the High Country Pathway, and straight ahead lie a beach and the cooling waters of Shoepac Lake.

If the day is hot, it's hard to resist the temptation to dash from the end of the pathway into the cooling waters of this most refreshing sinkhole.

56

Ocqueoc Falls Bicentennial Pathway

Place: Mackinaw State Forest

Total Distance: 6 miles

Hiking Time: 3 hours

Rating: Moderate

Highlights: Ocqueoc River and Falls

Maps: Ocqueoc Falls Bicentennial Pathway map from the Michigan DNR or MichiganTrailMaps.com

Trailhead GPS Coordinates: N 45° 23' 44.70" W 084° 3' 20.55"

While the Upper Peninsula has hundreds of waterfalls, the Lower Peninsula has only two, with Ocqueoc Falls being the most popular and accessible one south of the Mackinac Bridge. You can rush from the parking lot to the falls in a couple of minutes, but the best way to turn this stop into an adventure is to first hike the Ocqueoc Falls Pathway, a bicentennial project built in 1976.

This Mackinaw State Forest trail is shared by hikers and mountain bikers during much of the year and consists of four loops; 2.85, 3.5, 4.6, and 6 miles. More than just the falls, this is a very scenic area dominated by the river valley and forested by towering pines and hardwoods that are brilliant in early October. You begin by hiking along a ridge above the valley for some incredible views, and then return along the river, ending at the falls.

The first loop is not only the shortest but the most scenic, making it an excellent choice for families with children. But the entire pathway, a 6-mile loop, is an enjoyable hike and is the trek that is described here. To turn it into a weekend adventure, set up camp at the Ocqueoc Falls State Forest Campground, which features 15 sites on a forested bluff overlooking its namesake river.

The day-use area around the falls was extensively renovated in 2012 and can be a popular place in summer and fall. But once you on the trails, you will encounter few if any people, especially in the northern half of the system that forms the 6-mile loop as the majority of hikers seldom venture beyond the first loop.

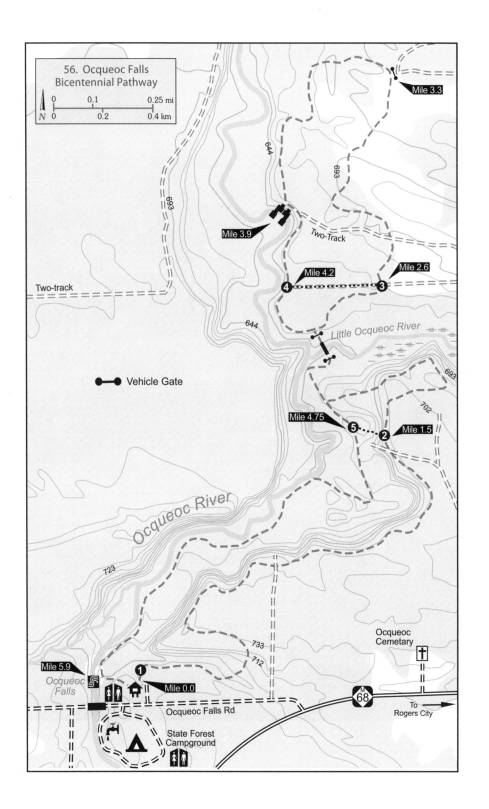

56. Ocqueoc Falls
Bicentennial Pathway

0   0.1   0.25 mi
0   0.2   0.4 km
N

Mile 3.3

644

693

Mile 3.9

Two-Track

Mile 4.2

Mile 2.6

④

③

644

Little Ocqueoc River

693

702

Two-track

●━● Vehicle Gate

Mile 4.75

⑤

② Mile 1.5

Ocqueoc River

723

Ocqueoc
Cemetery

733

712

Mile 5.9

Ocqueoc
Falls

①

Mile 0.0

Ocqueoc Falls Rd

M
68

To
Rogers City

State Forest
Campground

Ocqueoc Falls.

ACCESS

The day-use area for Ocqueoc Falls is well posted on Ocqueoc Falls Road, which can be reached from Rogers City by following M-68 west for 11.5 miles. When the state highway curves sharply to the south, continue straight onto Ocqueoc Falls Road to the entrance. On the south side of Ocqueoc Falls Road is Ocqueoc Falls State Forest Campground. A state park annual pass or vehicle permit is required to hike the pathway; there is a nightly fee for the state forest campground.

For more information, contact the DNR Gaylord Operations Service Center (989-732-3541).

TRAIL

The trailhead is marked in the parking lot with a locator map. The pathway is numbered in a counterclockwise direction, saving the small cascade for the end. At post No. 1 head east (right) and follow an old two-track through a red pine forest along a surface that is usually carpeted by pine needles. At *Mile 0.35* you make a short climb and then level out for the next mile as you skirt a bluff. At times you can look down into the river valley or across to the forested ridge bordering the Ocqueoc River on the west side.

The pathway will cross a number of old two-tracks throughout the day but in general is well marked and easy to follow. Just keep one eye out for blue DNR Pathway triangles on the trees or faded blue blazes. You cross one of the two-tracks at *Mile 0.8* and then at *Mile 1.5* arrive at post No. 2. To the west (left) is a very short downhill spur to post No. 5.

The 6-Mile Loop continues to the right and within a half mile makes a sharp swing to the west and descends off the bluff. At *Mile 2.1* you arrive at a T-junction and can head left for post No. 5 and the cascade or

The Ocqueoc River, seen often from the Ocqueoc Falls Bicentennial Pathway.

right to continue north. Heading north, you begin the two-way segment of trail, the result of the pathway being rerouted in the mid-2000s, and immediately arrive at a gate blocking motorized vehicles.

You descend to a steel bridge at *Mile 2.3* to cross the scenic Little Ocqueoc River and then climb out of the ravine, where you're directed right to continue the pathway in a counterclockwise direction. There is a confusing spot with a two-track at *Mile 2.4* and again when post No. 3 is reached at *Mile 2.6*. At the post the trail merges with another two-track but is well marked. The two-track is the crossover spur to post No. 4; the 6-Mile Loop heads left briefly to cross the two-track and then right to continue north.

At *Mile 3* you enter a meadow sprinkled with large trees that can be especially beautiful in the fall. Within a third of a mile you arrive at a series of large boulders used to block to motorized vehicles, particularly off-road vehicles (ORVs). At this point the trail, resembling an old two-track, swings west to begin its return to the parking lot. At *Mile 3.9* you emerge at what looks like a forest road cul-de-sac. Nearby is a bench perched on the edge of a high bank overlooking the Ocqueoc River. It's your first view of the river if you didn't sneak a peak of the falls in the beginning, and it's one of the best along the trail. You're looking down at a sharp bend in the Ocqueoc and a long stairway providing anglers access.

A steep downhill follows, and at *Mile 4.2* you arrive at post No. 4, where there is another bench and a partial view of the river. Here an old two-track heads east (left) for post No. 3 while the main trail, also an overgrown two-track, continues right along the bluff. Within a quarter mile you arrive back at the two-way single-track and use it to re-cross the Little Ocqueoc River and return to the T-junction at *Mile 4.5*.

This time continue straight along the more hilly terrain for post No. 5. You'll reach the junction at *Mile 4.75*, which is followed by another descent dropping you to the floor of the river valley. You reach the Ocqueoc River at *Mile 5* to begin the most scenic section of the trail. For the rest of the outing you remain close to the river to constantly catch views of gurgling trout stream through the trees. This stretch is one of the most beautiful river trails in the Lower Peninsula and ends with the Ocqueoc Falls, heard long before you see them.

While not big by Upper Peninsula standards, Ocqueoc Falls makes for the perfect place to end a hike or a ride, especially on a hot summer afternoon. The cascade drops 10 feet over a series of three ledges, making it easy in the summer for you to kick off your boots and wade in for a soothing foot massage that only Mother Nature could give. The parking lot is just 100 yards or so to the east.

57

Jordan River Pathway

Place: Mackinaw State Forest

Total Distance: 18 miles

Hiking Time: 2 days

Rating: Moderate to challenging

Highlights: Scenic overlooks, Jordan River, backcountry campsites

Maps: Jordan River Pathway map from the Michigan DNR or MichiganTrail Maps.com

Trailhead GPS Coordinates: N 45° 2' 48.08" W 084° 56' 12.24"

In the early 1900s the Jordan valley was little more than a sea of stumps, the telltale trademarks left behind by loggers. Today it is part of the Mackinaw State Forest, the site of Michigan's first National Scenic River, and one of most popular backpacking destinations in the Lower Peninsula, attracting thousands of hikers every year.

One of the reasons for the valley's popularity is the scenic Jordan River Pathway. The 18-mile trail begins on the top of Deadmans Hill with a panoramic view of the hardwood forest that has long since replaced the rows of stumps. From there the path quickly descends from the high bluff and for the most part is a walk through one of the most pristine watersheds in the Lower Peninsula. Along the way you skirt the cedar banks of the Jordan River, pass dozens of gurgling springs that feed it, and pause at small pools that are havens for brook trout.

The layout of the pathway also makes it ideal for a weekend backpack. The trailhead is just north of Mancelona, a four-hour drive from most major urban areas in southern Michigan. The trail is a loop, can be covered in two days, and features a hike-in campground conveniently located near the halfway point.

It's not an easy trek. You must be prepared to haul a backpack almost 10 miles each day and to constantly climb in and out of the valley. The trail is officially an 18-mile walk, but if you include a visit to the Jordan River Fish Hatchery, which many hikers do, then it's 19.5-mile trek. For those with only

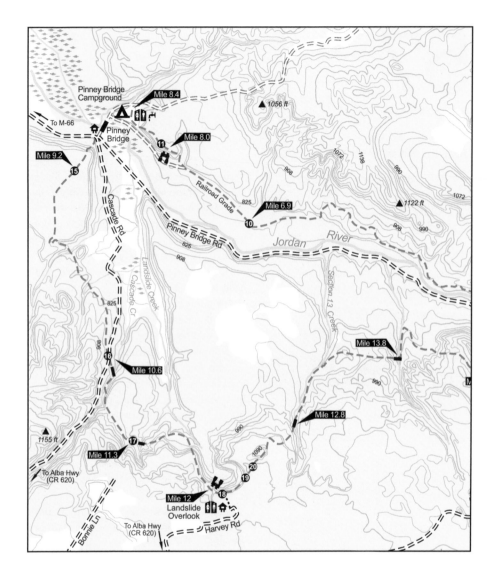

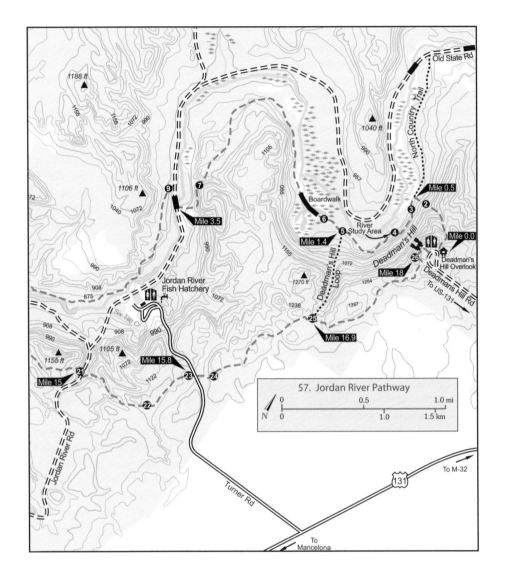

Map labels:

1188 ft
1040 ft
Old State Rd
North Country Trail
Mile 0.5
1106 ft
9
7
1040
1072
Mile 3.5
1106
Boardwalk
6
River Study Area
3
2
4
Mile 0.0
Deadman's Hill
Mile 1.4
5
26
Deadman's Hill Overlook
Deadman's Hill Loop
1270 ft
1072
Mile 18
1254
To US-131
Jordan River Fish Hatchery
Six Tile C
1238
1287
Deadmans Hill Rd
25
Mile 16.9
990
908
875
908
990
1072
Mile 15.8
23
24
1155 ft
1105 ft
21
22
Mile 15
1122
Jordan River Rd

57. Jordan River Pathway

N

| 0 | 0.5 | 1.0 mi |

| 0 | 1.0 | 1.5 km |

Turner Rd

131

To M-32

To Mancelona

an afternoon, there is also a cutoff spur that forms a 3-mile loop from Deadmans Hill.

But the effort of hauling a backpack to hike the entire trail is well worth it. The pathway's most enduring quality is that it is a refuge from the traffic-clogged city you just left. From the minute you leave the parking lot the Jordan River Pathway becomes a two-day escape into a woods that hasn't seen a logger's crosscut saw in almost a century.

ACCESS

Deadmans Hill is posted along US 131, 11.5 miles north of Mancelona or 6 miles north of Alba. From US 131 turn west on Deadmans Hill Road and drive 2 miles to the parking area and trailhead at the end. If you're driving north on I-75, depart at exit 282 and head west of Gaylord on M-32.

A state park pass is required to hike the trail and leave a car at Deadmans Hill. Just west of town on M-32 is the Department of Natural Resources Gaylord Operations Center (989-732-3541), where you can purchase the pass or pick up a trail map.

TRAIL

You begin at Deadmans Hill, a 1,336-foot-high ridge where logger "Big Sam" Graczyk was run over by an overloaded Big Wheel on the day he was to be married in 1910. It's also a steal-your-breath overlook where leaf peepers from all over the state swing by for a view of the Jordan valley during October.

First Day

Distance: 8.4 miles
On the north side of the parking lot is the trailhead with an intentions box and vault toilets but unfortunately no source of drinking water. From there a trail quickly drops off Deadmans Hill, a descent of almost 400 feet, before bottoming out in an open area on the valley floor at *Mile 0.5*, where you'll

find a posted junction with the North Country Trail (NCT). The NCT heads north (right) to merge into Warner Creek Pathway.

The Jordan River Pathway heads south (left) and reenters the woods to pass post No. 3 and skirt the base of Deadmans Hill. Post No. 4 marks an observation area, and at *Mile 1.4* you reach post No. 5. This post marks the junction of Deadmans Hill Loop, a 3.1-mile day hike from the trailhead. To continue on to Pinney Bridge Campground, head west (right); within a quarter mile you emerge at post No. 6, marking a beaver dam and a large wetland surrounding it. A boardwalk leads across the wetland and makes for an interesting place to look for wildlife.

The pathway before and after the boardwalk is a wide, dry, and arrow-straight trail through a wetland, the first sign of the area's logging past. The raised railroad bed was built in 1910 by the White Lumber Company so its flatbed cars could haul out the freshly cut timber to East Jordan. Now it keeps the boots of backpackers dry despite the beaver ponds on either side.

In the first 2 miles of the trail the terrain changes from forest to wetlands to beaver ponds to grassy meadows. But there's no Jordan River. Not until *Mile 3.5* into the hike do you see the river for the first time, when the trail descends to Pinney Bridge Road just after you pass post No. 7.

Designated a Natural Scenic River in 1972, the Jordan flows from the northeast corner of Antrim County to the south arm of Lake Charlevoix, forming a watershed of 101,800 acres. The outstanding feature of the river is the clarity of its water; it derives 90 percent of its flow from springs gurgling out of the hills and bluffs surrounding you. The runs and pools you pass are ideal habitat for eastern brook trout, which anglers find are numerous but generally small this far upstream.

A backpacker on the Jordan River Pathway.

You use the Pinney Bridge Road vehicle bridge to cross the river, and then follow the dirt road north briefly. At post No. 9 you leave the road and climb the bluff to the west. The trail descends to the Jordan River at *Mile 4.5*, and you skirt its banks for a half mile. This is a scenic stretch of the pathway where the clear and cold current of the Jordan swirls and weaves its way through a maze of grassy humps and islands, some supporting huge cedars, others little more than a bouquet of wildflowers in the spring.

At *Mile 6.7* the pathway merges onto railroad grade built by the East Jordan Lumber Company in 1918 and passes post No. 10 at *Mile 6.9*. You climb to a spectacular overlook at almost 1,000 feet, where post No. 11 at *Mile 8* marks an overlook and bench with a pleasant view of the Jordan River valley. There is no need to hurry here; Pinney Bridge Campground is less than a half mile away, reached at *Mile 8.4*.

In 1915 the campground was the site for Logging Camp Number 2 of the East Jordan Lumber Company. More than 60 men lived in the camp's barracks mounted on 60-foot-long flatcars so they could be easily moved. The hike-in facility has eight sites, fire rings, vault toilets, and a hand pump for water. There is a per-night fee to camp that you can deposit in a fee pipe in the campground.

Second Day
Distance: 9.6 miles, or 11.1 miles if you visit the hatchery

The second day is longer than the first, with much of it spent climbing in and out the ravines of those spring-fed creeks that make

The Pinney Bridge Campground, a walk-in campground for backpackers on the Jordan River Pathway.

the Jordan River so pure. Creeks with names like Cascade, Landslide, and Section Thirteen more than make up for the fact you are nowhere near the river the entire day.

From the campground, the trail crosses the Jordan on Pinney Bridge to Pinney Bridge Road near its intersection with Cascade Road. The pathway is clearly marked on the south side of Pinney Bridge Road and begins with a steady climb, reaching post No. 15 at *Mile 9.2*. The climb continues; at *Mile 10.3* a sign marks the 45th parallel, the halfway point between the equator and the North Pole.

At *Mile 10.6* you reach post No. 16 and then cross Cascade Road and descend to a footbridge over scenic Cascade Stream. The trail briefly follows the creek and then climbs out of the ravine the stream has cut. Post No. 17, reached at *Mile 11.3*, marks a footbridge over Landside Creek; there is a bench on the east bank. In the spring and early summer, this is another scenic stream with scattered pools that will entice anglers.

The steep climb continues until *Mile 12*, when you break out at Landslide Overlook. The overlook is marked by a railing along the edge of the ridge with a spectacular view of the valley below and post No. 18 nearby, marking the junction where the NCT heads south (right) to a trailhead and vault toilets on Harvey Road.

The pathway heads north (left) along the edge of the ridge, quickly passing post No. 19 and then post No. 20. The next 3 miles is the most rugged and remote section of the trail. You climb in and out of a ravine and cross three two-tracks before descending to cross Section Thirteen Creek at *Mile 12.8*. The creek is a delightful stretch to

walk as the trail skirts its bank, passing many pools along the way. After a half mile the trail swings away, but you'll reach a second stream at *Mile 13.8*, this one featuring a bridge and a bench. The climbing resumes but eventually the pathway levels out and at *Mile 15* emerges from the woods at post No. 21 on the side of Jordan River Road.

On the other side you follow a two-track up a hill and then continue on a wooded trail, passing post No. 22 and reaching post No. 23 on the side of paved Turner Road at *Mile 15.8*.

The Jordan River National Fish Hatchery, reached from post No. 23 by heading 0.75 mile north on Turner Road, makes for an interesting side trip. Constructed in 1962, the hatchery is used primarily for the production of yearling lake trout destined for Lake Michigan and Lake Huron. Two million yearlings are raised annually, living as fry and fingerlings in indoor tanks and outdoor raceways.

The hatchery (231-584-2461; www.fws.gov/midwest/jordanriver) is open 7 AM to 3:30 PM daily but has a 24-hour visitors center with displays and viewing windows along with bathrooms and drinking water. Even on the hottest day in the middle of the summer, this room is delightfully cool thanks to the 23,000 gallons of water in the building, kept at a constant 46-degree temperature.

On the other side of Turner Road the pathway climbs to post No. 24 and then levels out. Post No. 25 at *Mile 16.9* marks the junction with the Deadmans Hill Loop, and at *Mile 18* you arrive at the viewing area of Deadmans Hill. From there you follow a well-worn path 100 yards to the trailhead parking area.

58

Shingle Mill Pathway

Place: Pigeon River Country State Forest

Total Distance: 10 miles

Hiking Time: 6 to 7 hours

Rating: Moderate

Highlights: Backcountry campsites, over-looks, Pigeon River

Maps: Shingle Mill Pathway map from the Michigan DNR or MichiganTrail Maps.com

Trailhead GPS Coordinates: N 45° 9' 24.82" W 084° 27' 53.01"

One of the most popular campgrounds in Pigeon River Country State Forest is Pigeon Bridge. Located in the heart of this 105,049-acre tract, the campground has 10 rustic sites overlooking the Pigeon River, making it a favorite among trout fishers, who toss flies, spinners, and worms in an effort to entice brookies and browns.

But the campground is also frequented by hikers, because it serves as the trailhead for two well-known backpacking routes. Beginning and ending here is the High Country Pathway, an 80-mile loop that passes through four counties and the heart of Michigan's northern Lower Peninsula. Most backpackers need five to seven days to hike the entire circuit.

A little too long for you? Then also departing from Pigeon Bridge State Forest Campground is the Shingle Mill Pathway, a system of five loops that passes through some of the most scenic portions of the Pigeon River Country. Even better, the longest loops (10 and 11 miles) can be covered in six to seven hours by most hikers, making them ideal for an overnight trek. The first half of these loops shares the same trail as the High Country Pathway, where wilderness camping is permitted as long as you're 100 feet away from the trail or any body of water. You'll also find a pair of traditional dispersed campsites with one of them overlooking Green Lake, a very scenic spot to pitch a tent.

The hike described here is the 10-Mile Loop, the most scenic portion of the Shingle Mill Pathway, in my opinion, which allows you to spend a night at Green Lake. The

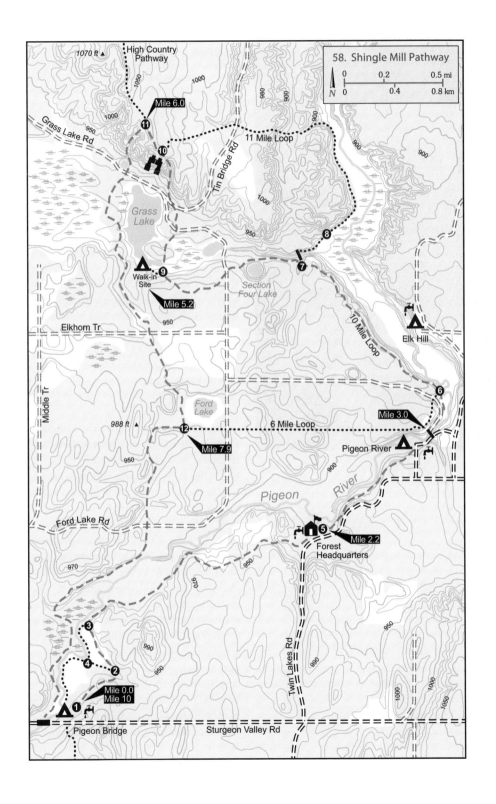

58. Shingle Mill Pathway

N

| 0 | 0.2 | 0.5 mi |
| 0 | 0.4 | 0.8 km |

1070 ft ▲

High Country Pathway

Mile 6.0

1050

1000

Grass Lake Rd

1000

950

11 Mile Loop

900

900

Tin Bridge Rd

1000

Grass Lake

950

8

7

Walk-in Site

9

Mile 5.2

Section Four Lake

950

10 Mile Loop

Elk Hill

6

Elkhorn Tr

950

Middle Tr

Ford Lake

988 ft ▲

12

6 Mile Loop

Mile 3.0

Mile 7.9

Pigeon River

950

900

Pigeon

River

Ford Lake Rd

5

Mile 2.2

Forest Headquarters

970

950

Twin Lakes Rd

900

3

990

4

2

950

976

1000

1050

Mile 0.0
Mile 10

1

Pigeon Bridge

Sturgeon Valley Rd

A trail sign for the High Country Pathway on the Shingle Mill Pathway.

From I-75, depart at exit 290 and head south for Vanderbilt. In town turn left (east) on Sturgeon Valley Road and follow it for 11 miles. The Pigeon River State Forest Campground is reached just after crossing the Pigeon River. To reach the state forest headquarters, continue east on Sturgeon Valley Road another 3 miles and then turn left (north) on Twin Lake Road. You'll pass the headquarters in a mile and reach Pigeon River State Forest Campground in 2 miles.

A state park pass is required to hike state forest pathways and leave a car at Pigeon Bridge State Forest Campground. For more information, contact Pigeon River Country State Forest (989-983-4101).

First Day
Distance: 5.2 miles
At the back of the campground you'll find a trail sign and display map for the Shingle Mill Pathway. The trail departs north and quickly reaches post No. 2, the junction for the 0.75-Mile Loop, and in a half mile reaches post No. 3, where the 1.25-Mile Loop heads back for the campground.

For the next half mile the pathway skirts the Pigeon River and then leaves the scenic trout stream to climb a wooded ridge. It's an uphill climb of almost 50 feet, but once you're on top you follow the edge of the ridge for more than a half mile—a scenic stretch of hiking in the fall—before descending to the Pigeon River Country State Forest head-quarters, reached at **Mile 2.2**. If the head-quarters, an impressive log lodge, is open, drop the packs and head inside to view the lobby displays on the elk herd and an impressive collection of wildlife mounts. Outside are benches, vault toilets, and drinking water.

lengths of the first three loops—0.75, 1.25, and 6 miles—make them better suited as day hikes, while the second backcountry campsite is along the 11-Mile Loop. You can also pick up the trail at several other places in the state forest, including the Pigeon River Campground, which would turn the northern half of the pathway into 6-mile day hikes.

From spring through fall hikers share the pathway with mountain bikers. On November 15 deer hunters arrive for the two-week firearm season, and in the winter Shingle Mill Pathway is a popular destination for cross-country skiers.

The Pigeon River Country State Forest headquarters, an impressive log lodge on the Shingle Mill Pathway.

From the headquarters, the pathway climbs in and out of the river valley before finally descending to Pigeon River State Forest Campground at *Mile 3*. The state forest campground has 19 rustic sites, many of them overlooking the trout stream. There are also vault toilets, picnic tables, and cold, clear drinking water from an artesian well.

Pigeon Bridge Road crosses the river near the campground, and at the vehicle bridge you can take off your boots and soak your feet in a pool that campers have dammed with rocks. Shingle Mill Pathway also uses the bridge to cross the river and then hugs the west bank to quickly reach post No. 6. At this junction the 6-Mile Loop heads southwest (left) to quickly cross Pigeon Bridge Road.

You head northwest (right) as the 10-Mile Loop immediately climbs a ridge bordering the west bank of the Pigeon River and then follows the crest of it for more than a half mile. Eventually you descend into a stand of red pine and reach post No. 7 at *Mile 4.3*. This junction marks the split between the pathway's 10-Mile Loop (west to the left) and 11-Mile Loop (due north to the right).

Head left for the 10-Mile Loop and in less than a quarter mile the trail passes beautiful Section Four Lake. This steep-sided, almost perfectly round body of water is an excellent example of the many sinkhole lakes found throughout this region of the Lower Peninsula. It's easy to stand on the edge of it and envision a hollowed limestone cave suddenly collapsing. Unfortunately you are not allowed to camp along the lake or fish it—it's being preserved for research.

The pathway continues west and crosses Ford Lake Road at *Mile 4.7*. On the other side of the sandy road is a blue-tipped post where the trail reenters the forest of hardwoods and pines, and in a half mile, or *Mile 5.2*, it reaches the backcountry campsite on Green Lake. It's situated in the middle of a stand of red pine, an open spot where you pitch the tent on a golden carpet of needles. And, other than post No. 9, that's all there is.

But what more do you need? Most likely you will have the spot to yourself, and in the evening you can stroll up the pathway for a clear view of Grass Lake and the huge beaver lodge that dominates the south end. Sit there long enough and the little engineers will eventually appear and most likely slap their flat tails at you.

Second Day
Distance: 4.8 miles
From the backcountry campsite the pathway swings north, skirts the south end of the lake, and crosses Ford Lake Road and then Grass Lake Road. Both roads are sandy, rutted two-tracks. On the other side of Grass Lake Road the trail cuts through a logged area and then climbs through a hardwood forest to post No. 10, reached at *Mile 5.8*.

The post marks the spot where the pathway's 11-Mile Loop merges back with the 10-Mile Loop. Also located here is a short spur to an overlook. A fire tower once stood here, and it's still possible to find the mounts. But even more impressive is the view. From this 1,000-foot perch, you can gaze down on Pigeon River valley or look southwest and see more than 20 miles of rolling northern

forest. What you can't see, ironically, is what lies at your feet, Grass Lake.

At post No. 10 you head left and in less than a quarter mile come to post No. 11, marking the junction where the High Country Pathway continues north (right). Head south (left) to stay on the Shingle Mill Pathway. The trail descends sharply and then breaks out of the woods to skirt Devil's Soup Bowl, another sinkhole lake, just before you cross Grass Lake Road again at *Mile 6.3*.

On the other side the terrain levels out considerably. Within a half mile the pathway crosses a footbridge as it passes within sight of Grass Lake, and at *Mile 7.8* it comes into view of scenic little Ford Lake. Keep in mind that some of these areas have been logged and laced with dirt two-tracks. Blue markers should keep you on course, however.

From Ford Lake, you climb to post No. 12, marking where the pathway merges with the 6-Mile Loop. Head right to hike through some old clear-cuts, and at *Mile 9* you will cross Ford Lake Road for the third time. In the final mile of the trek, you climb a ridge along the river, top off at 960 feet, and then descend into a wetland area. After crossing the small marsh, you're a quarter mile from Sturgeon Valley Road, which is used to cross Pigeon River to return to the state forest campground.

59

Lighthouse Ruins Trail

Place: Cheboygan State Park

Total Distance: 5.5 miles

Hiking Time: 2 to 3 hours

Rating: Easy

Highlights: Lake Huron beach, lighthouse ruins, rental cabins

Maps: Cheboygan State Park map from the Michigan DNR or MichiganTrail Maps.com

Trailhead GPS Coordinates: N 45° 39' 25.45" W 084° 24' 59.99"

Acre for acre, Cheboygan State Park might be one of most underused units in the Lower Peninsula, a park that contains almost 5 miles of Great Lakes shoreline yet attracts less than 50,000 visitors annually. For hikers who take the time to visit this park and are willing to endure soggy socks, that means a scenic beach walk and a bit of solitude with few if any other people around.

The 1,250-acre park features a day-use area and swimming beach in its southwest corner along Duncan Bay and a modern campground with 76 sites just north of it. Other than that Cheboygan for the most part is either low-lying forest and cedar swamps or Lake Huron beach and windswept dunes. It's a place where soggy trails often lead to spectacular sand.

The park has 6 miles of trails. This hike is the perimeter of the system, a 5.5-mile trek that begins and ends at the campground and includes what was once known as the Lighthouse Ruins Trail. Today the various trails are color-coded and labeled on park maps by their colors, but Lighthouse Ruins Trail remains a much more descriptive name for this walk.

The highlight of any hike in the park is the excellent coastal scenery, which includes several offshore lighthouses, miles of beach-combing, and the ruins of an 1859 lighthouse. The Red and Yellow Trails through the interior of the park are the wettest. If you begin at a trailhead along the park road, you can bypass these sections and combine the rest of the trails for a relatively dry 4-mile hike to Cheboygan Point.

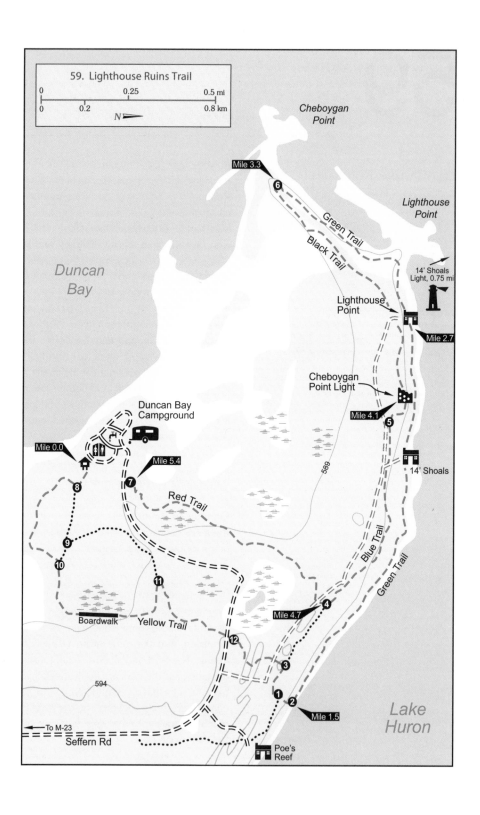

59. Lighthouse Ruins Trail

0   0.25   0.5 mi
0   0.2   0.8 km
N

Cheboygan
Point

Mile 3.3

6

Lighthouse
Point

Green Trail

Black Trail

14' Shoals
Light, 0.75 mi

Duncan
Bay

Lighthouse
Point

Mile 2.7

Cheboygan
Point Light

Mile 4.1

5

Duncan Bay
Campground

14' Shoals

Mile 0.0

Mile 5.4

8

7

Red Trail

589

9

10

Blue Trail

11

Green Trail

4

Mile 4.7

Boardwalk   Yellow Trail

12

594

3

To M-23

1

2

Mile 1.5

Lake
Huron

Seffern Rd

Poe's
Reef

Scattered along the trails are three rustic cabins that can be rented in advance. All three state park cabins are situated just inland from Lake Huron in the restricted portion of the park; only those who rent them are allowed to drive the rutted two-track along the north shore. Amenities include eight bunks, a hand pump, an outhouse, your own stretch of beach, and quick access to the trail system. For $65 a night, many people think this is the best summer rental in Michigan.

ACCESS

Cheboygan State Park is 3 miles east of the city of Cheboygan with a posted entrance off US 23. Once you're inside, follow the Seffern Road to the campground. You'll pass two posted trailheads with display maps along the road before reaching the campground, where the third trailhead is located next to site No. 54.

A state park pass or daily vehicle entry fee is required to hike at Cheboygan. Cabins and campsites can be reserved in advance (800-44-PARKS; www.midnrreservations.com). For more information or trail conditions, contact Cheboygan State Park (231-627-2811).

TRAIL

Hikers beginning in the campground might have to park near the contact station and walk through the campground to site No. 54, where the trailhead for the Yellow Trail is located. Yellow-tipped posts lead you into the woods, reaching post No. 8 within 100 yards. By staying right at every junction, you will follow the outside loop of the Yellow Trail and enjoy the most interesting section: the

Hikers following the trail in Cheboygan State Park.

Lighthouse Ruins Trail

Fourteen Foot Shoal Light, seen from Cheboygan State Park.

long boardwalk. Reached in a half mile, the planked trail leads a quarter mile through a cedar swamp that can be buggy in midsummer but is beautiful in the spring and fall.

Head north (right) at post No. 11. At **Mile 1.2** you break out at Seffern Road and cross it to post No. 12, marking the Blue Trail. This short segment returns to the woods and quickly crosses the dirt two-track that serves as the cabin access road to post No. 3. Head east (right) at the junction to quickly reach post No. 1, where a wide path parallels the dirt road to post No. 1. Head north (left) to pick up the start of the Green Trail, and at **Mile 1.5** you finally emerge at Lake Huron at post No. 2 just down the shore from the Poe's Reef Cabin. A bench is located here; you can take a break while viewing Poe Reef Light almost 3 miles offshore.

Head west (left) and follow the green-tipped posts for one of the most scenic hikes on the east side of the state. For almost 2 miles the trail is literally a walk along the beach in an area of the park that is open only to hikers and the handful of people who are renting the cabins. At **Mile 2.3** you pass Fourteen Foot Shoal Cabin and then come to a sign and spur leading to the lighthouse ruins, which you'll also pass on your return. Nearby is a bench with a fine view of Fourteen Foot Shoal Light less than a mile offshore.

You continue west along on a wide, sandy beach, and at **Mile 2.7** come to Lighthouse Point Cabin. This is the newest cabin and also the most spectacular. The two-room cabin sleeps eight and includes a screened-in porch; it's within view of the lapping waters of the Lake Huron beach.

Tip of the Mitt

The Green Trail remains on the shoreline as you pass the cabin and the fire pit just outside it, providing excellent views of Fourteen Foot Shoal Light. Within a quarter mile until you reach a bench at the base of Lighthouse Point and then cut across the point to return the beach until you reach post No. 6 near Cheboygan Point at *Mile 3.3*. Another bench is located here with a view of Fourteen Foot Shoal Light, while the Green Trail swings south to become the Black Trail.

The return on the Black Trail begins in open and grassy dunes before moving into the woods just before crossing the dirt road leading to Lighthouse Point Cabin at *Mile 3.8*. Within a third of a mile you reach the old stone foundation and partial rock walls that are the lighthouse ruins. Cheboygan Point Light was first built on a pier in Lake Huron in 1851 but lasted only a few years due to rough water and winter ice. In 1859

it was rebuilt on shore and was operated by the U.S. Lighthouse Service until 1930. The crumbling rocks that remain were the foundation of the lightkeeper's house that was attached to the tower.

Just beyond the ruins you arrive at post No. 5, indicating the start of the Blue Trail. After post No. 5, the Blue Trail begins paralleling the cabin access road. At times it's easier just to hike the two-track than to hunt for the footpath. At *Mile 4.7* you arrive at post No. 4, marking the junction with the Red Trail that heads south (right) for the campground. This 0.7-mile segment can be wet when it passes through some cedar swamps in the middle.

Toward the end you break out at a powerline clearing where the trail is still posted as Lighthouse Ruins Trail. The Red Trail then ends just up the road from the campground contact station.

60

Nebo Trail Loop

Place: *Wilderness State Park*

Total Distance: *8.35 miles*

Hiking Time: *3 to 5 hours*

Rating: *Moderate*

Highlights: *Mt. Nebo, rental cabin*

Maps: *Wilderness State Park map from the Michigan DNR, or Nebo Trail–Swamp Line Loop map from MichiganTrailMaps.com*

Trailhead GPS Coordinates: *N 45° 45' 17.50" W 084° 52' 38.10"*

Wilderness State Park at the tip of the mitt in Emmet County may have six cabins for rent, a boat launch, and two modern campgrounds, but for most visitors the outstanding feature is its undeveloped nature. The 10,512-acre unit, the largest piece of contiguous, undeveloped land in the Lower Peninsula, contains more than 26 miles of shoreline, a dedicated natural area, and a vast network of trails that attract those who want to photograph wildflowers, identify birds, or spend a day hiking through its forested terrain of pines and hardwoods.

How wild is Wilderness? The first wolves to appear in the Lower Peninsula since the early 1900s showed up here in the state park. In 1997 a Coast Guard pilot sighted a pair of along the shoreline, having just made the 5-mile trek across the frozen Straits of Mackinac. The pair have since evolved into a small but permanent population south of the Mackinac Bridge.

Winding across this vast park is a 38-mile network of trails with 11.4 miles designated as part of the North Country Trail (NCT), the national trail that winds from North Dakota to New York. Many of the trails are old forest roads. In the spring and after a heavy rainfall some wet sections can be encountered, but the mud is rarely impassable.

One of the most interesting day hikes in Wilderness State Park—and certainly the driest—is this loop, which combines Nebo Trail, Old South Boundary Trail, and the trail known as Swamp Line Road with several short nature trails. The entire hike is an 8.35-mile day hike, but it is well marked and there is little

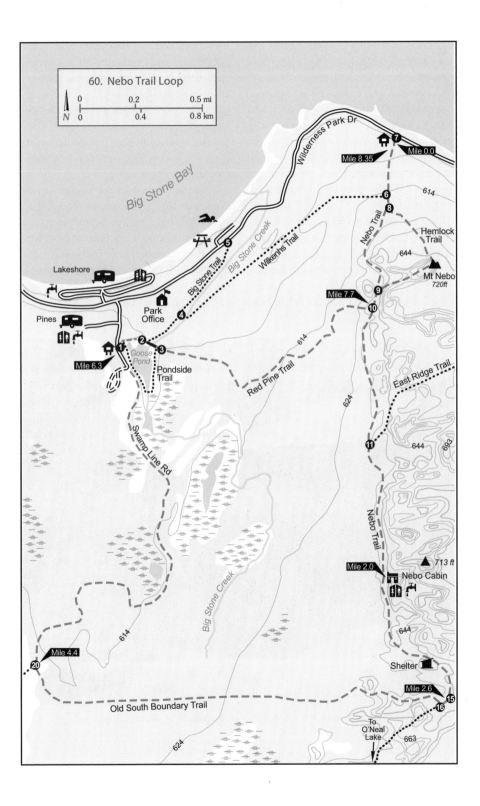

60. Nebo Trail Loop

N

| 0 | 0.2 | 0.5 mi |
| 0 | 0.4 | 0.8 km |

Big Stone Bay

Wilderness Park Dr

Mile 8.35   Mile 0.0   **7**

6   614

8

Nebo Trail

Hemlock Trail

644

Mt Nebo
720ft

Big Stone Creek

Wilkenhs Trail

Big Stone Trail

5

Lakeshore

Park Office

4

Pines

Mile 7.7   **9**

10

Red Pine Trail   614

East Ridge Trail

644   693

1   **2**   **3**   Goose Pond

Mile 6.3   Pondside Trail

11

Swamp Line Rd

624

Nebo Trail

713 ft

Mile 2.0   Nebo Cabin

644

20   Mile 4.4

Shelter   Mile 2.6   **15**

16

Old South Boundary Trail

To O'Neal Lake   663

624

elevation gain, making it an easier trek that most hikers accomplish in three to five hours.

Along Nebo Trail is a three-sided shelter—which makes a great place for an extended break or lunch if the timing is right—and Nebo Cabin, a classic log structure that can be reserved in advance. With a night in the cabin, you can turn the loop into an easy weekend backpacking trip with a 2-mile hike the first day and a 6.3-mile hike back to the trailhead the second.

The park also has 250 modern sites divided between two campgrounds. The Lakeshore Campground is situated along Big Stone Bay in a semi-open area, and among the 150 sites is a row right off the beach. Pines Campground is across Wilderness Park Drive and has 100 sites, most of them with paved pads and situated in a grove of mature pines. Both campgrounds tend to be filled weekends from early July to mid-August but usually have sites available midweek throughout the summer. The exception is the last week of August through Labor Day, when the park is filled daily due to the Mackinac Bridge Walk.

The description below begins at Nebo Trailhead along Wilderness Park Drive. If you're staying at the campgrounds, it would be easier to begin the loop at post No. 1 near Pines Campground. That would reduce the hike to 7.95 miles. Most of the route is open to mountain bikes with the exception of Red Pine and Hemlock Trails.

The Nebo Cabin, located along the Nebo Trail, can be rented for overnight use.

ACCESS

Wilderness State Park is 8 miles west of Mackinaw City and is reached by following County Road 81 and continuing west on Wilderness Park Drive after crossing Carp Lake River. The Nebo Trailhead is 1.5 miles east of the park office on Wilderness Park Drive.

Like all state parks, there is a vehicle entry fee at Wilderness. Cabins and campsites can be reserved in advance (800-44-PARKS; www.midnrreservations.com). For more information or trail conditions, contact Wilderness State Park (231-436-5381).

TRAIL

The Nebo Trailhead is well posted along Wilderness Park Drive and located 1.5 miles east of the park office. Within the parking area you'll find post No. 7 and a gate across the trail. Nebo Trail, like many trails in Wilderness State Park, is a two-track built by the Civilian Conservation Corps in the 1930s to access projects in other sections of the park.

Within a quarter mile are two junctions. The first, marked by post No. 6, is Wilkenhs Trail, which heads west (right) toward Goose Pond. Immediately following is post No. 8, marking one end of the Hemlock Trail. Head east (left) on Hemlock Trail.

This 0.6-mile spur leads pass some impressive hemlocks, more than 200 years old, and then to a steady but short ascent to the top of 720-foot Mt. Nebo. The "peak" is marked by a set of large stone blocks, the remains of a fire tower that the CCC built and used until 1949. If enough leaves have fallen, you can catch a glimpse of the Straits of Mackinac.

From the high point Hemlock Trail descends to the west to merge back into Nebo Trail. Nebo Trail immediately passes post No. 9 at *Mile 1*, marking the junction to Red Pine Trail, and then continues south

as a beautiful forest walk over slight rolling terrain. You pass post No. 11, marking the junction of the East Ridge Trail, and at *Mile 2* arrive at Nebo Cabin.

This snug, little structure was built by the CCC on a pine-covered knoll overlooking the trail. Outside are a vault toilet and drinking water; inside, five bunks, a table, and a wood-burning stove. The log cabin, a wonderful place to spend an evening or two, should be reserved in advance (800-447-2757; www.midnrreservations.com).

A half mile farther south is a gate across the trail and a three-sided shelter. The log shelter is another CCC project and features a massive stone fireplace and two picnic tables. It sits on top of a small rise overlooking the trail.

At *Mile 2.6* Nebo Trail reaches its southern end at post No. 15. Nearby is post No. 16, marking the junction of the O'Neal Lake Trail to the south (left) and Old South Boundary Road to the west (right-hand fork). With four trails merging, this remote corner of the park could be a confusing spot if it weren't so well marked with posts and locator maps. For this hike, just make sure you heading west from post No. 16 on Old South Boundary Trail.

Old South Boundary Trail, named because at one time it did mark the southern boundary of the state park, is a straight two-track that between *Mile 3* and *Mile 4* passes through a marsh area that can be wet at times and where there will be frogs jumping everywhere. Toward the end the trail swings northwest and arrives at post No. 20 at *Mile 4.4*, marking its junction with Swamp Line Road and Sturgeon Bay Trail.

Head north (right) on Swamp Line Trail, another two-track that within a mile passes an open patch of water surrounded by marsh. Just before the entrance to Pines Campground you reach post No. 1 at *Mile*

A hiker studys a pond along the Swamp Line Trail.

6.3, a major trailhead in the park. Head east. From this point there are several ways to return to the Nebo Trailhead, including following Big Stone Creek and a segment of the park road or Wilkenhs Trail.

The most scenic route, however, is Red Pine Trail, picked up at post No. 3 after skirting the north end of Goose Pond and crossing a footbridge over Big Stone Creek. Red Pine Trail departs east and immediately passes through a swamp area that is crossed by a lengthy stretch of boardwalk. In less than a half mile you climb out of the lowlands and follow the crest of a low ridge where it's possible to gaze down on both sides.

You pass two small ponds, descending to the second, larger one after first viewing it from above. Frogs will be croaking here and turtles scrambling off logs for the security of the water. If the bugs aren't too bad, it's hard not to pause in search of other critters. Beyond the second pond, the trail descends to post No. 10 at **Mile 7.7**, marking the junction with Nebo Trail.

Head north (left) on Nebo Trail, bypassing Hemlock Trail this time to return to Nebo Trailhead at **Mile 8.35**.